THE MORAL WISDOM OF ST. THOMAS

An Introduction

Peter A. Redpath, Ph.D.
St. John's University
Staten Island, New York

UNIVERSITY
PRESS OF
AMERICA

LANHAM • NEW YORK • LONDON

B
765
.T54
R 4164
1983

Copyright © 1983 by

University Press of America,™ Inc.

4720 Boston Way
Lanham, MD 20706

3 Henrietta Street
London WC2E 8LU England

All rights reserved

Printed in the United States of America

ISBN (Perfect): 0-8191-3145-8
ISBN (Cloth): 0-8191-3144-X

Augustana College Library
Rock Island, Illinois 61201

To my brothers, Jim and Bob, and to my sister, Kathy

ACKNOWLEDGEMENTS

I want to thank my friends, Dr. Richard Ingardia and Mr. Robert Marino, for the many helpful comments they made about the typescript of this book. I want to thank Kathy Monteverdi for her patience and her excellent work in typing the text. And I want to thank my department Chairman, Dr. Thomas Houchin and my Dean, Fr. Joseph Breen, C.M., for the encouragement they give me to do research. Without all the above assistance this book would never have come into print.

TABLE OF CONTENTS

PREFACE	ix
INTRODUCTION	1
CHAPTER ONE: THE NATURE OF MAN AND HIS PLACE IN THE COSMOS	11
THE RELATION OF ETHICS TO A "POWER PSYCHOLOGY"	15
POWER AND INSTINCT	18
THE ORDER CALLED "CREATION"	19
THE ORDER WITHIN THE PERSON	23
CHAPTER TWO: THE NATURE OF MORAL ACTIVITY	27
DISTINGUISHING A MORAL ACT---ITS SOURCE: REASON AND WILL	31
THE TERMINATING POINT OF MORAL ACTION: THE HUMAN GOOD	40
THE NATURE OF THE DISTINGUISHING HUMAN GOOD	47
CHAPTER THREE: MORAL ACTIVITY: ITS POINTS OF ORIGIN	55
1. POWERS AND APPETITES	55
2. EMOTIONS	59
3. DISPOSITIONS	63
4. HABITS	65
5. VIRTUES	67
6. GIFTS, FRUITS AND BEATITUDES	71
7. LAW AND GRACE	76
CHAPTER FOUR: EMOTIONS	79
THE PROPELLING EMOTIONS	80
1. LOVE OR LIKING	80
2. HATRED	85
3. DESIRE AND AVERSION	86
4. PLEASURE AND JOY	87
5. PAIN AND SORROW	102

THE CONTENDING EMOTIONS	108
1. HOPE AND DESPAIR	109
2. FEAR	110
3. DARING	113
4. ANGER	115
CHAPTER FIVE: LAW AND GRACE	121
GENERAL CONSIDERATION OF LAW	122
PARTICULAR CONSIDERATION OF LAW	125
1. ETERNAL LAW	125
2. NATURAL LAW	125
3. HUMAN LAW	128
4. THE OLD LAW	129
5. THE NEW LAW	132
GRACE AND MORAL ACTIVITY	135
CHAPTER SIX: THE PERFORMANCE OF MORAL ACTION	143
MENTAL AND VOLITIONAL FACTORS OF MORAL ACTS	143
MEASURING A MORAL ACT AND A GOOD MORAL ACT	152
EXTERNAL FACTORS OF MORAL ACTS AND OF GOOD MORAL ACTS	154
CHAPTER SEVEN: HUMAN HAPPINESS AND THE EXISTENCE OF GOD	163
CONCLUSION	167
ENDNOTES	169
QUESTIONS FOR STUDY AND DISCUSSION	191
BIBLIOGRAPHY	197
INDEX	199

PREFACE

The general aim of this book is to provide an introduction to the moral doctrine adhered to by St. Thomas Aquinas. Our intention is to give an exposition of this moral doctrine with a view to furnishing contemporary readers with insight into the nature of moral activity as St. Thomas understood it, and with a view to supplying a practical guide to the living of a reasonable life.

What has prompted us to write this work is an estimation that, more than anything else, the contemporary world needs such a work. People need right principles of action if they are to live together in peace. Yet in no area of human learning does the contemporary age appear to us to be more confused and bankrupt than in the area of discovering such principles. Instead of providing people with directives whereby they might make reasonable choices about how to live their lives, many contemporary ethicians analyze the meaning of words used in ethical discourse. And instead of combatting the approach taken by contemporary ethicians with an approach in which people, today, might estimate they might hope to find some truth and personal direction, more traditionally-oriented thinkers repeat hackneyed old teachings which have lost their meaning for modern ears.

We think there is an alternative to each of these approaches, however, and we think it can be found in the teaching of St. Thomas Aquinas in the First Part of the Second Part of his Summa theologiae. We think, moreover, that the bankruptcy which has befallen contemporary ethics is due primarily to two things: 1) a loss of the sense of the meaning of ethical, or moral, activity; and 2) the absence within contemporary ethics of guidelines for practical action. Beyond this, we are of the opinion that by examining the teaching of St. Thomas we can overcome this bankruptcy in a relatively readable work. For in this Part of the Summa theologiae St. Thomas engages in one of the most detailed analyses of moral activity which one can find, and, at the same time, he provides numerous insights into the workings of the human condition which can be used as practical guidelines for the living of a happy human life.

Before reading this work, however, we must give our audience a word of warning. Due to the fact that traditional modes of expression very often just do not mean anything to contemporary readers, we plan to take liberties with the language we use to convey St. Thomas's teaching even though some followers of St. Thomas might find this objectionable. In addition, for pedagogical purposes we might, at times, deviate from the order of presentation employed by St. Thomas himself. So, for these faults, we apologize in advance.

Finally, we wish to preface this work with one more observation. This work is intended to be an exposition of the moral doctrine adhered to by St. Thomas. It is not intended to be an apologetic, or a defense of St. Thomas's teaching against its detractors, if there be any. We are firmly convinced that there is a great deal of truth in the teaching of St. Thomas, and that St. Thomas was a profoundly wise human being. It is for this reason that we have entitled this book, The Moral Wisdom of St. Thomas. And it is for this reason that we wish this work to be understood as an exposition rather than as an apologetic. For we think that what St. Thomas says is, by and large, so true that he needs no defense from us. All he needs is the justice of an accurate and faithful report of his teaching in a language which is intelligible to a contemporary audience. We hope the following work will provide him with the justice of such a report.

INTRODUCTION

Why would anyone, today, write a book on the moral teaching of St. Thomas Aquinas? And why should anyone, today, read such a book? After all, the moral teaching of St. Thomas Aquinas is pretty much identified in the minds of many people with the natural law teaching of the Roman Catholic Church. Many, if not most, Roman Catholics have some familiarity with natural law morality. So such a book seems superfluous for them. And non-Roman Catholics would appear to be, by and large, uninterested in such a teaching. Reformed Christians might, we think, find such a moral teaching at variance with a propensity on their part to base moral living on faith in Christ. And religious people of non-Christian denominations might find such a moral teaching objectionable for reasons similar to those of Reformed Christians. That is, these people would, we think, be prone to consider the moral teaching of St. Thomas Aquinas to be at variance with some other principle upon which they base their moral activity. For while they might not base their morality upon faith in Christ, like Reformed Christians, they might base it upon the Old Testament or upon the Quran, or upon some other similar source.

The only audience left for a book such as this, then, would appear to be atheists, agnostics, and Catholics who either are ignorant of the moral teaching of St. Thomas, or who, while being aware of this moral teaching, are indifferent to it or who reject it. But surely most atheists and agnostics, especially those who read philosophy, would simply reject the moral teaching of St. Thomas as the ethics of the stone age. And what is left of our Catholic audience would not, we think, be very receptive to a book like ours.

Still, is all this really the case? Is a book about the moral teaching of St. Thomas really superfluous for many Roman Catholics because they already know this doctrine, unnecessary reading for some non-Roman Catholics because the moral teaching of St. Thomas is at variance with their own foundations of ethics, and antiquated material for still other Roman and non-Roman Catholics? We do not think so for several reasons.

First of all, we do not think that many people are really that familiar with the moral teaching of St. Thomas Aquinas.

Oh, sure, it is not uncommon to find people, especially those educated in Catholic schools, claiming that they have been exposed to the teachings of Aquinas; but we cannot help but be sceptical about the accuracy of such claims. And the reason for our scepticism is, we think, well-founded. For it is based upon certain recent statements made by both Professor Vernon Bourke and Father James Weisheipl.

A few years ago, in a special issue of the philosophical journal, The Monist, Dr. Vernon Bourke challenged the usual classification of St. Thomas's moral teaching as a "natural law" doctrine. In that article Professor Bourke argued:

> While the notion of natural law does play a part in Aquinas's teaching on morality, this does not seem to me to be a central role. Indeed there are many reasons why it might be better, today, to stop talking about natural law, both in the context of Thomistic philosophy and in the broader context of contemporary ethics. What I now advocate is the position that right reason (recta ratio) is the key theme in the ethics of Aquinas.[1]

At almost exactly the same time that Professor Bourke was making the above claim, Father James Weisheipl, in his highly respected and scholarly work, Friar Thomas D'Aquino—His Life, Thought and Work, contended that the understanding many of St. Thomas's commentators have regarding this moral teaching does not do justice to the thought of St. Thomas. What Father Weisheipl said was: "...many modern commentators have wrenched Thomas's teaching on natural law out of context and have distorted it;....The discussion of law in general and of natural law in particular does not constitute Thomas's full teaching on the foundations of natural law. In I-II, these are only preliminary questions for his principal interest, which is the Old Law and the New Law of the covenant which God made with his people."[2]

Now Dr. Bourke and Father Weisheipl are hardly what one could call "minor figures" in the area of St. Thomas's teaching. Both men are reputable and respected scholars when it comes to giving accurate reports about the thinking of St. Thomas. Yet one man says that we should stop talking about natural law when referring to St. Thomas's teaching, and the other says that many of St. Thomas's very own commentators have distorted his views on natural law, and adds that natural law is not even of principal interest for St. Thomas in the I-II of his Summa theologiae. St. Thomas's primary interest here, he contends, is not with natural law but with the Law of the Old and New Testaments!

If what Dr. Bourke and Father Weisheipl say be true, how can most people, Roman Catholic or not, claim to have an accurate understanding of St. Thomas's moral teaching? And whether or not one is willing to accept as true what St. Thomas has to say about moral activity, simply from his influence upon Catholicism, it is difficult to deny that this man's thinking has had an enormous influence upon the formation of subsequent moral thought. From the standpoint of simple historical importance alone, then, an accurate knowledge of the moral teaching of St. Thomas Aquinas is indispensible.

But this point does not seem to us to be the major reason why a book about the moral teaching of St. Thomas Aquinas is both timely to write and important to read. What makes such a work both timely and important seems to us to be this. St. Thomas Aquinas was a pre-Reformation thinker. As such, his teaching should be of interest both to Reformed Christians and to all Catholics. And this should be even more the case if St. Thomas's moral teaching has not been accurately reported by many of his commentators. For St. Thomas is still regarded as the pre-eminent theologian of the Catholic Church. Consequently, if his teaching on morality be open to re-interpretation, perhaps what he has to say might be of major importance to the ecumenical dialogue between Rome and Reformed Christians. Would not his teaching on morality, then, be of utmost importance to all Christians, and not just to Catholics?

But what about non-Christians? Would not they find the moral teaching of St. Thomas to be objectionable? Perhaps, but, once again, we do not think so. Some might not agree with various points which St. Thomas makes about the relationship of moral activity to revelation, but truth is non-denominational. And, as far as we can see, by and large, what St. Thomas has to say on the subject of moral activity is true. And this is another reason we would recommend his teaching to everyone.

Of course, we realize that by recommending the moral teaching of St. Thomas to others on the basis of its truth, we are presupposing that there is truth to be had in the area of morals. And to make such a presupposition is to be at variance with the popular contemporary habit of considering morals to be simply an expression of one's feelings, and to be devoid of factual content. We would not even pause to comment upon this situation were it not for the fact that this view seems to us to be widely held today, particularly among atheists and agnostics, but even among some people who claim to be theists. It would be unreasonable for us to expect people who reject ethics as a genuine area of human knowledge to be encouraged to study the moral teaching of St. Thomas because of its truth. It is encumbent upon us, therefore, to give some explanation as to why we think ethics, or morals, to be a genuine area of human knowledge and not an expression of personal preference.

Why, then, do we think that genuine knowledge can be achieved in the area of morals? Well, to explain our reasoning here, let us begin by pointing out what we think is the most widespread cause for contemporary thinkers to reject morals as a valid area of learning.

Ever since modern philosophy began in the time of Francis Bacon and Rene Descartes, the West has witnessed the progressive exclusion of objects and areas of learning, which were once commonly accepted to be genuine, from reality and from knowledge. The thinkers of the seventeenth century were men of genius who greatly augmented the development of an area of learning which, today, we call "experimental science," or "science." Unfortunately, however, it does not appear to us that these thinkers clearly understood the difference between the area of learning they were developing and learning as such. And, in so doing, they made a major mistake.

There are many ways by which we can come to learn about the world around us. One of these ways is by means of empirical observation, and by perception of effects made upon scientific instruments, which are evaluated from the perspective of mathematics. This way of learning about the world is the way proper to the area of learning which, today, many people call "science." It is not the only way to learn about reality, however. Yet many thinkers, today, seem to us not to realize this. Prior to the twentieth century, for instance, the terms "philosophy" and "science" were used interchangeably.[3] And prior to the seventeenth century, the term "knowledge" was readily applied to areas of learning to which mathematics was not applicable. From the seventeenth century to the present, however, largely due, we think, to the influence of Descartes and Newton, Galileo, Hume and Kant, the term "knowledge" has more and more become identified with "science," and "science" has more and more become restricted to the type of knowledge achieved in mathematics and physics.

To us the consequences of such a confusion are nothing short of disastrous. The words "knowledge," "learning," and "science" do not mean the same thing. We come to know many things without coming to know them by a process of discovery or investigation. And we know many things by means of a process of discovery or investigation without having to apply empirical observation and/or mathematics to our process of discovery or investigation. Properly speaking, when we "know" something we apprehend it as it is. When we "know" by "learning" we come to apprehend something by investigation. And when we know something "scientifically," understanding "science" to refer to "experimental science," we come to apprehend something through empirio/mathematical investigation.[4] Should we make the mistake of reducing all knowing to that which can be apprehended by experimental science, it appears evident that one may include something within the sphere of human knowledge and learning only to the extent that it is susceptible to analysis by means of experimental science. What, then, are we to do with traditional areas of learning like history, literature, art, the humanities in general? It would appear that either we must dispense with them as areas of learning or we must only study them the way empirical scientists study sense data.

A similar confusion has, we think, also developed along with the confusion of "knowledge" with "science." That confusion lies in the restrictive understanding which exists, today, regarding the meaning of the term "fact." Since the time of David Hume, and, more recently, since the time of Kant, the word "fact" has been, particularly in England and America, limited to objects of "experience," that is, to objects perceptible by the senses. The word "fact" is, we think, by and large, synonymous with the word "real." If such be the case, then, by restricting our understanding of the word "experience" to objects perceptible by the senses, we have, in effect, limited the factual and the real to the sense perceptible. And insofar as knowledge is genuine only to the extent that it has reality for its object, by reducing "fact" to the experienceable, and the "experienceable" to the sense perceptible, we have ruled out, a priori, any genuine knowledge of any non-physical reality. The result of such a restrictive understanding of the words "knowledge" and "fact" has, we think, been a major cause of the habit of many contemporary philosophers to consider ethics to involve a classification of the meaning of terms used in ethical discourse. For if the subject-matter of ethics be not something factual, then the proper role of the philosopher would lie beyond the realm of ethics. For a philosopher, at least in the Socratic sense, is an impartial observer. So if the subject-matter of ethics be not a fact, but rather a feeling, the philosopher might be a meta-ethician, but he should not be an ethician.

the realm of ethics. For a philosopher, at least in the Socratic sense, is an impartial observer. So if the subject-matter of ethics be not a fact, but rather a feeling, the philosopher might be a meta-ethician, but he should not be an ethician.

The reason for such confusion has its roots, we think, in the very complex political, philosophical and religious situation pervading the sixteenth century in Europe. The sixteenth century was filled with turmoil: religious wars, political intrigue, and philosophical scepticism. In order to help to put an end to all the chaos and conflict resulting from the sixteenth century, the Father of Modern Philosophy, Rene Descartes, and other thinkers coming after him who accepted some of his basic tenets, attempted to develop a new method of thinking. This method of thinking was supposed to eradicate doubt from the mind, and was supposed to be unquestionable. The outcome of these early attempts to develop a new method of thinking was what is now generally called "experimental science," or "science."

It was not without good intentions, we think, that the men of the seventeenth century sought to develop a kind of thinking which could replace previous kinds of thinking. Their intention was noble, given their historical situation, but, nonetheless, we think they over-estimated the boundaries of this new science. As a result of their over-estimation, and as a result of our fascination with the technological achievements made through the aid of empirical science, we have become over-zealous in our judgment about its area of application and about the extent of its possible achievements. We expect too much, today, from experimental science, and our exaggerated expectation is poisoning our ability to consider as real aspects of reality which are not apprehensible by the means and methodology proper to this science.

Certainly, no proposition about a matter of ethical behavior can be proved or demonstrated in the sense that one can immediately perceive ethical behavior, in the sense that one can perceive the effects of ethical behavior upon scientific instruments, or in the sense that one can mathematically measure ethical behavior. If by "fact" we mean something perceptible, and if by "demonstration" we mean empirical and/or mathematical verification, then, certainly, ethical behavior is neither factual nor demonstrative. But the use of the terms "fact" and "demonstration" in so restrictive a sense seems, to us, to be unwarranted. Even in contemporary physics and astronomy the word "fact" has a wider meaning than empirio/mathematical. For modern scientists themselves deal with "...objects that lie wholly outside the range of ordinary experience, because they cannot be directly perceived by us," objects like the "electron" in nuclear physics, and the "black hole" in astronomy. Scientific demonstrations for the existence of realities such as these are not strict empirical or mathematical demonstrations. Rather, they are arguments or inferences based upon empirical observations or upon scientific instruments.[5] Why, then, can we not simply say that when we use the word "fact" and the word "demonstration" in ethics and in experimental science we are using these words in a wide sense? That is, when, in the area of ethics we are talking about a fact, we are not talking about something directly observable by our senses. Rather, we are talking about some reality unobservable to our senses. But, in both the case of experimental science and of ethics, we are, at the very least, talking about features of reality. And when, in the area of ethics, we are talking about a demonstration, we are not talking about a controlled experiment or a mathematical proof. Rather, we are talking about a logically cogent argument whose truth can be affirmed with less certainty than is achieved in mathematical proofs, but which seems as certain as that achieved by an argument for electrons, or mesons, or for black holes.

Why, after all, are we justified in positing the existence of some reality or other? Does not the answer ultimately come down to the fact that, either directly or indirectly, our minds observe or apprehend that the reality in question does exist? For instance, by our power of seeing we see color, but we do not see sound. Nevertheless, we do not deny the reality of sound because we do not see it with our eyes. In a similar way, we hear people's voices. We do not hear their vocal cords touching together, but simply because this occurrence escapes our power of hearing, we do not deny its reality. Why not? Why does not our power of sight refuse to give equal credence to our power of hearing? Why does not our power of hearing refuse to recognize the reality of any feature not directly observable to it?

The reason seems to be that both these powers operate under the guidance of our minds. While we do not see what our ears hear, and while we do not hear what our eyes see, our minds judge that the existence of eyes and of color does not give an adequate account of the existence of hearing, and the existence of ears and of sound does not give an adequate account of the existence of seeing. Or take another example. Why are we justified in positing the existence of an area of learning called experimental science? How can anyone prove there to be such knowledge? Why do we not simply say that experimental science is not knowledge, but, rather, feeling, or guesswork? "Because we can test our knowledge," we might say, or "because we can accurately predict occurrences on the basis of our knowledge." So what? Observations are not real because we can predict them nor because we can test them. What makes consistent observations real and non-consistent ones not? They are both still observations and are not observations simply feelings?

Surely, most of us would consider responses like these to be unusual. And suppose some ethician were to come along and deny the reality of scientific knowledge because he could find no proof of its reality within ethics. Would not such an attitude be likewise unusual? What would make it unusual? Would it not simply be that the ethician, by virtue of his training, is not qualified to judge the reality or non-reality of scientific knowledge?

Now, if we should consider to be unusual responses like the ones just given in the examples above, why should we not consider to be equally unusual the claim that ethics cannot be a genuine area of learning because the subject it traditionally has claimed to study involves something not observable and not demonstrable by means of experimental science? After all, experimental science itself today posits the existence of realities which are not observable to one's senses, and the very _truth_ of the claim that the only kind of knowledge which is demonstrable is empirio/mathematical knowledge is not demonstrable in an empirio/mathematical way. Beyond this, one should recall that the scientific method did not exist prior to the seventeenth century. Does this mean that prior to the seventeenth century no one could have demonstrated anything to anyone else? Is not such a claim rather hard to accept? For suppose we were to go along with it. If demonstration were to be accepted as nothing but empirio/mathematical demonstration, the thinkers of the seventeenth century could not have demonstrated the truth of this kind of demonstration to anyone unless that person were already versed in an understanding of the techniques of empirio/mathematical demonstration.

But can anyone **really** accept this? Is this the way we come to accept the validity of scientific demonstration? By first understanding what such demonstration involves? Or is it not the case that many, if not most of us, accept the validity of scientific demonstration, that many of us have had its validity _demonstrated_ to us, without us having the foggiest idea of what scientific demonstration involves? That is, while most of us adhere to the validity of scientific demonstration, few of us do so because we have become convinced of its validity by means of empirio/mathematical demonstration. Rather, we accept its validity because of the achievements we witness its application to effect, or because of what we consider to be sound arguments given in its favor by people we trust, or for one or a host of similar reasons, none of which is a scientific demonstration, but each of which is a demonstration of some sort. Why, then, should we think that the men of the seventeenth century would have reacted any differently?

Well, then, supposing what we have just said to be true, we still have the problem of showing why we think ethics _is_ a genuine area of learning. How shall we resolve this problem? There are several ways we might be able to do this, but we think the easiest and most effective way is to give an accurate report of the moral teaching of St. Thomas. For we think that the moral teaching of St. Thomas expresses facts which are as cogent and compelling in their truth as facts which are found in any other area of human learning. This book itself, then, is our demonstration that ethics is a genuine area of learning. The content of this work is what we offer as our proof. For, clearly, if St. Thomas has constructed an ordered body of facts regarding the moral life which are as cogent and compelling in their truth as facts which are found in any other area of human learning, ethics is a genuine branch of human learning.

We wish, however, to caution our readers about one thing. While we propose to present an accurate report of the moral teaching of St. Thomas, we intend to do this in a condensed fashion, and without some of the more technical language used by St. Thomas. We think St. Thomas's moral teaching is profoundly interesting to read for someone who understands his use of language. Indeed, we find it nothing short of awesome. Yet the way some of his moral teachings have been transmitted to contemporary students by some of his disciples does, we are afraid to say, make him look like an enormous stuffed-shirt, or a medieval wind-bag. So, we cannot help but be sympathetic towards contemporary students and philosophers who might groan at the thought of another text on the moral teaching of St. Thomas, and who might view us to be "...proclaiming the beauty of Dulcinea del Toboso to a world that could see only an ugly hag being snatched from the grave."[6] In an age when even the most mundane things can be marketed in a way to capture the attention and interest of the buying-public, we hope it is possible for us to present the moral teaching of St. Thomas in a fashion which is vibrant, alive, rich and novel, rather than heavy, legalistic, bankrupt and burdensome to the human spirit.

After all, for St. Thomas, what ethics pursues is not some trivial or frivolous thing. The prize it offers is the summit of all human life. What it pursues is what is <u>most</u> <u>wanted</u> <u>by</u> <u>all</u> <u>human</u> <u>beings</u>. What it studies is what is of greatest interest to all of us.

If St. Thomas Aquinas has, as we think he has, penetrated more deeply than any other thinker into the nature of moral activity, how can what he has to say be dull, or unnecessary, or superfluous for any of us? And how can we fail to convey his genius, even in a condensed form, if we do him the justice of an accurate interpretation?

CHAPTER I

THE NATURE OF MAN AND HIS PLACE

IN THE COSMOS

In order for us to enable the moral wisdom of St. Thomas to begin to weave its way through the pages which follow, let us give this wisdom a general footing from which to start. Indeed, this is by and large what St. Thomas does when discussing moral activity within his Summa theologiae. Before beginning his discussion of moral activity, he gives his reader an overall view of the way he looks at the universe and the place of man in relation to the rest of reality.[1]

Of course, the treatment which St. Thomas gives to explaining his general world-view is much more detailed than we can hope to cover in a little book such as this. In fact, in the Ottawa edition of the Latin text of the Summa theologiae, this general world-view takes up over seven hundred pages.[2] Since we cannot hope to cover all this material leading up to St. Thomas's discussion of moral activity, let us try to summarize certain relevant points as best we can.

To begin with, let us place St. Thomas's moral doctrine within the more general context of his view of reality. St. Thomas, as far as we understand him, considered there to be a seven-fold division of reality, that is, a division of reality into: elements, composites, plants, animals, humans, angels, and God, which is arranged according to an order of inferior to superior.[3]

The world-view of St. Thomas is a view, then, which, from the start, might offend the democratic sensibilities of many of us. After all, how can he seriously claim that people are superior to animals, or that animals are superior to plants? Well, we think what caused St. Thomas to make this kind of judgment was something he noticed about the appearance, the behavior, the relationship to their environment, and the ability of things to influence others. What he noticed was simply that certain kinds of things closely resemble one another in all these ways, and less closely resemble other kinds of things. That is, he noticed more or less the same things that most of us tend to notice about the things around us. We see, for instance, that people tend to grow the same kind of peculiar-looking cellular structures within their bodies, things like eyes, ears, noses, hearts, livers, etc.. And we notice that trees do not tend to grow these things. We do not expect, for example, to harvest kidneys from kidney trees, or livers from liver trees, any more than we expect people to grow apples on the top of their shoulders in place of a head. We notice that stones never grow such peculiar structures, and, on the whole, we observe the existence of a stone to lack variety in its operations. We do not expect stones to bite mailmen, or people to marry oak trees, or chimpanzees to study anthropologists (although, come to think of it, it might be something worth considering). No, we do not, in general, expect any of these things to happen because, we say, the things in question do not have the power to do what we have been describing.

Well, St. Thomas noticed the same thing. What he noticed was that there was something within things which, in a vague way of speaking, marked out a territory for them. That is, there was something within things which created a boundary for their structure, and for their operations. It caused certain kinds of things to resemble one another in appearance, and to be able to engage in activities which resembled one another in kind. What this something was within things was something which, he thought, we could not observe by means of our senses, but it was, nonetheless, real. What he called it was a "nature," but for our purposes we might be better off calling it a "distinguishing power." And let us simply say that one level of reality was seen by St. Thomas to be superior to another because of the "distinguishing power" within it.[4]

For St. Thomas, then, there is present within certain beings the same kind of distinguishing power which causes them to resemble one another in appearance and to resemble one another in operation. And it is this distinguishing power which determines whether one kind of thing is superior or inferior to another. For one thing is generally considered to be superior to another in power because it exceeds another in the intensity of its power, in the extent of its freedom in its operations, and in the width of its sphere of influence.[5] For example, we tend to consider one person to be superior to another in political power to the extent that that person is more capable of determining the actions of others, in particular, of other people who have political or social power; to the extent that that person is able to determine the actions of many people, in particular, of many people with political and social power; and to the extent that, while that person is able to exert an influence on others, he or she is not subject to a similar type of influence directed against himself or herself. Or take another example. One person is considered to be superior in intelligence to another because that person is easily and quickly able to come to understand things which are difficult to know; because that person is able to do so habitually with regard to many such things; and because that person is taken to be an authority upon whom others depend in some way or other for their own education.

Relating all this to the seven-fold division of reality, St. Thomas considers one level to be superior to another because there is present within what he considers to be the higher level a distinguishing power which enables that thing, in general: 1) to engage in kinds of operations which, for their performance, require less dependence on beings existing outside of that thing than do the kinds of operations engaged in on a lower level; 2) to engage in a variety of such kinds of operations; and 3) to exert an influence on the operations of others, particularly on those kinds of things which, like themselves, have a power to influence the operations of others. Thus St. Thomas does not think that plants are superior to stones because plants have a greater height than stones. He thinks plants are superior in their power to engage in operations over which they have some direction and control.[6] Stones have very little power to be the initiating cause of operations over which they have direction and control. They spend most of their time just holding their parts together, unless someone comes along to write on them, or to throw them through a window, or to skip them along the top of a lake. And over the latter kinds of operations they have little control, except with respect to what kinds of instruments can be used to write on them, or how far they can be thrown. Certainly not much of an existence, is it?

When one contrasts to this what plants do, how can one deny the superiority of plants to stones with respect to their power to initiate and to control actions on their own? Why, plants can do a variety of things which stones cannot, things which originate within the power of the plant, and which enable the plant to have some say over what it is going to do with its life, and what it can do to others. For instance, plants can seek out food with their roots, they can grow a multiplicity of peculiar-looking structures within their bodies, they can give off odors, give rise to beautiful colors - they simply can give rise to numerous kinds of actions which stones cannot. Still, like stones, most plants cannot decide to get up and move out of the neighborhood if they get tired of their surroundings. Nor can they run away from beings who wish to uproot them.

So, while one might say that plants have within them some power whereby they are able to do many things which are internally determined, and whereby they have some say in what they are going to do with their lives, this is not much of an existence either. Notice how much a plant depends upon its immediate physical surroundings for the performance of its operations. Contrast this to the way an animal depends upon its immediate physical surroundings. Plants tend to be tied into ground. As St. Thomas puts it, it has its head in the ground and its feet in the air.[7] The most simple changes in its environment can radically alter its destiny. An animal, on the other hand, is not rooted in the ground, and its distinguishing power, or nature, provides it with ways of operating which enable it to grow and to develop in a manner which, when compared to the growth and development of a plant, is less susceptible to determination by its immediate physical environment. The animal does not have to attach its head to the earth to get its food from a very small geographical radius. Its nature has provided it with organs which enable it to determine from within itself what it does, how it will do it, why and when it will do it. So how it eats, when it eats, where it eats, why it eats, or how, when, where or why it reproduces, is more under its control than are the same activities under control of the plant. Notice, too, how an animal tends to have organs of sensation and of reproduction on the outside of its body. By means of its sense organs an animal can survey its environment. It can, within certain limits, determine what it takes into its perception and what it leaves out. It can turn its head away, run, cover its eyes, ears, mouth or nose if it wishes not to be influenced by its surroundings, and by virtue of these organs it can engage in operations which initiate from within its own body and which contribute the maintenance and growth of itself within existence as an independent and free being.

Of all the operations in which it engages the ones least under an animal's control are the ones it shares with plants: nutrition, growth, and reproduction. The drives within the animal to grow, to eat, and to reproduce are not within it by deliberative choice. They are there by what we call "instinct." And these instinctive drives are the most difficult ones for an animal to control. Nonetheless, each tends to be more under control of the animal than it tends to be under control of the plant. This is most obvious in reproduction where one animal tends to generate its kind in the body of another animal with which it has chosen to mate, and not by casting its seed to the wind.[8]

Yet despite all the sophistication in operation we notice among animals, we note the same degree of self-mastery among humans and, beyond this, a kind of self-direction wholly lacking among animals. In a way, animals act by choice. For they do make decisions. But they do not make logically calculated decisions. The sheep seeing a wolf will spontaneously run away. It will not do so because it has reasoned that all wolves are dangerous to sheep; this is a wolf; this is dangerous to sheep. And the ape in the zoo cage trying to get a banana hung from the ceiling will, by trial and error, figure out how to get it, but the same ape does not have the ability to distinguish between true and false, right and wrong, good and evil. He does not have the power to train people to do tricks, or to develop arts and sciences, to comprehend abstract principles in light of which logical deliberation takes place, or, on the basis of such deliberation, to determine whether or not he will follow his instincts. He simply lacks the power which makes one capable of doing such things, and this is true of all animals.[9]

The Relation of Ethics to a "Power Psychology"

The point we have been trying to make thus far in this chapter is that St. Thomas considers one kind of reality to be superior to another on the basis of the presence of a distinguishing power within itself whereby it can initiate and control its own action. We think it is particularly important for our readers to understand this because we think that the contemporary decline in our understanding the nature of ethics is founded upon our inability to understand that ancient and medieval ethics was based upon a "power psychology." This inability, we think, is intimately connected to our contemporary habit of attempting to understand everything from the perspective of experimental science. That is, from the perspective of experimental science, what is of principal concern about a reality is that which can be directly observed through our external senses, or through instruments which are extensions of these senses, to the degree that these observations are capable of mathematical measurement. Thus something like human intelligence, from the perspective of experimental science, consists of actions performed on an I.Q. test, or "anger" is a word used to describe an observable set of actions a person engages in when we call him angry. Now, to many of us, there is more to human intelligence than a set of mathematically measurable actions, and there is more to anger than empirically observable behavior. Intelligence, we think, for most of us, is viewed as a power within us whereby we know, and anger is, for most of us, viewed as an appetite which causes us to feel dislike and a desire for revenge. Moreover, we think that most of us would say that we "experience" our intellectual power and our anger. We do not experience these directly through our external senses, but we experience them, nonetheless. And much in the same sense we experience people to be kind or nasty, generous or stingy, magnanimous or petty.

The problem we seem to be faced with, then, is this. To us the reality of ethics rests upon the reality of a power psychology. Ethics appears to us to be misunderstood today, not because there is anything unreal about ethics, but because we have been trying to observe this subject from the wrong perspective. In order for us to re-establish the worth of this subject, we think it is necessary for us to appreciate, once again, in the history of ethics the need for a power psychology.

Now suppose what we are saying be correct. Suppose we are right in claiming that contemporary philosophy cannot observe ethical behavior, cannot recognize it, because it tries to approach this behavior from a perspective which is totally blind to it. What makes us so sure that there is any way of observing reality other than by means of our external senses and scientific instruments? Well, it seems to us that if we do not admit this we become confronted with a host of problems. For even the simple observations of science are not so simple. They require the use of memory. Even the grasping of a simple sentence requires that we recall the first part of the sentence when we come to hear the last. But we do not apprehend our memories by means of our external senses. In addition, in the act of sensation our organs do not directly do the sensing. They are instruments of sensation. Thus even when they are being acted upon by external stimuli, we are not aware of this unless we turn our attention to sensation. If we should be under hypnosis, or should we just plain not be paying attention, the stimulus goes unnoticed. And what about organ transplants? If the act of perception were the property of the organ, how could one be fitted with artificial organs which are able to renew the activity in the subject which had the deficient organ? Moreover, unless one says that one has the power to see, how can one say that one sees? Does one say the person in question is doing what he has not the power to do? This hardly seems intelligible. When you come right down to it, unless we admit the reality of powers in things how can we ever talk about anything doing anything?[10] If, for example, John has not the power to see, or to think or to hear, to what are we attributing the activity when we say that John sees, thinks or hears? How can John see, stop seeing, and see again unless when the act of seeing disappears from John the power to see remains in him? And if the power should not remain within him, how can these intermittent activities be attributed to a common subject?

Beyond all this, how can we explain the existence of science itself without a power psychology? Where does science exist? Is it not a human activity? St. Thomas would consider science to be a habit of a power called the "intellect."[11] Now, if there be no power called the human intellect, to what does science belong?

Clearly, one cannot say that science belongs to people because people _commonly agree_ that science belongs to people. Nor can one rationally contend that science belongs to people because people _say_ it belongs to people. Views like these make no more sense than the view that people possess the activity of hearing because people _commonly agree_ that the act of hearing belongs to people, or because people _say_ it belongs to people. And the reason why such views make no sense is clear -- common agreement and verbal attribution are incapable of causing the activities in question. Hearing and science are activities performed by humans. As such, they must belong to human beings. And they can only belong to human beings to the extent that they are caused by human powers.

Well, if such be the case, how can moral activity belong to human beings, how can it be a human activity, unless it issues from a human power? Surely, it cannot. There simply seems to us to be no way to establish the existence of a reality like moral activity without a power psychology.

Of course, we are well aware of the fact that many modern and contemporary philosophers have attempted to deal in their own ways with some of the problems we raise here. In pointing out these problems we are not saying that ways of looking at the world might not be devised to answer some of these objections we raise. We just have not found any which we consider worthwhile. And we find that most of these responses come from thinkers who look at the method of experimental science as the only method of apprehending reality. In our

"Introduction," we pointed out that we think this procedure is absolutely wrongheaded and, consequently, many of these responses which, in and of themselves, appear to us to be weak, appear even less strong when viewed as logical outgrowths of this kind of context.[12] Finally, we think that the moral doctrine of St. Thomas is among the best arguments we have for the superiority of the traditional approach to the study of ethics over the modern approach. We will let the reader be the judge, after having finished reading this work, whether or not St. Thomas had a method of observing reality which escaped the vision of modern science.

Power and Instinct

Now, if this notion of power be so important to understanding St. Thomas's moral teaching, to what does it refer? Well, to tell the truth, the notion is not easy to elucidate, but in a rather vague way of putting it, St. Thomas understands by a "power" what many of us today would understand by a "conductor." That is, a power is a principle or source of an operation.[13] It is what we, also, might today call a "force." In the case of human beings, it is a force which, in most cases, operates in conjunction with an organ, and the power may be either receptive or active.[14] Of course, this might sound confusing, so let us give an example to make our point clear. Sight, for St. Thomas, is a power which has the eye as its organ. It is the power through which we engage in the act of seeing. So it is a power which becomes operative, that is, it is a causal force which is brought into act, when in conjunction with its organ (the eye), it is presented with a stimulus or an input which, in a sense, "turns it on." Insofar as it can receive and conduct the stimulus or input which makes it operative, it is being acted upon; it is passive. Insofar as it is made operative by the input it conducts, when once the input is received, the power is active. Or to put it in another way, active powers resemble tubes in a T.V., or electrical wires, inasmuch as they can cause actions to occur, but only with the help of some electrical input being received into themselves.

Aside from the concept of a power, there is another concept which is essential to understand if one wishes to comprehend St. Thomas's moral teaching. The concept to which we are referring is what today we call an "instinct" (inclinatio).[15] And what he is referring to is this. Powers, by virtue of the organs through which they operate, and for other reasons

which are not necessary for us to go into, because they are
not needed to grasp the point and may only tend to confuse,
are limited in what they can do.[16] The organ acts as a conductor for the power, and what the power can do is limited
by the organ. Thus by sight we can see, but we cannot breathe.
We need lungs for that. Furthermore, in addition to the
limitation found within the power, there is, also, found what,
today, we might call a "tropism." That is, there is an unconscious and spontaneous gravitation or attraction within
the power to respond to the stimulus which activates the
power. And this spontaneous gravitation, as something akin
to a magnetism within a power being conducted by an organ, is,
like the power, limited in its attraction, and in its response,
by its organ.[17] Thus the power of sight gravitates towards
light as the stimulus towards which it responds, but in doing
so it gravitates towards light according to the ability of
its organ, the eye, to conduct light to the power. The organ
has a range of receptive ability for light beyond which it
cannot be taxed. It is receptive to light within certain
limits. Too much light will destroy the eye. Thus the magnetism within the power is attracted towards light according
to the receptive range and condition of its organ, and it is
repelled by the activating stimulus when this exceeds the
limits of its organ or power.[18] So, in short, an instinct
is much like the attracting and repelling force within magnets.
And, we submit, it is something we <u>observe</u> to be present
within things, except that it is a <u>magnetism</u>, in the case of
human beings, which we observe to be present within living
powers. And we think, moreover, that we have as much evidence
to claim that we observe such an attracting force to be present
within things we call organs, like our stomachs in their attraction for food, as the empirical scientist has the evidence
to claim he observes the reality of attracting and repelling
forces to be present in lifeless magnets or in falling bodies.

The Order Called "Creation"

Another way of understanding St. Thomas's notion of power
and his view that one kind of power can be superior to another
can be attained by taking a look at St. Thomas's view of reality
from top to bottom, rather than from bottom to top, the way we
have been doing. Looking at it in this way, we can easily see
that, for St. Thomas, reality is an order. (For St. Thomas
an order exists whenever a multiplicity of beings hold positions
of varying closeness and distance to one and the same point.)[19]
The common point to which created beings hold relations of

varying degrees of proximity and distance within this order is, of course, for St. Thomas, God.[20] And what acts as the foundation of the varying relations of creatures to God is God's support of the world through His causality.[21] So, we may say that, for St. Thomas, reality is a causal order.

When he tries to express what he means by "God," St. Thomas refers to God as <u>ipsum esse per se subsistens</u> (the subsisting act-of-existing itself).[22] Upon hearing this some readers might be prompted simply to close this book and to go on to something intelligible. But if they will simply bear with us for a moment we think we can give them some idea of what St. Thomas has in mind when he speaks in this way. Imagine for a moment an electrical force. Whenever we experience electricity we experience it through some medium or conductor, like copper wires, water, appliances, tubes, and so on. Well, God, for St. Thomas, resembles an electrical force which needs no conductor to support His existence (<u>esse</u>). He is a self-conducting act.[23]

Everything other than God, on the other hand, exists by means of a force, which St. Thomas calls its act-of-existing (<u>esse</u>), which is not a self-conducting act.[24] But what kinds of things are there other than God, and what does it mean to say that these kinds of things exist by means of an act which is not self-conducting? Well, some of the other kinds of things which exist we have already mentioned, namely, elements, composites, plants, animals, and humans. In addition to these, the only kind of real being needed to complete the population of St. Thomas's created order is the angelic being. Of course, many contemporary readers might prefer that we omit angels from our description of St. Thomas's created world. Unhappily, despite the bad press they have been getting lately, we simply cannot leave them out. St. Thomas did consider them to be real, and even though this might offend the sensibilities of some contemporary readers, we think that by taking a look for a moment at St. Thomas's understanding of angels, we can more easily explain to our readers St. Thomas's overall view of reality.

The real order, for St. Thomas, consists of seven kinds of beings arranged in a hierarchical order according to their power to exist on their own. God is at the top because He is the force which causes all others to be by supporting them in existence. He is the only being in reality who is an act-of-existing which is self-conducting. Just below God in this order lies a series of specifically distinct beings, angels, which receive their existence from God. To understand why St. Thomas considers angels to be superior in existence to beings below them, all one need understand is that their superiority lies in the resemblance their kind of existence has to the kind of existence possessed by the most perfect being in reality, that is, to the kind of existence possessed by God.

Well, just what kind of existence resembles God's in this way? To explain this let us, once again, make an analogy. Imagine, one more time, an electrical force. This time, however, instead of imagining it as self-conducting, imagine it to be received into an appliance. The appliance we have in mind is one which needs electricity to operate, but it is different from the ordinary, run of the mill, everyday appliance. For once it receives an initial electrical impulse, the electrical force within it can never be lost. An angelic nature is a being like this. It is a being which receives its act-of-existing from God. There is nothing within it which can ever cause it to lose its existence, however. It has within itself only a power to exist. It has not within itself a power not to exist. It is not self-conducting with respect to its act-of-existing because its conducting power is other than the force which causes it to exist, but once it does exist there is no deficiency within its conducting power which can cause it to lose existence.[25] So, unlike an ordinary appliance, there are no tubes or wires within an angelic nature, which can wear it out or break it down in its continual reception of existence from God.

Beings below angels in the order of reality are, like angels, not self-conducting in their existence, but, unlike angels, there is something within the nature of these beings which can dissipate their conductive capacity. What this something is, is matter. St. Thomas looks at matter as a king of secondary conductor which exists through a primary conductor, which he calls a "form." If the form of a thing be a perfect conductor, as in the case of angels, then there is no need for that thing to have a secondary conductor, that is, matter, to assist in the conduction of that thing's existence. Unlike the form, which is a power to conduct existence, matter is a power to conduct form, and, unlike form, which only can be, matter can cease to be.[26]

The first of those beings below angels in existence are human beings. They are inferior to angels inasmuch as humans are material. Being material they are not perfect conductors of their act-of-existing.[27] They need matter to be able to receive existence, but, for St. Thomas once they receive existence, like angels, the forms they possess become complete in their own conductive capacity, and cannot lose their act-of-existing.[28] The form of a human being is not the same as a human being. It is the soul of a human being.[29] A human being is what results from the joining together in existence of a living, intelligent form and a matter capable of supporting living, intelligent life. A human being, for St. Thomas, can lose its existence, and this makes a human being inferior to an angel. But a human being has within itself a force which can exist on its own when its physical existence is lost.[30] So, in this respect, the existence of a human being more closely resembles the way God exists than does the existence of animals, plants or composites.

One way in which, we think, we can easily come to understand St. Thomas's view of human nature is by comparing his view to the view of Plato. One might say that up to St. Thomas's time the Platonic view of a human being, largely because of the respect St. Augustine had held for Plato, had dominated the Christian West. Now, while St. Thomas was a great respecter of St. Augustine, he thought there was something basically wrong with Plato's view that a human being is a mind whose only connection to the body lay in operation.[31] That is, the way St. Thomas understood Plato, Plato thought that a human being to be a mind which is related to its body as a motor. For Plato the unity which joins together mind and body is not a unity of existence, but a unity of operation.[32] For St. Thomas, such a union is insufficient. A real unity between mind and body, according to St. Thomas, must be a unity in existence rather than a unity in operation.[33] For unless there be such a real union, St. Thomas thinks, for instance, it would be impossible for Plato to consider sensation as natural to man, since sensation requires a body. But if a human being should be considered to be a disembodied mind what need would it have of sensation?[34] Indeed, a human being would become what St. Thomas would call an "angel."[35]

While St. Thomas disagrees with the view of Plato regarding human nature, he is somewhat sympathetic to Plato. He thinks that Plato went wrong not in his view that a human being is an intellectual substance. He thinks Plato went wrong in considering a human being to be a complete intellectual substance. St. Thomas thinks that a human being is an intellectual form, or a mind, but an incomplete one. So, to be complete in its nature, a human must have a body joined to its form.[36]

For St. Thomas the only way a form can conduct the act-of-existing is if that form is complete as a conductor. The form of a human being, however, is incomplete as a conductor. Hence it needs matter to be joined to it in existence so as to make it complete as a conductor. Once a human being exists this conductive completeness immediately ensues and the body is no longer needed for the soul to remain in existence.

To put all this in another way, in a person neither the soul nor the body is complete. A human person is what results from the joining together in existence of an intellectual soul and a matter capable of sustaining intellectual life. In a human being the soul conducts the act-of-existing to the body. The body does not conduct the act-of-existing to the soul. For this reason the body depends upon the soul for its existence as a living human body, but the soul does not depend upon the body for its existence as a soul. In the person the body is joined to the soul not to enable the soul to exist as a soul. It is joined to the soul so that the soul might become __complete__ as a human soul, because the body provides the soul with the means whereby the soul can engage in operations which make it a complete intellectual substance. That is, a complete intellectual substance is a substance which is not merely capable of engaging in awareness. It is a substance which __is__ actually aware.[37] Much like a complete power to see is one which actually does see. But one could imagine such a power to see being able to exist, but never becoming operative because some obstacle stood in the way of its apprehending its appropriate stimulus. Well, if one could envision a human soul prior to its being joined together in personal existence with a body, the human soul would pretty much resemble the power to see which is not operative because of some obstacle standing in its way. And in this way man is unlike the angel. By their very nature, St. Thomas thinks, angels possess objects of awareness, much like, for Plato, human beings have a natural awareness of forms. But human beings, St. Thomas thinks, must gravitate outward beyond their souls to find objects which are capable of activating awareness within their souls. The only way a human being can do this, however, is with a body. So a human being must either possess a body, which is an organ suitable for acquiring the objects of intellectual activity, or he must remain forever devoid of awareness.[38]

The Order within the Person

Thus far within this chapter we have been emphasizing the importance of the notions of power and instinct for understanding the moral teaching of St. Thomas. Within the last section of this chapter we examined St. Thomas's view of creation in order to introduce another element into our explanation of St. Thomas's moral teaching. That element is the notion of "order." For St. Thomas the nature of a thing is its distinguishing power. It is that which locates that thing on one level of reality or another. The nature, in addition, is the generating cause of the powers and instincts within a thing. For St. Thomas within every kind of power there is an instinctive drive to exercise its activity. That is, every kind of power within reality spontaneously strives to exist in act and to maintain itself in act. It seeks, in other words, its own mature and complete development as a power. Furthermore, as we have already pointed out, the powers which are found within reality are of diverse kinds. Some, like elementary natures, can act in only one way. Others, like human natures, can engage in a variety of operations. What makes this possible is that the power which is the human soul generates within the human body an order of sub-powers. That is, the way the human soul follows its instinctive drive to exercise its own activity is by generating within the person a set of powers which are instinctively subservient to the existence in act of the person. These sub-powers which are generated by the soul, like all powers, possess instinctive drives. And, like all instincts, these drives exist for the preservation and completeness in operation of their powers.[39] The point, however, is that the instincts which exist within the sub-powers of the soul strive not only to maintain their powers in act, but they, also, strive to adhere to the order of priority established within these sub-powers by the soul.[40] Thus, for St. Thomas, man's soul operates on the human body on three hierarchically ordered levels. Every human being has a power to live, a power to sense, and a power to understand.[41]

How well these powers are exercised by us varies, but most of us, we think, would agree we all possess these powers. And, we think, most of us would agree that each of these powers operates within certain limits, and that each power has a tendency to operate in a certain way. Our vegetative power, for instance, itself a sub-power of the soul, is divided into its own sub-powers of nutrition, growth and reproduction.[42] Our sense power is divided into the internal sense powers (consisting of powers like imagination and memory) and the external powers (consisting of sight, hearing, smell, taste and touch).[43] And our intellectual power is divided into the active intellect and the power of understanding.[44]

On the vegetative level we do not teach ourselves how to grow or how to consume food. On the sense level we do not teach ourselves how to see, how to hear, how to imagine or how to remember. <u>We know how to do</u> all these things by the spontaneous inclination inherent within our powers. And we do not teach ourselves to tend to value one power over another, but we tend to do so nonetheless. Thus we tend to be willing to sacrifice an organ to preserve a power, and to sacrifice a power to preserve our person.[45] No one teaches us to do this. We tend to act this way instinctively.

The human person is thus composed of an order of powers, not of just one power. The instinctive drive on the part of the human being is to maintain <u>itself</u> in existence. Now, for St. Thomas, this means that a human being has an instinctive drive not simply to exist, but to exist <u>as a human being</u>, that is, by maintaining itself in existence through the most suitable ordering of all of the powers at its disposal. And this is true not only of human beings, but of all living things.[46] A plant, for instance, has an instinctive drive to live like a plant, not like a stone or a Washington bureaucrat. This means that there is an unconscious drive within a plant to stay in existence as a plant by exercising all of the powers in its possession in an order most suitably disposed for the maintenance of a well-developed plant life. And the same can be said of an animal. An animal unconsciously develops certain powers and instincts by which it is enabled, more than is a plant, to be the initiating cause of a variety of operations, to influence others by its own initiative, and to be less likely, than is a plant, passively to suffer from the adversities of external circumstances. This is true in fact, however, only to the extent that the animal exercises its powers and instincts in an order which gives priority to its sense powers and sense instincts in the initiation and direction of its operations.

Most of us, we think, recognize this. It is for this reason that we do not bury Fido in the back yard and water him periodically, and we do not walk our plants on the end of a leash every morning and evening. For Fido to thrive as a dog he has to do more than vegetate; he has his best shot at living a good dog-life by not confusing himself with a petunia. It would, therefore, not be in his best interests for Fido to use his vegetative powers to be the ultimate initiator and director of his choices and of his destiny. Hence Fido instinctively subordinates his vegetative powers and appetites to his sense powers and appetites. Well, the same is true, <u>mutatis mutandis</u>, of human beings. With respect to the initiation and direction of their choices and their destinies, all human beings have an instinctive drive to subordinate their vegetative powers and appetites to their sense powers and sense appetites, and their sense powers and appetites to their intellect and will.[47] Fido pursues and avoids things because he finds them pleasureable or painful, useful or useless, not because he finds them true or false, or judges them to be good or bad. But human beings instinctively tend to initiate and direct their choices on the basis of deliberative decisions, not merely of utility, pleasure and pain, but of right and wrong, good and evil. Thus the mere sight of something does not incline us to pursue or to avoid it, nor does the sight of it plus the knowledge that it is pleasureable or painful. What initiates our decision to flee or to remain is the knowledge that it seems good or bad, or right or wrong, to stay or to go.[48]

This power within the person to initiate and to control his choices and to work out his destiny through his own deliberation causes the human person to occupy the top position within the physical universe of St. Thomas.[49] This, however, can only be clearly understood when it is viewed within the context of St. Thomas's views of power, instinct, order and creation. For within this context one can appreciate the fact that St. Thomas is singling out superiority in freedom as the mark of superiority within the order of the universe.[50] Hence, to sum up the point of this chapter, the human person occupies the apex of creation because of the presence within the human person of a power whereby he surpasses all other physical beings in his freedom. And this, moreover, is the mark, for St. Thomas, of the moral character of human life.

CHAPTER 2

THE NATURE OF MORAL ACTIVITY

It is one thing for us to say that, for St. Thomas, it is the presence of a power within the human person by which he surpasses all other physical things in his freedom which gives to human life its moral character. It is quite another thing to try to show why, for St. Thomas, the moral life is the free human life. Part of the problem lies in trying to understand what is meant by the word "moral." We use this word a great deal, but very often with not too much clarity. Most often, we think, the word is used, today, to refer to right human behavior, or to human behavior which is worthy of praise or of approval. Now, for St. Thomas, the word "moral" does not mean right human behavior, nor does it mean human behavior which is worthy of praise or of approval. And the fact that the word does not have this meaning for him is, perhaps, one of the most important things to recognize for someone who wishes to understand St. Thomas's view of morals. St. Thomas would find no problem, for instance, in talking about murder as a "moral activity," but, in the ordinary way we use the word, today, if someone were to say that murder is a "moral activity" we would be prone to consider him to be a screwball. So, because of the difference in the way we commonly understand the word "moral," today, and the way St. Thomas understood this word, we had better get some sense of what St. Thomas understood this word to mean before going into explaining why the moral life is the free human life.

So what is it, then, that St. Thomas means by the word "moral"? To what does it refer? Well, St. Thomas is pretty clear in his Summa theologiae about what he understands to be signified by the word "moral." In the First Part of the Second Part of this work, St. Thomas says that the word mos is the Latin equivalent of the Greek words ĕthos and ēthos. That is, the one Latin word, mos, translates two Greek words (one with a short e and the other with a long e), one which refers to custom (consuetudinis), and the other which refers to a natural or quasi-natural inclination (inclinatio) to some action. In this latter sense, Thomas states that brute animals are said to have "morals." And it is from this latter sense of the word that St. Thomas understands moral virtue to be signified.[1]

27

The extended use of the word "moral," extended to apply both to animal actions and to virtuous actions, is something which might strike the contemporary reader as peculiar. Yet we think that St. Thomas's wide use of the word "moral" here can be understood when one recognizes what St. Thomas intends to be meant by the word "natural."

For St. Thomas the nature of a thing is the distinguishing characteristic, or essence, of some thing insofar as this distinguishing characteristic, or essence, moves its subject to action. In moving a subject to action the nature of a subject inclines, or bends, the action of a subject in a certain direction. So, for St. Thomas, the word "natural" refers to that which agrees, accords, or to put it a little more colloquially, "heads in the same direction," as the direction established in a subject by some nature. Natural actions are, thus, actions which are put into movement by some nature, and which, while being put into movement by some nature, are caused by the nature to head in a certain direction. Or, to put it in another way, natural actions are actions which agree with the direction caused in a subject through its nature. And the direction which natural actions possess, to some extent, therefore, manifests the directing activity within the subject in its nature.[2]

An example of a natural agent, for St. Thomas, would be something like an element, or a stone, or a plant. For St. Thomas every physical thing which exists has within it a starting point, or source, of movement or change, which sets boundaries, and establishes an order of development for the kinds of actions in which a thing can engage. This principle is, once again, a thing's nature. Elements, for instance, can act together to generate stones. Stones, in turn, have within them a nature which causes them to maintain themselves in existence as stones, and to resist decomposition into their elements. This same nature, so to speak, holds stones together, and determines what stones can do, how they can do what they do, determines what can be done to stones, and how what can be done to stones can be done to them. (Thus stones, when dropped from the hand, fall to earth, not through custom, but because the nature of the stone establishes within the stone a receptive capacity to respond to the pull of gravity.)

Or take an apple tree, for example, or an animal. An apple tree is headed in a certain direction by its nature. It is headed in the direction of growing apples. And animals are headed, by nature, in the direction of being animals. And both apple trees and animals are directed to mature operation according to an orderly development of parts. In addition, both of them agree with, or follow, the direction in which they are headed by their natures when they perform the respective functions they are bent by nature to perform. But an apple tree cannot agree with its nature by some internal propensity to follow this push of nature. It cannot bend, lean or dispose itself in the direction of following its nature because it has no alternative open to it.[3]

Such is not the case for animals or for people, however. To some extent, by comparing alternative courses of action open to them, and by deciding to follow one course rather than another, both animals and human beings can direct themselves to follow the directives of their natures. In a manner similar to plants, both human beings and animals, by nature, possess tendencies, or "instincts," to direct their activities in definite ways. A tendency like the instinctive drive to pursue food, to avoid pain, to grow, and so forth are examples of natural tendencies. We possess these tendencies "by nature." That is, we are born with them as drives within our powers. We do not possess them by some decision on our part that we would like to have them. (In this sense, they are absolute. Like them or not, we are stuck with them.) But, in addition. to such tendencies there resides, to some extent, within both animals and humans a tendency to direct themselves in the way they follow their natures. Apple trees do not decide how they are going to follow the directive of their natures to grow apples, but it is characteristic of humans and of animals to direct themselves to follow the directives of their natures by some sort of decision.[4]

A natural activity, then, for St. Thomas, is an activity which agrees with a natural instinct. A moral activity, on the other hand, is a special type of natural activity. It is an activity which agrees with a natural instinct, but which does so by some sort of decision on the part of the agent as to how it will agree with its instinct. Since such a type of decision-making process is present within both animals and humans, St. Thomas thinks the word "moral" can, to some extent, be applied both to animals and to humans.[5]

Now does this mean that, for St. Thomas, animals can, properly speaking, be called "moral agents"? No, it does not. In fact, St. Thomas goes so far as to claim that, "...moral acts and human acts are the same."[6]

But how is this possible? How, on the one hand, can St. Thomas hold that the word "moral" can refer both to brute animals and to virtue, and, on the other hand, hold that moral acts are human acts?

Well, the answer to the above question seems to be this. As St. Thomas sees it, the more an individual is capable of directing itself in the way it follows activities initiated by its own nature, the more an individual is capable of shaping the character of the way it responds to its own natural direction, the more it is proper to call its action "moral." This, in turn, means that the more an action withdraws itself from dependence upon factors external to an individual's own ability to initiate and to direct its own response to its own natural activity, the more such an action can properly be called "moral."[7]

This, then, is the reason St. Thomas can use the word "moral" to apply both to brute animals and to virtue, and, at the same time, he can say that moral acts are human acts. For by moral acts St. Thomas means nothing less than "free acts."[8]

And by free acts St. Thomas means acts which are self-initiated, self-directed and self-mastered. That is, free acts are acts which an agent, by virtue of some power within itself, directs to agree with the directives of its nature. Since both animals and humans can, to some extent, decide to direct their actions to follow the bent of their natures, to some extent both animals and humans are free.[9]

As St. Thomas sees it, however, freedom is more fully realized within humans than it is within animals. The reason for this is that it is by virtue of reasoned choice that humans bend their actions to agree with the bent of their nature, whereas when an animal pursues something it perceives, in some way, to be agreeable to its nature, it does so, for St. Thomas, by a type of spontaneously derived decision.[10]

So, for St. Thomas, the word "moral," or "ethical" is what he would call an "analogous term." That is, it is a word which is used in an analogous way to refer to some characteristic, feature or reality which can be present in different kinds of things in varying intensity, but which is most fully realized in one kind of being rather than in another.[11] For St. Thomas the words "moral" and "ethical" refer to special types of natural acts which are bent by an agent into agreement with its instincts. Now, since among all the creatures in the physical universe the human being is the one which most stands out as "master of his own acts" par excellence, it is, therefore, to human beings that St. Thomas principally and primarily attributes the words "ethical" and "moral."[12]

Distinguishing a Moral Act -- Its Source:
Reason and Will

Having identified moral acts with human acts, it becomes necessary at this point to explain more fully what it is which gives to acts the character of being human. Human acts are acts performed by humans, of course. But are all acts performed by humans human acts, or are only some acts performed by human beings human acts? All this seems rather puzzling. So perhaps we had better consider for a moment what we mean by action, and then we might understand more clearly what St. Thomas means by human acts.

Think of some action, any action, something like talking or building, or pitching a ball. What is going on? Some sort of movement, right? But what sort of movement? What is it that makes the sort of movement we call "pitching" to be pitching? Do we call someone a "pitcher" if he habitually misses something at which we see him throwing? Not usually, but it really depends upon who is throwing, and upon whether or not he is aiming at the object at which he is throwing. Suppose, for instance, you happened to come across someone tossing a baseball at an object a few feet away, and he kept missing it, over and over again, by just a few inches. Would he be pitching _at_ it? Perhaps. But suppose that person were a famous ballplayer, like Nolan Ryan, for example. What would you say then? Would the action be one of pitching _at_ the target or pitching a little _away_ from it? Well, it seems likely in this situation that the latter would be the case. But the easiest way to tell would be to ask the pitcher. He would be the only one who would know with absolute certainty because he is the only one who knows what he is aiming to do.

Or take another example. Suppose you were to come across two people who looked like they were fighting with one another. How would you know they were fighting and not just fooling around? If you were to come in in the middle of the apparent dispute, you would have some difficulty determining this, would you not? But suppose you came in at the beginning or at the end. Most of the time it would be easier to figure out what was going on, would it not? Why is this? Is it not for the simple reason that there are three elements which are involved in action. One is the thing which acts. The second is a movement proceeding from the thing which acts. And the third is the thing in which the movement terminates. Thus the action called pitching involves a person causing a ball to move toward something. If any one of the three be missing, the target, the pitcher, or the ball in movement, one might have something resembling pitching, one might even call it "pitching," but one would not, in a complete sense, be describing the action which is usually signified by us when using this word. We would be using the word in an unusual or extended sense.

The point we are trying to stress here is that a movement starts to become definite to us, to be distinguished by us, and to be made intelligible to us as one kind of action rather than another, only to the extent that we know both the source of the change and the terminating point of the change. So something like the movement of fire becomes intelligible to us as the action of heating only when there is a recipient of some force proceeding from the fire, be it air, water, a person, or something else. Thus any action can be considered from the perspective of the one who initiates the action or from the perspective of the one in whom the action is realized. Hitting can be the movement of the hitter or the movement of the thing hit. Heating can be the force emitted from the fire or the change being effected in the recipient of heat. But the point is that to gain the most complete understanding possible of the nature of an action, one needs to know both the source of the movement and the terminating point of the movement.

When we relate what we have been saying about action to human action, it becomes clear that an action becomes intelligible to us as human to the extent that we know the source of human action and to the extent that we know the terminating point of human action. Now it is obvious that the source of human action is a human being, but what is it about actions proceeding from human beings which causes us to distinguish them as human? And what is the terminating point of human action?

Perhaps by giving an example we might better be able to answer these questions. Suppose, instead of talking about human action, we talk about police action, or military action, or nightclub action for that matter. What are we talking about? Breathing? Talking? Walking? No, it does not seem so. Well, all these are parts of police action, and military action and nightclub action. Why not distinguish these actions by these movements then? The answer seems to be that the actions of talking, walking and breathing do not, in and of themselves, enable us to distinguish military action, police action and nightclub action, one from another.

So, when talking about the latter kinds of action, we are talking about actions which proceed from a power or characteristic which is present only in one person, or in one group, and not in another. Thus police or military action would involve characteristic behavior proceeding from people acting by virtue of some specially vested authority and involving some kind of subject which can come under the influence of such behavior. And nightclub action would describe characteristic ways of behaving which are engaged in by people who frequent nightclubs. Of course, once again, one could use these words, "police action," "military action," and "nightclub action" to describe entirely different things from what we have been describing.

One could, of course, use "police action" to describe baby-sitting, or "military action" to describe playing canasta. The point we wish to make is simply that, while there are a host of ways we can use words, when St. Thomas uses the words "human action" he is using these words in the way we commonly use them to distinguish, and to make intelligible to others, one kind of action from another. That is, in using this phrase, St. Thomas is referring to action which is "distinctively human," to action which proceeds from some power within humans which is not found within animals or plants.

What, then, is human action? Well, from the way St. Thomas talks about it, and from what we have just been saying, human action is an action which belongs to a human being by virtue of some power within the human which is distinctively his. That is, a human action is not just any old action capable of being performed by a human being, like sleeping or eating. Rather, once again, it is an action which is found only in humans, and not in animals or in plants. Consequently, it might help to avoid confusion if, instead of referring to this action as a "human action," we refer to it as a "distinctively human action." This will enable us to differentiate more easily actions which are "distinctively human" from actions which are "performed by humans," but which are not unique to humans by virtue of some particular power possessed by them and not possessed by other beings.[13]

And having agreed upon this use of terminology, when is human action "distinctively human," rather than just an "action performed by humans"? Well, as we pointed out a little while ago, a movement becomes intelligible to us as one distinct kind of action rather than another to the extent that we know both the source of the action and the terminating point of the action. In the case of distinctively human action, St. Thomas tells us that the source of such action is the power of will and of reason.[14] That is, for St. Thomas, the distinguishing mark of human action is self-directed action.[15] It is action which is started by some power within the human person, and which issues towards its completion under the direction of some power within the same person. What enables a human being to dominate his actions, to be master of what he does, is, for St. Thomas, the presence within him of the power of will and of reason.[16] For the power of will and of reason cause some actions on the part of human beings to be more than reflex responses to causal stimuli, and cause the person acting to be able to determine the nature of his action by his own command.

The powers of reason and of will are, like any and every power, caused to be operative by some stimulus other than the power itself. What makes these powers unique is that through them a human being can choose whether or not to pursue that which stimulates his power, or whether or not to engage in the operation activated by the stimulus.[17]

To make some analogies which might make the point clear consider, first, what happens to a flower in the morning when stimulated by sunlight. Why, its petals spontaneously open wide. There is no interruption on its part in its response to the stimulus. That is, it does not wink its petals at the sun, pause, turn away, turn back, open its petals again, just a little bit, and, then, after all this, finally open them wide to the sunlight.

Compare to this the way an animal, a lamb, for instance, reacts to certain stimuli. There are some actions on its part which involve no interruption in its response to a stimulus, the action of digestion or of fighting off disease, for example. There are other actions, however, which can cause an animal to pause slightly and, then, to initiate some action from within itself. Suppose that our lamb be confronted by a wolf. The lamb will first perceive the wolf through the lamb's external senses; then it will try to flee from the wolf. Why does it do this? Because of the wolf's color? No, but the color of the wolf is what causes the lamb to see the wolf. The wolf's color causes an immediate and spontaneous reaction in the animal's sense of sight. But the lamb does not flee from the wolf because it finds his color repugnant or because it finds the noise the wolf makes to be annoying. That is, the wolf's color and sound do not over-tax the lamb's sense powers in the way that a bright light or a loud noise will cause an animal to turn away its head or to cover its ears.

The animal reacts to some stimuli as does a plant, that is, spontaneously. But, unlike the plant, the animal is aware of whether or not the stimulus over-taxes the receptive capacity of its sense powers. A stimulus which does this, the animal finds unpleasant, and avoids simply as unpleasant, that is, as unconducive to its sense powers. The lamb, then, not only sees the wolf's color, but since there is nothing unconducive to the lamb's power of sight in the color of the wolf, there must be something else about the wolf which causes the lamb to flee from the wolf. What the lamb perceives about the wolf is that the wolf is harmful to itself as a lamb. And such a perception is more involved than is the perception that something is pleasant or unpleasant. One perceives a sound as unpleasant or pleasant simply by consciously receiving the sound into the power of hearing. But one perceives something as dangerous by joining to some sense perception, which one finds pleasant or unpleasant, the added feature of being harmful. Thus the latter kind of perception involves a kind of comparison not found on the level of the external sense powers. Hence when the lamb perceives the wolf to be dangerous to itself, there is a momentary pause in its activity. It sees the wolf, hesitates for a moment, and flees.

This, to St. Thomas, suggests that the animal is possessed of a power of estimation which can instantaneously perceive particular things to be fitting or unfitting, useful or useless, harmful or safe. In perceiving something as harmful or safe, useful or useless, fitting or unfitting, the animal makes some instinctive responses. These responses are common to the members of a species and appear to us to be almost programmed. A bird which needs a place to rest will build a nest, and the nests built by the same kinds of birds look pretty much the same. One is not a split-level, another a ranch, a third a cape-cod. The same goes for bees, which nest in places like trees or in the ground, and for ants, spiders and so on. Each can perceive something to be useful, but in responding to a situation which demands some sort of comparison or estimation, their responses are limited to a few standard and highly predictable ways. Furthermore, the more an animal becomes pressed by necessity to respond to a situation of utility or danger the more predictable and standardized its behavior seems to get.[18]

Notice how different is this kind of response from the response found within humans to situations of utility and harm. Human beings, like animals, have some stimuli to which they respond spontaneously, like food in the stomach, or disease in the body. Yet just as animals are able to recognize something in a stimulus, like a pleasant feature, or something useful, which is unrecognizable to the plant, so human beings can recognize features of a stimulus which are unrecognizable to an animal, features like its goodness or evil. Hence, not only do human beings instinctively pause to estimate a thing's utility, or safety, or fittingness, the human being also pauses to figure out in his mind, to deliberate, and to decide upon the most conducive course of action to pursue by relating ideas back and forth within his mind.

An animal will pursue something which it finds conducive to its sense desires, that is, something pleasant. In addition, it will pursue something which it finds conducive to the execution of a desired operation, that is, something useful. It does not pursue these, however, because it has engaged in some sort of sophisticated activity of comparison or relation. That is, instinctively it concludes that something is pleasant, and spontaneously, almost automatically, pursues it, in a way that looks programmed for it. Instinctively, it estimates something to be harmful, and immediately avoids it, in much the same programmed-like way. The ordering of its actions in response to the stimulus does not appear to come from any sort of investigation or process of discovery whereby it decides to position its actions in one way rather than another because it understands that one way of positioning its activities is more conducive to it than is another.

In other words, the immediate and standardized way in which an animal responds to a harmful or unpleasant stimulus indicates that the conclusion to position its actions in one way rather than in another is not arrived at by a process of investigation and discovery. The bird which builds its nest in the way it does orders its activity; it positions its operations. It does one thing, then, another, and another, and so on until the nest is complete. But it orders or positions its activities in the way it does not because it has come to understand by investigation that there is a causal connection between ordering its operations in this way and the production of its nest. It **does not** observe the causal connection.

Human beings, on the other hand, react to a stimulus in a way which indicates that they do understand a causal connection to exist between their experience of the stimulus and the way they position their activities in response to that stimulus, and that they, also, understand what this connection to be.[19]

If you stick your hand out to take away a bone from a dog which is chomping away on the bone, you can more or less predict the dog's reaction. Perceiving the action to be unpleasant or harmful, you are likely to find the dog will leave some teeth-marks in your hand. The same kind of response on the part of a bank executive to a waiter at the Waldorf Astoria under similar conditions would, on the other hand, be less predictable. One would not expect, however, the bank executive to bite the waiter's hand because the banker can recognize things about the waiter's actions which are unrecognizable to the dog. The dog's reaction results from a conclusion on the dog's part, jumped to spontaneously through immediate estimation that the person's action is threatening. The banker's reaction results, also, from a conclusion on his part, but this is a conclusion arrived at with some interruption to consider what the waiter is doing and why he is doing it.

Notice the difference: the dog's reaction is dictated by immediately jumping to the conclusion that the action is not fitting or suitable for it. The banker's reaction is dictated by his own searching within his mind, by his own ability to piece together the parts of the waiter's action in relation to his dinner in order to draw a conclusion from his own mental piece-work. The animal instinctively fits bits of actions together without understanding or seeing _what_ these actions, done in this positional way, or order, contribute to the work as a whole. The human being, on the other hand, recognizes how and why positioning one's actions in a certain way contributes to what is being done. What is distinctive about human action, then, appears to be this. Human beings have a power and an appetite within them whereby, in reaction to certain stimuli, they are able to weigh alternatives before drawing a conclusion as to the most conducive way to position their actions when reacting. That is, they are able to react with reason. Human beings are rational.[20]

Now we realize, in saying this, that the immediate reaction of many readers will be something like, "Oh! sure, humans are rational. Well, I know a lot of people who are not the least bit rational." And we can appreciate why many people would react this way. Nonetheless, we think such a reaction is presumptuous and is an over-reaction to a confused notion of what we mean when calling human beings "rational." When we define something we do not define it in terms of what that thing in fact does. We define the thing in terms of what it uniquely _can_ do. For example, substitute for our definition of a human another fairly popular one, say, that humans are tool-using animals. Well, we know a lot of people who never use tools. And even if they did, would they have to use them every instant of their lives in order to be human? We hardly think so. Hence when we say that something gives human action its distinctive character, what we mean is that human action is unique because it is caused by a <u>power</u> which is found only in certain kinds of living beings which we call "human." Distinctively human action is action which bears the stamp of a power within humans whereby before they decide to react to a stimulus, they hesitate, not just for a moment, but very often for a good long time.

Certainly animals make decisions. They fulfill their wants on the basis of those decisions. But notice how quickly they decide to do what they do. They do not argue with themselves about the various alternatives open to them. They do not debate with themselves about why this way of acting fits better than that. Human beings, on the other hand, compare prospective actions one to another. And they consider the extent to which, more or less, the prospective actions can contribute to the achievement of what they want. No matter what kind of action we are talking about, be it playing a guitar, building a house, hitting a baseball, or just plain thinking about any old thing under the sun, such action is rational to the extent that it employs a power which can put things in one place rather than in another in light of directives arrived at through some such process of comparison.

All human reasoning, in one way or another, involves a power to put things in their proper places, to put things where they belong. Something as simple as hitting a baseball is a rational activity to the extent that the way we position our actions in response to a pitch is a habit developed by our bodies under command of our reason. When we run the bases we put one foot in front of the other. We position the movement of our legs and arms. We go to first base, then to second, then to third, and, finally come to home plate. Something as simple as thinking involves putting ideas together which belong together and separating ideas which do not. That is, thinking correctly involves joining together, through our ideas in the judgments we make, features which exist joined together outside the mind, and not joining together, in the same way, features which do not exist joined together outside the mind.

Now for human beings to be able to position their activities in ways such as we have been describing, they have to have some sense of part/whole relationships. That is, they have to be able to see the bits of action which they are joining together to be related as parts of some bigger plan. It is in light of the bigger plan, of the action to be completed, of the finished whole, that the parts are compared one to another and are judged to fit together or not to fit together. It is in light of the action to be completed that people hesitate and argue with themselves, that they weigh alternatives, develop strategies, seek help from friends, and try to figure out how they should direct their movements to complete the action they desire.[21]

Animals do not direct their behavior on the basis of decisions arrived at the way human directives are derived. Animals do not derive their directives in such a way. When a bird builds a nest it positions its actions the way it does, getting one piece of grass now, then a twig, and so on, because of some spontaneous decision to do so. It does not position its activities in this way because it has figured out through study and investigation that this is a conducive way to piece together the activities in order to get the job done. It does not arrive at this directive because it has figured out through a comparison of their relative merits for contributing to the building of a nest that twigs work better than stones. When did you ever see a bird try to test the suitability of stones for the building of a nest? The bird's behavior is self-directed in the sense that there are commands or directives internal to it in light of which it does its work. The bird is like a human being with amnesia. It knows how to build its nest, but it has no idea how it arrived at the conclusion to build nests the way it does. What is distinctively self-directed or self-mastered about human action, on the other hand, is that the directives which determine the way a person positions his actions in response to a stimulus are directives which are derived by the human being through a process of comparing alternative actions like parts to a whole.[22]

The human being does not have to direct his actions by virtue of an impulse which is just there, commanding him to act. The human being can choose his own directives. He can choose to violate directives he has decided are the only ones which will get him what he wants. He knows more or less where he got his directives. He knows more or less why they contribute to the achievement of what he wants, and what they contribute to the same achievement. Animals know none of these things. Deliberatively derived directives do not impel animals to act; they impel only humans. Only humans engage in moral activity in the sense that they possess a power through which they can choose, on the basis of some comparison as to why they are fitting or suitable, directives which impel them to act. Only human beings can elect to develop a second nature, that is, a series of customary or habitual responses, in light of a power to judge certain actions, more than others, to contribute to the fulfillment of their wants. It is in this sense that human action is self-directed, self-mastered and uniquely free action and animal action is not. Animals order their responses through directives within themselves, but not within themselves as derived by them through a process of comparison which enables them to recognize why these should be followed. Their directives are imposed upon them by an immediate decision of suitability or unsuitability. Thus more than to any other being in the universe self-directed, self-mastered and free actions belong to humans.[23]

The Terminating Point of Moral Action: the Human Good

Having determined what gives human action its distinctive character from the perspective of the agent, it now remains for us to examine human action from the perspective of its terminating point. For, as we said above,[24] a more complete understanding of an action is to be gained by considering that action both from the perspective of its source and from the perspective of its point of termination than from one of these perspectives alone. The initiating source of distinctively human action is, for St. Thomas, the power of reason and of will. It is by virtue of these powers that humans can impel their responses according to deliberatively derived directives. But what is the terminating point of human action? And what does it contribute to our understanding of a moral act?

In order for us to answer these questions it will be necessary for us to consider what St. Thomas means by the word "good." For the terminating point of an action is what St. Thomas would refer to by means of the word "good."

So, then, to what does the word "good" refer? Well, we know this is going to sound silly to some people, but, from the way St. Thomas speaks of the word "good," it seems to us that the word refers to something akin to a spatial notion. That is, when we say that something is "good," it seems to us that the meaning we wish to convey is closer to the type of meaning conveyed by the words we use to give things location in place and position than it is, as many, if not most, contemporary philosophers think, to an emotional or subjective meaning.

When we say a thing is in a certain place, we relate the distance or closeness of the thing in question to the surfaces of the bodies which surround it, and we give to those surrounding surfaces a kind of immobility in relation to the thing in place.[25] Thus we can be riding in a plane going from New York to Chicago, and our place in the plane can remain the same while we go from one city to another. In much the same fashion we can relate the parts of a thing to its surrounding surfaces, and, thereby, we can recognize relations of proximity and distance between those parts and their surrounding surfaces. Hence a person can remain in his room yet he can walk about from one part of the room to the next. In doing this we could say he is in the same place, insofar as the surrounding surfaces, that is, the walls of the room, remain the same. At the same time, he has changed his position in relation to those walls.[26] The relations of proximity and distance which are essential elements of our ideas of place and position are real, but hard to grasp. A person living in California does live farther from New York than a person living in Chicago. And what allows one to locate a thing's distance in relation to these places is the fact that the places remain stable in their distance from one another. If such were not the case, if California and New York were constantly, and at random, shifting their distance one from the other in great amounts, we could never pinpoint more or less just where, at any moment, something moving between these two points happened to be.

Now that which we call "good," we think, fulfills much the same function for the things to which we attribute it as what we call a "surrounding surface" fulfills for place and position. That is, the word "good" establishes a relation of proximity or distance between things by establishing itself as a fixed point in relation to them. Thus, like the terms "position" and "place," we cannot make sense out of the word "good" unless we understand it as an aspect of a thing which sets up some relation between a thing, or parts of a thing, and something else.

But what kind of feature are we talking about in calling something "good"? Well, in a rather vague and general way of speaking, for St. Thomas, the word "good" refers to that which fulfills or completes a power's appetite as the terminating point instinctively pursued by the power. That is, the good is that which fulfills or completes an appetite, striving, pursuit, demand, desire, or the like. Thus it is that which not only terminates a pursuit, demand, etc., but also gives direction to these. And, in this fashion, it resembles for us, as we said above, a spatial notion. The good, for St. Thomas, is primarily a point of fulfillment pursued by some power through its appetite.[27]

So, as far as we see it, when we call something "good," in the most complete sense, we are saying that this thing fulfills or realizes what, in some way or other, is sought after by another as fulfilling for itself. These two aspects, then, being sought after and being fulfilling, seem to complete the notion of the good. Consequently, as we just noted, that which is good not only terminates a striving by fulfilling it, it also gives specific direction and order to the pursuit: specific direction because that which is pursued determines and limits the approaches and options required to be used by the pursuer; and order because the proximity and distance of a thing headed in a specific direction toward a fixed point is determined for that thing by the nature of the point of termination. For example, if someone has a specific desire to become a doctor, if this be that point which will put his desire to rest, the way he positions his actions will be directed by this desired object, and how close he gets to becoming a doctor will be determined by whatever features cause a doctor to be a doctor.

Another way of explaining what St. Thomas understands to be meant by the word "good" would be by saying that, for him, the word refers to that which fulfills a requirement. One need not think of the word as referring only to some conscious act of willing, to something like "getting what you want." For St. Thomas the word "good" can be applied to any kind of situation in which features can be related in such a way that one fulfills another. The good is that which completes that which is receptive to completion, or conducive to it. That is, the notion of completeness, which is essential to anything good, contains within it, cannot be understood apart from, notions like compatibility, suitability and fitness. One thing can complete another, can fulfill it, only because it somehow is compatible with, suitable, or fitting for that other. That which is good, in a sense, then, is that which puts things in their proper places. It fits things together which belong together. Hence it both fits and fulfills whatever, in any way, is conducive to fulfillment.

Certainly we realize that some of our readers might not find our description of the good to be either fitting or fulfilling. Nevertheless, we think this is about as complete as we can be. Concepts like suitability, compatibility, fitness, fulfillment, completeness, etc., are not very exact and clear. So it is easy for us to see why some people would almost automatically relegate these concepts to the area of the subjective. If, however, one will, once again, recall that St. Thomas is working within the context of a metaphysics (sorry, but we just cannot avoid using this word here) and a psychology which considers powers to be real, and which looks at powers much in the same way that we view conducting forces, one should have an easier time understanding the above notions to express realities and not just subjective states. Certain forces are suitable for, fitting, compatible with, fulfilling, etc., for certain powers and not for others; much like a pair of pants fit one person but not another, and one kind of food is conducive, or fitting, for one person's digestive power and not for another's.

Even though we realize that some people might have difficulty accepting the reality of features like the ones we have been describing, we think they have no choice but to do so if they wish to adhere to the reality of moral activity, scientific activity, or to the reality of any human knowledge whatsoever for that matter. To prove this, consider for a moment that the features we have been talking about are features we commonly describe not only in ethical discourse but in other types of discourse as well. We often use the words "good," "bad," "fitting," "unfitting," "fulfilling," "unfulfilling," etc., to describe not only ethical behavior but other kinds of behavior as well. And while it is true that very often we do use these words to refer to things, or to situations, or to statements about which we have some feeling or emotional leaning, we, at the same time, use them to refer to things, situations and statements about which we have no such leaning or feeling. In other words, these terms are not the peculiar property of the jargon of ethics, but they pervade many areas of human discourse. For instance, we often talk about "good books," "bad movies," "suitable responses," "fitting things together," "fulfilling jobs," and "incomplete work." When we use these terms under these circumstances, are we referring simply to our feelings about the subjects themselves? We would say that the latter is the case, and we think that if we restrict the subjects signified by these terms simply to different feelings we cannot account for the impartiability of knowledge of any kind, not just of ethical knowledge.

What we mean by the above statement is this. Human knowledge is a complex operation which involves, at its very core, an ability to isolate, to distinguish, one factual feature from another, and simultaneously in the apprehension of these features, involves an apprehension, by a comparing activity of the mind, of features possessed by things only in relation to other features. To elucidate our point let us examine for a moment what appear to us to be two radically distinct ways in which every human being comes to know. One way is immediate, and presupposes no prior foundation in knowing. And the other way is mediated, and presumes some prior and immediate apprehension of reality. The first kind of knowing is the kind proper to a child when he first passes from not knowing anything to a judgment that there is something which exists which he knows. The second kind of knowing is the kind proper to investigation, experience, study, and learning, and involves a process of reasoning and searching on the part of the knower. The latter kind presupposes the former, and both involve, it seems to us, both a receptive process, whereby features of things are isolated by the mind, and an evaluative process, whereby features are compared one to another.[28]

When a person knows he does so by making a judgment, a judgment which is correct. And prior to making a judgment there is no conscious knowledge in a precise sense. To give an example to make our point clear, consider for a moment an activity as simple as scratching. When does one know that one is scratching? One might be scratching one's face, or hands, or arms without knowing it, but when one says to oneself, "I am scratching myself," one immediately becomes aware of both the idea and the activity. The idea does not come first in awareness, and then the judgment; they seem to coincide.

Thus even the most simple act of knowing involves a complex process of comparison, or a process of evaluation. That is, even the most simple act of knowing requires a recognition on the part of the mind, a simultaneous knowledge, that, in forming an idea or in making a judgment, a person must put the parts of the idea or judgment where they belong; that he must include within his idea only elements which belong there, which are, that is to say, fitting or suitable; and that he must terminate his judgment as a judgment only when he recognizes that the judgment is complete, that is, when he recognizes that there is nothing missing which is supposed to be there.

In every act of knowing, therefore, it appears that there is demanded of the human mind an ability to distinguish and to compare not only the features it grasps, but, also, features of its very act of knowing, as to what belongs and what does not belong, what is suitable and unsuitable, what is complete and what is incomplete. That is, every act of knowing involves the ability to position and to place different elements together in light of some ordering principle. A knowledge of positioning and placement requires a knowledge of distance and proximity to some stable point. When we know something we position or place our ideas in relation one to another. We say to ourselves that these two ideas belong together or that they do not, that they fit or they do not fit.

For example, what makes an answer to a question a good answer? The fact that it fulfills the demands of the question, is it not? Now, when we give an answer to a question, do we not locate the parts of our response in a certain order, putting one part in one place and another part in another? And is not the question itself asked in some sort of orderly fashion? Someone, say, might ask, "Who was the first president of the United States?" And a good answer, an answer we could also call "right," would be, "George Washington was the first president of the Unites States." Suppose, instead of having framed the question in the above fashion, our enquirer had asked, "States of the who was United president?" and our response had been, "The of was United Washington president States." How could we possibly make heads or tails out of what the question or answer meant, and whether or not the answer was right? Unless we know with certainty and immediately that there is a right way and a wrong way to form questions and answers, a good and bad way to construct ideas and to make judgments, there seems to be no way to do this. Knowledge, thus, requires not simply the possession of ideas, it also requires the ability to place those ideas together on the basis of a comparison of the degree to which those ideas are more, less, or equally suitable for each other. It requires that parts of a judgment can be fit together with other parts which are suitable for each other, and are agreeable with what we understand a complete judgment to be. What it means to be complete as a judgment, therefore, dictates how the parts of a judgment can be organized.

We do not want in this work to get involved in a long, drawn-out analysis of the meaning of judgments, ideas and the like. Analyses like these are more properly reserved by philosophers for the study called "epistemology." We have brought up issues like these within the context of our study of the moral act because, according to St. Thomas, to understand any act in as complete a fashion as possible, one should consider the act in question both from the perspective of the power from which it originates, and from the perspective of its point of termination; and because, once again, according to St. Thomas, the point of termination of a human act is something which St. Thomas calls "good," and is something which he considers to be real.

In our own day and age we think that popular opinion and philosophical attitudes might not be able to get a clear grasp of St. Thomas's views because, today, many, if not most of us, tend to make some sort of distinction between "facts" and "values," which is, in a vague and general way, we think, supposed to separate what is studied by science from what is studied by ethics. What we are trying to argue here, in our roundabout sort of way, is that this kind of distinction simply will not stand up. One cannot, that is, say that ethics does not deal with facts or reality because ethical judgments are judgments of value, and that science does deal with facts and reality because judgments of science are not judgments of value. And the reason one cannot say this is because the judgments of both are judgments of value, and are, also, judgments of fact. We would say that the judgments of science are judgments of value because every judgment in some way or other involves a fitting together of parts on the basis of a comparison of their suitability or unsuitability for fulfilling the requirements of a complete judgment. And if value judgments are mere subjective preferences, then it would appear that the death knell has sounded not simply for ethics but for science as well. For science can no more be an impartial observer of facts and reality than can ethics. There is no way, then, it appears to us, that one can disqualify a knowledge of values from the status of being real on the basis of the observations of science. The reality of judgments of science depends upon the reality of judgments of value. The reality of judgments of value does not depend upon the reality of judgments of science.

Having expressed our views about the inability of science to be an impartial and competent judge about the reality of what we call "good," and having explained, as well as we can, what we understand St. Thomas to mean by the word "good," it remains for us to get back to explaining what is distinctive about human action from the perspective of its point of termination. What is it, then, which is instinctively pursued by human beings as their distinguishing human good? Well, whatever it is, it is something which completely satisfies a human being because St. Thomas tells us the good is what puts an appetite to rest. Since, moreover, for St. Thomas, what puts every appetite to rest is the perfect operation of its power, the distinguishing human good should reside in the perfect operation of the human person. That is, whenever any power reacts to a stimulus as something to be pursued, it does so because it apprehends within that stimulus some feature which, in some way, can contribute to maintaining that power in existence in complete operation. And since a human being is caused to be human by virtue of the possession of some distinguishing power within it (as we pointed out in Chapter 1), the maintenance of this power in complete operation would appear to be the distinguishing human good.

The Nature of the Distinguishing Human Good

Such a description of the distinguishing human good, however, appears to be so vague as almost to be meaningless. Besides a lot of people would simply disagree with our claim. After all, it seems we are saying that there is some sort of overriding good pursued by all human beings. Yet, if we look around us, not only do many people appear to pursue many different goods, but one and the same person, at various times, appears to pursue different goods. For example, some people spend their whole life long working to accumulate wealth. Others work to get political power. Still others seek physical pleasures like sex and booze - while others want big reputations - the fame and glory of a movie star, for instance. And one and the same person may at various times, or even at the same time, be pursuing one or more of these goods. And we must admit that each of these has something to say for itself. Why, then, do we claim, with St. Thomas, that the distinguishing good of people is of the same kind for all human beings?

Well, for someone to understand why we hold this it will be necessary for one to recall what we said in the latter part of Chapter 1 about there being an order of powers within a human person.[29] For St. Thomas the person generates an order of sub-powers through the soul. The human person, then, in a rather vague and general way of speaking, is a power instinctively pursuing its own mature and complete development in existence. To develop itself it generates sub-powers which, in turn, have within themselves an instinct for their own mature and complete development in existence. But, in addition, and this is the important point, this instinct within the sub-powers is not only to develop themselves, but, also, to subordinate themselves to the directives of reason. And the power of reason instinctively subordinates itself to the good of the whole person, that is, to the maintenance and preservation of a complete and mature personal life. Not only is there, then, an instinctive subordination of powers within a human being, there is, also, an instinctive subordination of instincts. Thus human beings by instinct subordinate sense organs to sense powers, and sense powers to intellectual powers, and intellectual powers to personal preservation.

To show the truth of this, consider our immediate and spontaneous reaction to the thought of sacrificing our eyes to keep our sight. Our reflex reaction, we think, is that we instinctively value our sight more than our eyes. We would instinctively rather prefer to sacrifice our eyes to preserve our sight than we would prefer to sacrifice our sight to preserve our eyes. And instinctively we intellectually value the power of sight more than any other sense power.[30] Still, we instinctively value sanity more than sight.[31] Our immediate reaction to the thought of giving up one to preserve the other is that we would spontaneously prefer to lose our sight to preserve our sanity rather than to lose our sanity to preserve our sight.

None of this seems to us to be unusual. The organ instinctively subordinates itself to the directives of its appetite; its appetite instinctively subordinates itself to the directives of its power; and the power instinctively subordinates itself to the directives of the person. The organ exists for the good of the appetite; the appetite exists for the good of the power; and the power exists for the good of the person. We have stomachs to fulfill the appetites and powers of nutrition and growth. And we have the powers of nutrition and growth so that we might live as people. We have stomachs to live as people. We do not live as people in order to have stomachs. In short, what every human appetite and power instinctively pursues, aside from its own good, is the subordination of itself to the good of the person. And what this means is that there is one highest good instinctively pursued by all people. That is, if all people exist as people by virtue of the possession by them of the same kind of distinguishing power, and if this distinguishing power generates in them an order of sub-powers, each of which instinctively seeks its own fulfillment, yet, at the same time, instinctively subordinates its good to the good of the whole person, then the good of the whole person is the one highest good instinctively pursued by all people. This good is *most* *wanted* by all people.

But how can we really accept this? How can we claim that all people most want one and the same kind of thing? Well, while we realize that the claim does seem a little outlandish at first, nonetheless, we think it follows. After all, a want one possesses even though one never chose to want it, is a stronger want than one possessed by choice. For it imposes itself upon a person whether one wants to have it or not. Instinctive wants, however, are wants which we have whether we choose to have them or not. Since the good is that which fulfills a want, the highest good is that which fulfills a highest want. Now the want which <u>most</u> imposes itself upon all other human wants, which orders and directs all other human wants (those of sub-powers, and of human choice) to subordinate themselves to it, is the highest human want, namely, the instinctive want of a person to live the life of a complete person.

And while this statement, too, appears somewhat vague, it tells us at least this much. It tells us that there is a kind of good most wanted by all people, and it tells us that this good is not our most wanted good because we choose to have it as our most wanted good. This automatically rules out the possibility that the highest human good, what most of us, in our everyday way of speaking call "happiness," can lie in the possession of wealth, or sex and booze, or reputation, or political power, or any other things like these. For all of these are goods pursued through wants we possess by choice, or are instinctive wants which are instinctively subject to direction by reason and will.

It is not an instinct common to the human species to pursue political power or fame as the greatest want of human life. If people do pursue these goods as goals in life, they do so because they have, through their own free decision, chosen to make these goods to be the goods they most <u>choose</u> to seek after. But what one most chooses to seek after is not one's highest human good. It is one's most highly <u>chosen</u> good, whereas the highest <u>human</u> good is one's most instinctively pursued human good.

No matter what one chooses to set up as personal goals in life, these goals do not eradicate the instinctive goals we all have. And while some people can choose to make other things, like sex, or booze, or wealth, to be their highest goals in life, since each of these is, in a sense, a good pursued by instinct (we instinctively pursue pleasure and bodily goods even though we might not choose to fulfill our sexual instincts, or to drink alcohol, or to amass a great fortune), each of these goods somewhat pursued by instincts is pursued by subordinated instincts. None of us instinctively most wants happiness in order to get sex or wealth. We instinctively pursue the latter in order to get the former. Hence neither can these be the highest human good.

Of course, there may still be some people who are having trouble understanding the justification we have been giving of St. Thomas's view of the distinguishing human good. So, for any of those who may still be lost, let us make the following analogy. Suppose you were born with a set of instinctive urges. You did not choose to have them, but you had them nonetheless. And suppose this set of urges was an ordered set. That is, suppose that one urge was stronger than another, was instinctively wanted by you more than another, and could control, to some extent, the movement of the urge below it. Now suppose the strongest urge you had was to live in Buffalo, New York. You did not decide to choose this place as the only place to live which would completely satisfy your instinctive urge, which would put it to rest, but, still, the most dominant urge you had was to live in Buffalo. In fact, every choice you made, and every other urge you had, was made and had by you so that some day you might live in Buffalo. And while you were born with the urge to get to Buffalo, you were not born with a knowledge of where Buffalo was.

You were provided, however, with a set of compasses of different sizes which were inserted directly into the urges you possessed. That is, inserted into your strongest urge was the largest compass (a will) pointing you in the direction of Buffalo. And inserted into your other urges were smaller compasses pointing you, not in the direction of Buffalo, but pointing you in the direction of things you needed to use to get to Buffalo, or to get to Buffalo more easily. For example, one of these smaller compasses pointed in the direction of obstacles to your journey, and to things you might use to overcome these obstacles if and when you did become confronted by them. Another smaller compass pointed to things you needed to have in order to make the trip, things like money, clothes, food, cars and so on, or to friends, or to the ability to influence others. And still another compass helped you to see, hear, feel, and so on, where you were going.

At the beginning of your journey, and at every point along your journey, you had four choices: 1) to take the trip or not to take it; 2) to let your largest compass be your guide; 3) to ignore the direction of your largest compass and to set out on your own using no compass whatsoever; or 4) to follow the direction of one of your smaller compasses. And whichever choice you made, once it was made, the more difficult it would become to change direction. In addition, if you chose either to ignore the direction pointed to by the largest compass or to follow the direction pointed to by one of the smaller ones, as if these would get you to Buffalo, the longer you did so, the more blurred would become your vision of the direction pointed to by your largest compass. In fact, at some point you would no longer be able to see the latter at all.

Imagine that the first choice you made was to ignore your largest compass, and was to set out on your own. That is, even though you did not know what Buffalo looked like, you decided you did not need this compass. So you set out on your journey and you got lost. Instead of going to Buffalo, you wound up in Beverly Hills, California.

Now what do you do? Do you look at your largest compass? Do you compare the place you are in to the direction pointed to by your biggest compass? Well, perhaps. You might say, "This does look like Buffalo, but I still have this wanderlust." If so, more likely than not, you head out on your own in some other direction. But wait a minute. All is not lost. At this point you recall that your will is not your only compass. You have others, too. You have compasses which point you in the direction of all those things which you need to have in order to make your trip as trouble-free as possible.

After travelling around on your own for a while, you get tired of this. You decide that perhaps you made a mistake. Perhaps instead of going somewhere, all that you wanted more than anything else was to acquire those things you needed to have in order to make a trouble-free trip. Or perhaps you did this right off the bat. That is, perhaps you decided, since you did not choose to go in the direction pointed to by your will, that is, by your biggest compass, that you would simply go about collecting things for your future trip. Consequently, you set about collecting automobiles, and money, and friends, and reputation and power (to get more money and more friends), and so on. And after doing this for a while you decided that you did not choose to have this nagging urge to get to Buffalo any longer to be one of your urges. You chose to have it become something different. Therefore, you decided, by an act of your own choosing, you were going to make some other good be your ultimate good. But no matter how you connived, no matter how much you manipulated, you could not turn this chosen good into your instinctive ultimate good. Your instinctive desire to get to Buffalo simply would not accommodate you. It would not go away.

We think this analogy expresses in a more concrete fashion St. Thomas's understanding of the distinguishing human good. This good, which we call "happiness," is, for St. Thomas, an instinctively sought-after good. It is not a good sought after by choice. We want it whether or not we want to want it. So, much like birds, or lambs, or dogs, or any other living being, human beings have instincts which direct their behavior. What radically distinguishes human action from the action of such animals is not that these animals have instinctive drives and humans do not. What radically distinguishes human action from the action of such animals is that human beings can decide not to follow the direction of their instincts. They can freely choose to go in a totally different direction, or not to go anywhere at all. If a swallow is instinctively directed to go to Capistrano, it goes to Capistrano, at the appointed time, in the appointed direction. But the same thing would not at all be true in the case of human beings. Instincts point powers in the direction of their good. To the extent that we pay attention to the direction in which an instinct points a power, to that extent we know the "right" direction to head in, and we can choose a path which agrees with the direction of our instincts, a path which, thereby, becomes the "right" path. For that which is right is little more than that which is headed in the direction of a striving toward some sought-after point. Since human happiness is what is most pursued by human beings, and since what is most pursued by any power is perfect operation, viewing human beings as kinds of powers, human beings instinctively pursue their own perfect operation as their happiness. And since human beings exercise their operations in a living way, human happiness resides in living a perfect human life.

But what is a perfect human life? Well, it is a life which exercises all of the powers within a human being in accord with their instinctive drive to subordinate themselves to reason, so that human reason might be able to give the best service it can to the maintenance of human life as self-mastered, independent and free. Human happiness, for St. Thomas, is nothing other than the living of a perfectly free human life. And this, as we said at the end of Chapter 1, is what marks human life with its moral character.

Does this mean that, for St. Thomas, human happiness lies in doing as one pleases? No, it does not. And by this time we think that this point should be clear to most of our readers. Today, we tend to understand freedom in a negative way. That is, we tend to consider freedom to lie, in one way of another, in acting without restriction. Thus when we speak of a "free lunch," or a "free admission," or a "free ride," we think of a lunch, or an admission, or a ride which requires no payment. And it seems to us that we tend to look at freedom in this way today because we have lost our sense of the meaning and reality of what St. Thomas calls a "power." For St. Thomas a free act is not an act which is unrestricted. Rather it is an act which originates within the power of an agent, and which conforms with this power's instinctive manner of directing its actions to completion.[32]

For example, if someone were physically to overpower you, to place your hand on a gun, and, then, to pull your finger on the trigger in order to shoot someone, the action could not be called free on your part. Or if, using the same example, you had picked up the gun on your own, and, after having picked it up, someone, then, had forced you to shoot, the action would in one sense have been free and in another would not. What you contribute to an action under your own power and under your own direction is free. What you do not so contribute is not free. For St. Thomas an act is not free because it is without restriction. It is, in some sense, without restriction because it is free. That is, a free act is an act without external and violent restriction. An act which you start, but which you then lose control of, is unrestricted, but is it a free human act? What makes the act free, it seems is that it originates within a power through a command of the power, not from a command outside the power, and that, once originated, this same act is brought to an end under the direction of the power, and not under the direction of some other power. Human happiness, then, does not lie in living an unrestricted life. It lies, for St. Thomas, in living a self-mastered life, a perfectly self-mastered life. To explain how this is done and what it entails will be our project throughout the rest of this work.

CHAPTER 3

MORAL ACTIVITY:

ITS POINTS OF ORIGIN

In our identification of human happiness with the living of the perfectly free human life, we took care to emphasize that by "free" we meant self-mastered. The question which arises now is, "What is meant by a 'self-mastered' human life?"

The answer to this question is not simple, and to give ourselves some foundation from which to start our explanation, let us begin by recalling that, for St. Thomas, moral activity is a special kind of natural activity. It is the natural activity of a moral, or human, being. That is, it is the type of activity performed by a being with a nature, or power, which is inclined to direct its own activities through the deliberative choices of its reason and will.

To understand the acts of any power, however, it is necessary, as we have pointed out in previous chapters, to understand: 1) the point of origin of such activity; 2) the movement which originates from this starting point; and 3) the terminating point of the activity. In this chapter we will give a synopsis of St. Thomas's views on the first of the above points.

What, then, is the point of origin of human activity? Well, it is the nature of a human being. But because a human being has a composite nature, the origin of human activity cannot be simply explained. That is, the origin of human activity resides in a number of co-operative elements. These co-operative points of origin for human activity within a human being are reduced by St. Thomas to the following: 1) powers and appetites; 2) emotions; 3) dispositions; 4) habits; 5) virtues; 6) gifts; 7) law and grace.[1] Each of these plays a role in stamping an action with its moral character.

1. Powers and Appetites

As a natural activity, moral, or human, activity involves moving a subject to act. A study of moral, or human, activity, therefore, must involve what moves a moral, or human, subject to act. What moves a human being to act, however, is human powers and human appetites. A study of moral activity must, therefore, involve, for St. Thomas, a study of human powers and of human appetites.[2]

The human powers and appetites which moral activity involves, for St. Thomas, are powers and appetites which, in some way, come under control of the direction of human reason. For moral activity is distincitvely human activity, and distinctively human activity is activity which occurs under the deliberative direction of human reason. These powers and appetites, then, are the sense powers and sense appetites, and the intellectual power and its appetite, the human will.[3]

a. Sense powers and sense appetites

On the level of sense life St. Thomas understands a human being to be possessed of five external sense powers (touch, taste, smell, hearing and sight) and four internal sense powers (general sense, imagination, cogitative sense, and sense memory).[4] St. Thomas thinks a human being possesses all these powers in order to lead a complete human life. The five external sense powers are not alone sufficient for such a life, for St. Thomas, because, for him, to live a human life it is necessary to apprehend things not only when they are present, but even when they are absent.

A human life, for St. Thomas, is the life of an intellectual being. Without some movement towards that which is absent, he thinks people would never come to know anything, because coming to know begins with that which is absent. To move towards that which is absent requires, however, that people possess faculties for the reception and the retention of absent things.[5]

So, for St. Thomas, to receive sensible features people have the five external senses and the internal, general sense. To retain and to preserve sensible features people have the imagination, which is a storehouse for features received through the external senses and through the general sense. Finally, for the reception of features not attained through the five external senses and through the general sense, people have a cogitative reason, and for the preservation of these features people have a sense memory.[6]

A person, one should recall, is, for St. Thomas, an intellectual substance. A human person is an intellectual substance which achieves complete intellectual life through the activity of reasoning. Reasoning, however, requires comparing. Complete intellectual life cannot be achieved for a human being, therefore, without faculties which enable a human being to engage in the act of comparing.[7]

In addition, as a reasoning being with a living body, complete intellectual life cannot be achieved for a human being without the preservation of one's bodily existence. So, for St. Thomas, to maintain the process of rational investigation necessary for the complete life of a human being, a human being has to be able to compare realities which relate both to his intellectual life and to his personal preservation.[8]

But to be able to do this a human being has to have powers beyond the five external senses. By virtue of the external sense powers people successively apprehend disconnected portions of reality. Through their eyes they see a portion of color at one moment, through their ears they hear a bit of sound the next moment. Now, without some interconnection between these disjointed sensations, how is it possible to compare one color to another, or to compare color to taste, or taste to odor? The answer, for St. Thomas, is that it is not possible. As he sees it, human beings require a general sense and an imagination to be able to make such comparisons. And such comparisons require that there be people in existence to make them. Hence, people need powers whereby they can seek and avoid things which are safe or harmful, pleasureable or painful, useful or useless to themselves as reasoning, living beings. And these powers, for St. Thomas, are the powers of cogitative reason and of sense memory. By virtue of the former a human being is able to compare and to estimate sensible realities as to their utility, advantage, and sensory suitability. And, by virtue of the latter, a human being is able to recall the information reported to it through its cogitative reason.[9]

In addition to the external and internal sense powers, St. Thomas understands human activity to find its origin in sense appetites. For, like all powers, there is present within the sense power an inclination to be receptive to certain activities and to be resistant to other activities.[10] The sense appetite which is attracted to what is conducive to the conducting capacity of the senses, and which avoids what is not amenable to the senses, St. Thomas calls the "concupiscible appetite." (We will refer to this appetite as the "propelling appetite.") The sense appetite which resists whatever is not conducive to its sense power St. Thomas calls the "irascible appetite." (We will refer to this appetite as the "contending appetite.")[11]

b. Intellectual power and intellectual appetite

The powers and appetites we have been talking about above are, for St. Thomas, present not only within humans but also within higher forms of animal life. In both man and animals the sense appetites are triggered into action by the estimative reason (in humans St. Thomas refers to this as "cogitative reason" or "particular reason").[12] Thus in animals the immediate estimation that something is pleasureable or painful, useful or useless, advantageous or disadvantageous, causes a natural response in the animal's appetite. In an animal the appetitive power is the highest court of appeal with respect to whether or not it will respond to a stimulus with one sort of activity or another. In a human being, on the other hand, the appetitive power is subject to another power as to a final court of appeal. In a human being the sense appetite is commanded and directed by reasoning, by comparing particular desires to general considerations.[13]

The role played by the intellectual power in moral activity, then, is primarily one of comparing and commanding. By comparing particular sense desires to some general judgment as to what befits the situation, we direct and control our appetites. The intellectual activity which we employ to move our minds in such comparing activity St. Thomas calls "reasoning." Hence moral activity requires rational activity.[14]

The diversity embraced by reasoning gives to a human being options for action not open to an animal. Similar options are made available to human beings by virtue of the possession of an intellectual appetite, which St. Thomas calls "the will." The sense appetite has no choice but to pursue or to avoid particular objects once they are perceived to be conducive or non-conducive for an animal. The will, on the other hand, is not absolutely determined to choose any particular good. For what triggers the operation of the will is not some sensation of pleasure or pain, or of some perception of utility or advantage.

The human will responds to something in which it finds suitability or fitness much like the eye responds to color. But to such an object the will can respond in at least four ways. It can desire that object or not desire it. It can choose to pursue that object or not choose to pursue it.

About desiring or not desiring an object, the will, then, has no choice, any more than the power of seeing has a choice about whether or not it will respond to light. The will has to desire what reason judges to be good. This is the feature of reality to which it responds: overall fitness, overall suitability. But the will need not <u>choose</u> to pursue that which it desires as fitting or as suitable.[15]

In this respect the possession of a will makes human beings distinct from animals. Animals have no choice but to follow their appetites with regard to what they spontaneously estimate to be useful, or pleasureable or advantageous. The judgment by which a sheep decides to flee from a wolf is not a free judgment, or an act of free choice, because such a decision, or choice, is not the conclusion of a process of rational comparison. And it cannot be the conclusion of such a process of comparison because animals are unable to evaluate fitness or suitability in an abstract way. That is, an animal cannot compare a particular object which it senses to be fitting or suitable in some particular way to some overall notion of what it understands the word "suitable," or "fitting," to mean. For it lacks the ability to abstract its sense awareness and its desire from the particular situation. A human being, on the other hand, can calm himself down, or can arouse his appetites, by relating his sense awareness and his particular desires to some abstract awareness and desire. Thus, by reasoning things out, a human being can alter his appetites and his choices.[16]

The human will, therefore, is not determined to choose any particular thing which it judges to be good because rational choice (<u>electio</u>)[17] always involves abstract comparison. Human choice always follows the conclusion of a deliberative process, of a process of approximation.[18] That is, rational, or "free," choice is the terminating point of a process of measuring the proximity or distance one object has to another in relation to fulfilling a want. Where there is no comparison of alternative ways to fill a want there is no free choice. The choice is determined since there is only one way to act.[19] Human choice, as free choice, can never be absolutely determined to select any one thing in particular, then, for St. Thomas, because free choice, as following the terminating point of a process of reasoning, or of comparison of alternative options, by nature and definition, presupposes the ability to act in more than one way.[20]

2. Emotions

We are all aware of various ways in which we react to things we find pleasant or painful, useful or useless, advantageous or disadvantageous. If we find an object pleasant, useful or advantageous, we tend to like it and desire to have it.

If we find, because of certain conditions, circumstances or obstacles, that we cannot get it right away, we hope to achieve it in the future. If our hope be fulfilled, we feel pleasure. If not, we feel pain. If we strongly desire to have it, and find no hope of getting it, we feel despair. If, on the other hand, there be hope for our obtaining something we strongly desire, but if there be some formidable obstacle standing in our way, we might proceed with fear or with daring. In either case we might experience anger.

If we find an object unpleasant, useless or disadvantageous, we might react in pretty much the same way, except that our initial reaction would be one of dislike rather than one of attraction. That is, when we find an object unpleasant, we try to avoid it. If we find we can avoid it rather easily, if the object be not grossly unpleasant, and if there be no formidable obstacles standing in our way, we experience pleasure. If, however, we find ourselves confronted by grossly unpleasant objects, and major obstacles to our overcoming these obstacles, we experience despair, fear, anger and sadness.[21]

In both the above situations we might notice something else—these reactions are accompanied by physiological changes within us.[22] When experiencing love, desire, hope and pleasure, we might find our muscles loosening up, our eyes dilating, blood rushing to the top of our head and the bottom of our toes, and a warm feeling all over. When experiencing aversion, despair, fear, or sadness we might find just the opposite bodily reactions tending to occur. That is, we might find our muscles contracting, or a sweating of the palms, difficulty in breathing, and a cold feeling all over. And when we are angry we might find that we tend to see a combination of these bodily reactions.

The reactions we have been talking about above are what we generally call "emotions." St. Thomas calls them by a different name, "passions,"[23] but the general account we have just given regarding the emotions is pretty much the analysis of St. Thomas. St. Thomas's analysis of the human emotions is, we think, an incredible exercise in introspection, detail, precision and brilliance. We have found nothing comparable to it within the history of philosophy. Because of the profundity of his views in this area we will have to devote a separate chapter to his treatment of human emotions. At this point, however, we would like to explain what St. Thomas means by what we call an "emotion," and we would like to explain how St. Thomas relates the emotions to a self-mastered human life.

What, then, does St. Thomas mean by an "emotion"? Well, for him, an emotion is a reaction caused within either the propelling or contending sense appetite by the suspicion that something is pleasant or unpleasant, useful or useless, safe or harmful, and accompanied by some physiological change. He says that there are six propelling emotions, and five contending emotions. The propelling emotions he lists as: love and hatred, desire and aversion, pleasure and pain. The contending emotions he refers to as: hope and despair, fear and daring, and anger.[24]

Propelling emotions, Thomas states, are reactions to objects which are perceived simply as fitting or unfitting in relation to sense desire. This distinguishes them from contending emotions in which an object is not only perceived as being appealing or unappealing to a sense appetite, but, in addition, is perceived as being difficult to attain or to avoid.[25] The mark of a contending emotion, then, is much like the mark of a contender in boxing. It must overcome an obstacle to achieve what it seeks.

These emotions, according to St. Thomas, are not just experienced at random. They arise in a definite order: "...first occur love and hatred; seond, desire and aversion; third, hope and despair; fourth, fear and daring; fifth, anger; sixth and last, pleasure and pain, which are consequents of all the emotions..."[26] First, in the order of actual occurrence, one is either attracted towards something or not. So love and hatred come before all other emotions. Depending upon whether or not one is attracted by the object, one either pursues it (desires it) or avoids it. If the object in question be difficult to attain or to avoid, one experiences hope or despair; then, depending upon the difficulty encountered, fear or daring, and, then, anger.[27] Minor obstacles, perceived as minor, do not generate fear or daring.[28] And what causes anger is a perceived evil which is both difficult to overcome and present at hand. When one realizes that an evil is both difficult, unavoidable and at hand, fear or daring become accompanied by an impulse to attack. This impulse is anger.[29] The only emotions left are either pleasure or pain. Which one is achieved depends upon the outcome of one's actions.

Certainly, St. Thomas realizes that one need not, at any one time, experience all these emotions. All he is contending is that if certain emotions do occur certain others must, also, be present. Anger and daring cannot be present without love or hatred, desire or aversion, hope or despair. But all of the latter can be present without anger or daring, or pleasure or pain for that matter.[30]

In addition, St. Thomas realizes that emotions, in and of themselves, are neither morally good nor morally evil. Moral action, it should be recalled, deals with how a human being is moved to act. For a human being is a moral agent. And moral activity is a kind of natural activity. Nature, however, is what moves a subject to act. A human being is moved to act through powers, and appetites and emotions. Hence moral activity involves emotional activity. What makes emotional activity moral activity, then, is the fact that it is the emotional activity of a moral agent. But moral agency is determined by the subjection of activity to reason and will. Consequently, morally good and bad emotional activity is determined by the extent to which emotional activity is subjected to well-ordered reason and will. Emotions which are morally good generate within us favorable appetites towards things which are _really_ good for us and unfavorable appetites towards things which are _really_ bad for us. And emotions which are morally evil do just the reverse. They generate within us an unfavorable appetite towards something _really_ good for us and a favorable appetite towards something _really_ bad for us.[31]

This, then, is how the emotions are related to the self-mastered life. Emotions cause us to react to things which are _really_ good and _really_ bad for us. Good emotions are appropriate appetitive reactions to real sense goods and to real sense evils. Thus a person who reacts with fear and anger to something really unpleasant, or really dangerous, and difficult is emotionally well-ordered, if his reaction be directed by a well-ordered reason. But a person who reacts with fear and anger to _apparently_ unpleasant, or _apparently_ dangerous and difficult threats is emotionally disordered. And the same can be said for a person who reacts emotionally to real dangers but does so without a well-ordered reason. For such persons have no good reasons for such reactions. And it is precisely good reasons which measure whether emotions are good or bad.

Emotions, it should be recalled, are reactions to perceived estimates that something is pleasant or unpleasant, useful or useless, dangerous or safe. Such estimates are instinctively derived conclusions. They occur spontaneously within us. For example, we hear a loud noise and spontaneously estimate, or sense, danger. This sense of danger can cause in us an emotion of fear. But whether or not fear is a good emotion for us to feel cannot be determined by us by the mere presence before us of something we have instinctively estimated to be dangerous. For our sense appetites do not grasp the cause which connects the instinctive estimate of danger to the loud noise. What makes a loud noise dangerous? Are all loud noises dangerous or are only some? If only some loud noises are dangerous, what is the cause for these loud noises being dangerous? These are questions we have to reason out.

As the philosopher David Hume so perceptively noted a couple of hundred years ago, our senses do not grasp the causal connection between two sense events.[32] We would agree with Hume here, but we would add that, nonetheless, we do grasp causal relations between sense events. This is not something we grasp with our appetites, however, but with our reasoning power.

By rationally comparing our sense estimates to the things we know to be causing those estimates we can determine whether or not an emotion we might be feeling is reasonable or not. Because our reason can recognize something about a situation which our emotions cannot, namely, the cause for our feeling such an emotion, reason has control over our emotions. This is why one of the best remedies for altering an emotional state is to reason, in an abstract way, about the causes of our situation, or perhaps, about some entirely different situation. And the truth of what we say here is something anyone can experience for himself.[33]

For St. Thomas, then, emotions play an essential role in the living of a self-mastered life because they are gauges of real sense goods and of real sense evils. An emotion, for Thomas, is not a purely subjective preference or feeling about something. Rather, it is a reactive impulse to real goods and real evils which are perceived through our appetites. Our appetites grasp aspects of the world which escape our five external senses, aspects like danger. Our emotions cause us to move in one direction or another in response to the estimates made by our appetites. But which way we move we have to determine by reasoning. When used under the direction of correctly employed reasoning, then, our emotions become more educated to the real goods and real evils around us for they become habituated to respond spontaneously to the direction of reason. When so used, indeed, the emotions become inseparable from the living of a moral life.

3. Dispositions

In our discussion of emotions we just noted how, when emotions become habituated to respond to the direction of correct reasoning, these emotions become inseparable from the

living of a moral life. The inseparability of emotions from
the living of a moral life, therefore, depends upon our ability
to habituate emotions to respond to reasoning. For St. Thomas,
however, habits usually presuppose dispositions. Hence, before
going into an explanation of what is meant by habits, we have
to consider what is meant by a "disposition."

To explain what St. Thomas means by a disposition let us
recall for a moment what St. Thomas means by nature and by
instinct (<u>inclinatio</u>). The nature of a thing is the starting
point within a subject of a subject's activity. Within the
nature of every thing there is what we described in Chapter 1
as something akin to a magnetism, or a gravitation, which bends
the acts of a nature in a definite direction.[34] This quasi-
magnetism, or quasi-gravitation, is what we mean by an instinct.

Now, for St. Thomas, while all subjects are headed, through
their natures and instincts, in the direction of some definite
activity, some subjects can follow the directive drive of their
nature in several ways, others can only do it in one way.[35] That
is, some subjects are determined to act in one way in the pursuit of their natural activity while to other subjects several
ways of acting are open. In the case of the former, the question
of dispositions is irrelevant. For a subject which acts in
only one way cannot direct, or order, the response of its acts
to its nature. Yet such adaptation is precisely what is suggested by the word "dis-<u>position</u>." A disposition is an ordering
of parts.[36] In the case of moral activity it is, for the most
part, an acquired leaning, or tendency, to act in one way rather
than in another. As St. Thomas understands it, then, a moral
disposition is an inclination to arrange, or to order, activity
in relation to one's reason and will.[37]

Such an inclination, for St. Thomas, is required before
the acquisition of a habit because it is through the con-
ditioning activity of a disposition that a power becomes capable of exercising a habit.[38] For example, take something
like the activity of swimming. Such an activity appears to
us to be a habit of a person who has the power to swim. Before
having developed the habit of swimming in the right way, such
a person first had to dispose the various parts of his body to
a certain order of co-operative action. He had to condition
his body, or get it into shape. That is, he had to incline his
body to position the movements of its various parts (hands,
feet, etc.) to be responsive to the direction of reason. Well,
St. Thomas sees this to be pretty much the case with practically
every habit we human beings develop through our reason and our

sense powers. Habits are acquired, by and large, through the help of dispositions within these powers. And these powers can become mature in the exercise of their activities only through the development of appropriate dispositions and habits.[39]

4. Habits

This, of course, leads us right into the next question, which is, "What is a habit?" Well, for St. Thomas, a habit is a disposition, but it is a disposition which endures. It is not a tendency which is here one minute and gone the next. It is a disposition, also, which is not easily removable. It is tightly held.[40]

The specific kind of disposition which is a habit is one which arranges the order of activity of a power in relation to the nature, operation and goals of its subject. A habit is an adopted tendency to order a power's activity in relation to a natural disposition instinctively inherent within a subject.[41]

The powers to which habits belong are those powers capable of engaging in more than one particular activity; namely, the external and internal sense powers, the sensory appetite, man's rational power, and will.[42]

a. The external and internal sense powers and appetites

It might seem a little unusual to include the external sense powers among powers to which habits belong, for, after all, these powers act by instinct to perform one particular activity. In response to light, for instance, eyes see, and, in response to physical contact, hands feel. This is something which St. Thomas realizes. It is not, then, in the above respect that external, or internal, sense powers for that matter can possess habits. On the one hand, external and internal sense powers act instinctively to perform a particular activity. But, on the other hand, these same powers act instinctively to subordinate the direction of their respective activities to human reason and will. And it is in this respect that both can be habituated.[43]

As an example of habituation of the external sense powers, take the case of a musician or of a basketball player. A musician is a person who has habituated his eyes, ears, hands, and perhaps his mouth or feet even, to respond to ordering certain activities performed through these organs to the direction of reason. A musician's reason is, in a sense, in his hands, eyes, ears, etc. And the same can be said of a basketball player. Basketball is a rational activity, but it is a rational activity which requires that reasoning order the response of feet and hands to split-second reaction. A basketball player is, thus, someone who has developed the habit of directing his physical activity as commanded by his mind.

As an example of habituation of the internal sense powers, think of someone who is good at remembering, guessing, or imagining. A memory-expert does not work at random. Nor does a fairly consistent winner at card-playing, or a good storyteller. Each has developed the inclination of ordering actions of some internal sense faculty according to the direction of reason.[44] Each has a gimmick of some sort to assist him in his activity so that it can be done with consistency and precision.

As far as the sense appetites go, both the propelling and the contending appetite instinctively subordinate themselves to direction by the will. Hence all of our emotions can be habituated to control by reason. For the will is the rational appetite, and the emotions are activities of the sense appetites. There is, then, a way of arranging our emotional reactions to sense desires so that these reactions have rational direction.[45]

    b. Reason and will

Even the power of reason itself is, for St. Thomas, capable of habituation. The reason for this is that reason is a power of a human being. It is generated by human nature to cater to the needs of the human person. And it is a power which can exercise its activity in more than one way. So, as is the case with every such power, to insure that it is exercised in a way which fits the needs of the person, the order in which it exercises its activity must be made receptive to being arranged by the natural disposition of the person. But this is to arrange such powers by reason. Hence reason itself must be disposed by reason.[46]

St. Thomas points to science as a habit of reason, and also to wisdom and understanding.[47] What St. Thomas means is that the way we order our judgments, or parts of our judgments, in relation to knowledge disposes our power of reason to achieve knowledge or not to achieve it. Logic is thus, for instance, a habit of the mind. It is a habit of ordering our judgments in a right order, that is, in an order which achieves knowledge and truth rather than ignorance and error. And philosophy is a habit whereby we apply logic to problems discoverable by reason so as to come up with right answers. For a person to become logical or scientific, or grammatical, even, he must arrange his thinking to be disposed in a permanent way to definite types of activity. Such dispositions are habits of reason.[48]

In a similar way, for a person to be just, he must arrange his desires in a certain way. That is, just as there are habits of reason there are habits of will. Justice is one such habit.[49] As a habit of the will it requires an ordering of desires and choices in relation to reason. And as a rightly ordered habit it is a virtue.[50]

5. Virtues

In referring to justice as a virtue we have used a word which has become, in our estimation, both increasingly less used and increasingly misunderstood within twentieth-century America. For many Americans, we think, the word "virtue," today, necessarily connotes something moral. But, for St. Thomas, this is not the case. For him the word refers to a disposition which *strengthens* a power in the exercise of an activity it is directed to perform.[51] As a disposition, virtue orders the operations of a power to fit together with the natural disposition of the power. So St. Thomas distinguishes virtues according to the powers to which they belong, and according to the manner in which they are received into these powers.[52] There are, for him, four different kinds of virtue: 1) intellectual; 2) moral; 3) cardinal; and 4) theological.

a. Intellectual virtues

Intellectual virtues are, for St. Thomas, habits which perfect the intellectual power in the apprehension of knowledge, or in the application of knowledge.[54] According to him, there are five intellectual virtues: understanding, science, wisdom, art and prudence. Understanding, science and wisdom perfect the mind's ability to apprehend knowledge. Art and prudence perfect the mind's ability to apply knowledge.[55]

For St. Thomas knowledge can be achieved either through an immediate apprehension of some truth, or by means of reasoning to the apprehension of some truth. Understanding is a virtue related to knowledge achieved in the former way, and science and wisdom are virtues related to knowledge achieved in the latter way. Understanding, that is, is a habit whereby the intellect is perfected in its ability to grasp immediately knowable truths. Science is a habit whereby the intellect is perfected in its ability to reason rightly to the apprehension of knowledge. And wisdom is a habit whereby the intellect is perfected in its ability to grasp those truths most difficult for the human mind to know.[56]

Wisdom, science, and understanding perfect the mind's ability to make right judgments about things to be known. Art and prudence perfect the mind's ability to make right judgments about things to be made and about things to be done.[57]

b. Moral virtues

In order to live a perfectly self-mastered life, St. Thomas holds that more is needed than the right disposition of reason through intellectual virtue. What is needed is that human appetite be rightly disposed through the habit of moral virtue.[58] The reason for this is that moral activity involves the habit of making right choices. For right choices to be made, however, two elements are necessary. First of all, one needs a right appetitive disposition towards some fitting good. And, second, one needs to deliberate rightly about the means of obtaining this good. Right deliberation, therefore, involves the intellectual virtues of understanding and of prudence. For to deliberate rightly one must understand the good aimed at, and one must reason prudently about the means to achieve this good. But, in addition to right deliberation, to make right choices one must have the appetitive disposition to "listen to reason." A self-mastered life, then, requires moral virtue. For through moral virtue human appetites are perfected in their ability to be directed by reason.[59]

For St. Thomas there are three principal moral virtues because there are three appetites which can be directed by human reason. These appetites are the will, the propelling appetite and the contending appetite. The three principal moral virtues are justice, temperance, and courage, and, together with the intellectual virtue of prudence, they make up what St. Thomas calls the "cardinal virtues."[60]

St. Thomas refers to these as the "cardinal virtues" because he thinks that when we speak about "virtue" without being more definite about the kind of virtue we mean, we are understood to be referring to moral virtue.[61] Moral virtue in the complete sense, however, requires not merely perfection in one's ability to do something rightly, but also perfection in bending one's desire in the direction of causing a good act to be brought into existence.[62] So the principal, or "cardinal," virtues cover rightness of appetite. Rightness of appetite is required of justice, temperance, and courage, because these are the good habits of the various human appetites. And prudence, in a way, is related to rightness of appetite because it is intellectual reflection about things to be done.[63] That is, moral acts demand correctness in choice, and correctness in choice demands both correctness in appetite and correctness in reasoning about the order of things to be done.[64] The cardinal virtues are of principal importance, then, to the performance of moral activity.

These four cardinal virtues do not exhaust the number of virtues Thomas relates to moral activity, however. For each of these is a virtue to the extent that it is directed by rightly ordered reason.[65] But reason directs the powers and appetites in a certain order. As St. Thomas sees it, an object which stimulates an emotional response can do so as apprehended by an external sense, by imagination, or by reason, and as apprehended as relating to the soul, to the body, or to external things.[66] For example, someone might apprehend one and the same object as pleasureable to touch, useful for one's body, good for one's mind and helpful to others. Each of these aspects has a different relation to reason, however. Hence each calls for a different virtue. In addition, "any virtue which causes reason to consider rightly may be called 'prudence'; any virtue which causes actions to be due and right may be called 'justice'; any virtue which controls and restrains the passions may be called 'temperance'; and any virtue which strengthens the soul in any way against the emotions can be called 'courage'."[68]

c. Theological and infused virtues

In considering the theological virtues we are not, it should be noted, stepping outside the realm of moral activity. Moral activity, for St. Thomas, encompasses more than natural moral virtue. For, as we noted above,[69] moral acts involve acts of free choice. Choice, however, is an act of reason and will which presupposes some end. That is, choice requires a reasoned comparison of objects in order to determine which is more likeable in relationship to some desire of ours. Without something desired, then, there can be no choice. Nor can there be any choice unless the recommendation arrived at through reasoned comparison be accepted by the will.[70] That which is desired by human beings, however, is, as we noted in Chapter 2, happiness or self-mastery. Human happiness, however, for St. Thomas, is twofold. One, human beings can achieve through acts not surpassing their powers. The other can be achieved only through acts surpassing human powers, through acts of divine power, and by a kind of participation in divinity.[71]

That St. Thomas should hold such a view should not take many readers by surprise. After all, he is called "Saint" Thomas. Hence it should not be surprising to find him including the virtues of faith, hope and charity among the virtues related to moral activity, and to call these "theological virtues."[72] For these virtues are called "theological" because God is their object, because they are infused in human beings by God alone, and because they are communicated to human beings through divine revelation in Sacred Scripture.[73]

Of course, St. Thomas's contention that there are theological virtues presupposes that there is a God, and that there is a divine revelation. For him theological virtues play the same sort of role in helping a person achieve the human good which surpasses human powers as the intellectual and moral virtues play in helping a person achieve the human good which does not surpass human reason.[74]

Moral activity requires the habit of making right choices. This is the case whether one is talking about the moral activity achievable by human powers or the moral activity which surpasses human powers. And, as we have already noted in this chapter, right choices require a right appetitive disposition towards some fitting good, and they require right deliberation about the means of achieving this good. In the case of moral activity achievable by human powers, the virtues of justice, temperance and courage serve to fill the former requirement, and prudence fills the latter requirement. In the case of moral activity surpassing human powers, faith fills the latter requirement, while hope and charity fill the former requirement.[75]

The natural moral and intellectual virtues cause the human mind, will, and appetites to dispose themselves to be directed by rightly ordered reason.[76] The theological virtues cause the human mind, will, and appetites to dispose themselves to be directed by God.[77] Faith causes the human mind to seek attachment to God. Hope causes the will (and, through the will, the sensory appetite) to overcome obstacles to the achievement of attachment to God. And charity causes the will (and, once again, through the will, the sensory appetite) to delight in divine union by attaching the will to God through love.[78]

While the theological virtues fulfill a role similar to the role fulfilled by the intellectual and natural moral virtues, there is a major difference between how these virtues are caused in human beings. The intellectual and natural moral virtues can be caused by repetition of intellectual and moral activities, but the theological virtues can be caused only by God. Thus St. Thomas calls them "divinely infused" virtues.[79]

Divinely infused virtues are virtues which cannot be acquired by repetitive activity of human powers, and, at first sight, they might appear to be identical with theological virtues. But St. Thomas does not think so. For him all theological virtues are divinely infused, but not all divinely infused virtues are theological. Just as there are acquired virtues of prudence, justice, courage and temperance, there are infused virtues of prudence, justice, courage and temperance.[80] And these virtues, for St. Thomas, differ in kind.[81] The acquired moral virtues, for him, for example, demand that acts measure up to standards set directly by human reason. The infused moral virtues, on the other hand, demand that acts measure up to standards set directly by God.[82] So, for instance, with respect to eating, Thomas says, "...a measure is established by human reason so that the food consumed might not harm the health of the body, nor impede the act of reason; however, according to the rule of divine law it is required that 'a man chastise his body, and bring it into subjection' by abstinence from food and drink, and from other like things."[83]

The infused moral virtues differ from the acquired moral virtues, then, in two respects. First, and most evident, is that infused moral virtues cannot be acquired through habituation. They are infused in human beings through the theological virtues, and disappear from human beings with the departure of the theological virtues, in particular, of charity.[84] And, second, the infused moral virtues are more demanding than the acquired moral virtues because they require that we not only measure up to our own power, but surpass it.[85]

6. Gifts, Fruits and Beatitudes

Aside from the infused moral virtues, there are other effects which St. Thomas thinks are caused in a person through the possession of the theological virtues of faith, hope and charity. The first of these St. Thomas refers to as "gifts."[86] The second he calls "fruits."[87] And the last he names "beatitudes."[88]

Gifts, for St. Thomas, are, in a way, like virtues because, like virtues, they perfect a person for right action. They differ, however, from all the virtues, even the theological ones, in this respect. Gifts dispose a person to be readily receptive to a special type of divine activity which St. Thomas calls "inspiration," while virtues cause a person to be responsive to reason.[89]

The theological virtues, for instance, cause a person to be responsive to God through that person's reason. For a person to direct himself to God, however, St. Thomas does not think that direction through his own reason is enough. Rather, a person must thoroughly consent to have his direction to God be determined by God. Hence a person has to have all of his powers disposed to submit to God's direction in all of one's actions.[90] Such a disposition is achieved by seven gifts which come to a person possessing the theological virtue of charity. These gifts are: understanding, wisdom, counsel, science, piety, courage and fear of God. The first four dispose man's intellect to divine direction and the last three perfect a person's appetite to the same.[91]

We realize, of course, that such talk about "theological virtues" and "gifts" might not find a very receptive audience among readers in the twentieth century. Why, such talk is liable to make even many a contemporary Catholic theologian turn a deaf ear. Imagine, then, what it should do to a less theistic listener! No doubt, to some it must sound like a bunch of medieval hocus pocus and mumbo jumbo.

But if one will stop for just a moment to consider the character of St. Thomas, one might perhaps gain some insight here into the message of Christian moral teaching. St. Thomas was a Christian theologian, and his moral teaching is that of a Christian theologian. The happiness sought by a Christian is a supernatural one, and the method by which this is achieved is a supernatural one.

What St. Thomas appears to us to be doing is spelling out for his readers what happiness is, and how it is achieved, as understood by a Christian. Happiness, for a Christian, lies in union with God. It is through this union that, as a Christian sees it, a person achieves perfect freedom or self-mastery.

Of course, this kind of happiness differs markedly from the kind of happiness pursued by many, if not most, people. For many people happiness lies in some other kind of achievement related to one or more of the human powers and appetites. That is, happiness for these people is something they pursue in a "natural way," and not something they pursue in a "supernatural way." The happy life, in this natural sense, lies, for

St. Thomas, in a perfectly moral life. That is, it is a life in which a person, through his own free decision, has developed the habit of ordering his choices in agreement with an instinctive natural disposition within the human person. And that instinctive natural disposition is to direct one's powers and appetites by a reason which adheres to natural law.

Well, transpose yourself for a moment from a natural happiness to a supernatural one. If God exists, happiness resides in God. To become happy, then, one must find God.

But how is one to find God when God cannot be found by human reason? Well, God must, in some way, lead a person to Him. And, for St. Thomas, God must not violate a person's freedom in the process.[92]

How, then, is this to be achieved? The answer, to Thomas, is by raising the human personality to a level of perfection where it can find God, and can freely choose to be disposed by God.

The theological virtues of faith, hope and charity enable a person to find God. The gifts enable a person to allow his powers and appetites to be arranged by God.

The gifts, then, cause an alteration in the human personality and in human behavior. The result of the presence of these gifts within a person cause that person to have: charity, joy, peace, patience, long-suffering, kindness, warmth, mildness, trustworthiness, moderation, continence, and chastity. These are the twelve results, or "fruits," of the inspired gifts.[93]

That a person's behavior should change as a result of a change in a person's view of happiness is not surprising. It should not be surprising, then, that a person who seeks happiness in a supernatural good should possess behavioral qualities different from the natural norm. To St. Thomas most people are not charitable, joyous, peaceful, patient, long-suffering, kind, warm, moderate, continent, and chaste. And how many people do you know like this?

The reason, for St. Thomas, that most people are not like this is because to be like this is to be somewhat abnormal. Normal people do not tend to withdraw from things which attract their sense powers and appetites. Normal people do not tend to withdraw from seeking happiness in riches and honors. But because they do not tend to withdraw from things like this,

normal people often become violent and aggressive, seeking
security for themselves by killing their enemies in fights
and wars, and seeking consolation for life's troubles in
pleasures like sex, drink and drugs. And normal people often
have an inordinate love for their own good. Some of them not
only do not give to others their due, but they steal what
belongs to others. That is, normal people often are never
satisfied. Life to them is filled with misery.[94]

It is the abnormal person, abnormal in the sense of
"super-normal" rather than "sub-normal," who escapes from the
transient and fleeting happiness of the multitude. The best
life a normal person can achieve is a life of imperfect moral
virtue. He can become somewhat just, prudent, temperate and
courageous. What such a person cannot become, as St. Thomas
sees it, is habitually charitable.[95]

Now, of course, there are people who would disagree with
St. Thomas here. They might point to the fact that a lot of
people who claim to be supernormal, or "supernatural" are not.
There are a lot of "believers" who are not joyous, peaceful,
kind, warm, etc.

But such a point would not, we think, be relevant. For
it is not by faith or hope that one becomes supernatural. A
person receives these inspired gifts only to the extent that
he has a living faith, that is, a faith impressed by charity.
Hence a person can believe in God and still be a wretch in his
dealings with others.[96]

Also, one should consider what St. Thomas says in light
of history. Did the pre-Christian Greeks and Romans extol the
fruits St. Thomas talks about? Oh, sure, the Stoics and the
Epicureans would recommend moderation in choosing one's pleasures,
but does moderation for the Stoic and for the Epicurean mean
moderation determined by a God with the character of a Christian
God? And what about the most virtuous of ancient Greeks and
Romans? Were they any more decent than an average old man or
woman saying a rosary? Can they come anywhere near a St.
Francis or a Mother Teresa in their self-mastery and love for
others? We think not.

There are certain benefits, then, as St. Thomas sees it,
which come to a person of charity. These benefits are spelled
out in the famous eight beatitudes given in the Sermon on the
Mount.

The eight beatitudes are:

1. Blessed are the poor in spirit.
   For theirs is the kingdom of heaven.

2. Blessed are the meek.
   For they shall inherit the earth.

3. Blessed are those who mourn.
   For they shall be comforted.[97]

For St. Thomas these first three beatitudes are related to withdrawing from things which attract our sense powers and appetites, from those things which we desire without inspiration of the Holy Spirit. Without the benefit of divine gifts people seek happiness in riches and honors. The first beatitude recommends shunning this in order to grow in spiritual goods. Without the benefits of divine gifts, people are violent and aggressive, seeking security for themselves by killing their enemies in fights and wars. So St. Thomas finds that the second beatitude refers to the security and tranquility possessed by those who seek eternal goods. And without the benefits of divine gifts, people seek consolation for life's labours in the pleasures of the world. To those who shun such consolation St. Thomas thinks the third beatitude promises comfort.[98]

4. Blessed are those who hunger and thirst for justice's sake.
   For they shall be satisfied.

5. Blessed are the merciful.
   For they shall receive mercy.[99]

For St. Thomas the fourth and fifth beatitudes relate to works which order a person rightly with respect to his neighbor. Without the benefit of divine gifts, he thinks that people draw back from acting rightly towards their neighbor. For they have an inordinate love for their own good. Some people do not give others their due. In fact, they take what belongs to others. Such people are never satisfied. Whereas, to those who act rightly towards others, the fourth beatitude promises satisfaction. Other people do not practice mercy towards their neighbors because they do not want to be troubled by other people's problems. To those who act mercifully towards others, therefore, the fifth beatitude promises freedom from misery.[100]

6. Blessed are the pure of heart.
   For they shall see God.

7. Blessed are the peacemakers.
   For they shall be called sons of God.[101]

The sixth and seventh beatitudes indicate the rewards promised to people rightly disposed to God through the gifts of divine inspiration. The sixth beatitude promises to such people a vision of God. The seventh beatitude promises them perfect union with God because to be a peacemaker one must be rightly ordered--that is, at peace.[102]

8. Blessed are those who are persecuted for righteousness' sake.
   For theirs is the kingdom of heaven.[103]

This last beatitude is, to St. Thomas, a kind of confirmation in all the beatitudes. For there is a certain order to the beatitudes. The more a person is fixed in the gifts of divine inspiration the more he goes beyond his own gratification in physical goods, the more rewarding become the goods accorded to him. To possess the kingdom of God as a son of God is the highest reward for man, for St. Thomas, because it is the most complete union with God.[104]

7. Law and grace

The last of the principles of moral activity lie in law and in grace. Each of these in some way contributes to the performance of moral action. We need not spend too much time on St. Thomas's teaching on grace because what he says about this is not very lengthy. What he has to say about law, however, is quite elaborate. So we will examine both these issues in a separate chapter.

For now let us just preface that chapter by saying that, for St. Thomas, complete moral activity takes place within the context of a community. That is, for St. Thomas, people, by instinct, seek to develop as moral beings by living together with other people. Now, for this to be possible, law is necessary. For law directs co-operative living among people.[105]

Hence to get a complete picture of the moral teaching of St. Thomas, one has to consider moral activity in relation to five types of law St. Thomas examines in the Summa theologiae: 1) eternal law; 2) natural law; 3) human law; 4) the Old Law; and 5) the New Law.[106]

Each of these kinds of law plays a role in moral activity. What role is played by each, and why each is important to human life will reveal key elements in our understanding of the moral

teaching of St. Thomas, and in our understanding of the meaning
of a "self-mastered" human life.

CHAPTER 4

EMOTIONS

What we attempted to do in Chapter 3 was to single out for special consideration the starting points St. Thomas finds to be present in moral activity. Our purpose in doing this was to introduce our readers to certain basic ingredients which contribute to what St. Thomas means by a "self-mastered" human life. In this chapter, and in the next chapter, we will examine in greater detail two of the ingredients we considered within Chapter 2--namely, emotions, and law and grace.

The reason for our proceeding in this manner is twofold. On the one hand, we hope to acquaint our readers with a better understanding of what these principles contribute to complete moral activity. And, on the other hand, we hope that through an understanding of St. Thomas's teachings about the emotions and about law and grace, some of our readers might derive practical benefit in the living of their own lives. For, as Aristotle says regarding the nature of the study of ethics:

> The purpose of the present study is not, as it is in other inquiries, the attainment of theoretical knowledge: we are not conducting this inquiry in order to know what virtue is, but in order to become good, else there would be no advantage in studying it. For that reason, it becomes necessary to examine the problem of actions, and to ask how they are to be performed. For, as we have said, the actions determine what kind of characteristics are developed.[1]

To understand human actions, however, it is necessary to understand the sources of human action. Several of these sources we think we have covered as thoroughly as we can, namely, powers and appetites, dispositions, habits and virtues. But emotions and law are so misunderstood today, and yet play such a large role in moral activity, as St. Thomas understands it, that more detail has to be spent on each of these.

Certainly, in the case of emotions, most people would, in practice, recognize a major influence on their behavior. For who has not, in some way, been prompted to action by love or hatred, anger, fear, hope, or the like? Indeed, distinctively human activity is inseparable from the emotions. For distinctively human activity is free activity, that is, deliberatively chosen activity. And deliberatively chosen activity always involves appetitive preferences and reactions. For without movement of the appetite no choice can be made.[2]

A knowledge of our emotions, therefore, is inseparable from human happiness. Such being the case, let us take a look at the propelling and contending emotions to see what effects they have upon human behavior.

The Propelling Emotions

1. Love or Liking

Best selling novels are written about it. Songs are composed about it. Movies are devoted to it. Products are marketed by means of it. And scores of people hover around T.V. sets in the afternoon to watch soap operas dealing with it. What is "it"? Why, love of course.

In fact, so much of human energy is devoted to this theme that one might think we should have exhausted the topic by now. Certainly, one might expect that with all we know, today, from psychology, sociology, anthropology, T.V. and science that some thirteenth century Catholic friar could not tell us anything we did not already know about it. Well, let us take a look at what St. Thomas has to say, and, then, let us judge.

First of all, "love" or "liking," as we commonly use the term, refers, for St. Thomas, to wanting good things for someone, either for ourselves or for someone else. Thus love has a twofold object: the good thing which is wanted by someone, and the one for whom it is wanted.

Secondly, St. Thomas distinguishes between two types of love. One he calls "love of friendship" and the other he calls "love of desire." Love of desire differs from love of friendship in that in the love of desire the object loved is not loved for its benefit, but is loved for ourselves or for another.[3] When someone, for instance, loves candy or ice cream he often loves it because of a certain satisfaction it produces within his sense appetite. He does not love it in order to impart some good to the ice cream through his love. But when one person, say, loves another person with a love of friendship, that person not only loves the other because the other makes him feel good, but because through his love he might impart a good to the other.

Suppose, for example, Vinnie loves Marie. And suppose, because he loves Marie, he wants to buy Marie an engagement ring. Vinnie is obviously attracted to Marie in a different way than he is attracted to the ring. He <u>loves</u> Marie, but he just <u>likes</u> the ring we might say. That is, he desires Marie in a twofold way, but the ring only in one way. He is attracted to the ring through Marie, because he associates it with her. Marie possesses the good which he wants, then, not the ring. And in liking, or loving, the ring Vinnie is not attempting to transfer a good to the ring through his love. But in loving Marie he seeks to transfer a good to Marie through this love.

a. The causes of love

Love, for St. Thomas, is an emotion. As such, it is located in an appetite. In an animal it is located solely within the sense appetite. In a human love resides both within the sense appetite and within the will. What causes response to an object in both the sense appetite and the will is an estimation or judgment that something is, in one way or another, fitting or suitable for a person. What makes a thing attractive, then, is its goodness (for the good is what is fitting), and one's knowledge (for estimation and judgment are species of knowing).[4]

Two of the causes of love, then, for Thomas, are knowledge and goodness. For a person can only love something which, in some way, he knows, and which, in some way, "fits" his appetite.[5] A third cause of love, as St. Thomas sees it, is likeness.

Things can be alike in two ways, however. They can actually possess something the same, or one can have in actuality what another has in potentiality and as an object of inclination.[6]

The first kind of likeness, St. Thomas thinks, causes love of friendship because the affections tend into one another. For they find a good in another which is identical with one in themselves. So in loving the other they love something in themselves, and in loving something in themselves they love something in another. For instance, if a person is attracted to himself because he has a certain color hair, he is likewise attracted to that color if found identically in someone else.

The second kind of likeness, for St. Thomas, causes love of desire because the object loved is not loved for actually possessing something with which a person identifies as being attractive in and of itself. Rather, the thing desired is desired in order to realize some potential in the lover. It is only in relation to this potential actualization, then, that the object is loved. So this kind of similarity can also give rise to a friendship based upon pleasure or convenience, but not to a perfect friendship where one loves another to share something with him rather than to take something from him.[7]

b. Effects of love

St. Thomas lists several effects of love. Most of them seem to us to be hardly what one would expect from a medieval friar.

The first effect St. Thomas lists is union. People in love are united in one way by being present to one another. In another way, people are united only by inclination and feeling. That is, they share in the love of some good. For, at the very least, people in love want something good for themselves. And if the love be a love of friendship they want good things for the other person as they do for themselves. So, St. Thomas says, "a friend is said to be another self," and quotes St. Augustine's description of a friend as "half of one's soul."[8]

The second effect of love which St. Thomas describes is "mutual inhesion." Lovers, as St. Thomas sees it, inhere in one another in mind and in desire. For the person loved is constantly on the mind of the person in love. The person in love, on the other hand, is in the mind of the person loved in the sense that the person in love "...is not content with a superficial understanding of the person he loves, but he strains to probe the details of the person loved and to enter into the depths of his mind."[9]

The person loved is constantly in the desire of a _person in love_ through the pleasure present within the lover's feeling for the beloved. When the person loved is present, for example, the person in love takes delight in the beloved, or in goods associated with the beloved. When the person loved is not present, on the other hand, the person in love feels a longing for the beloved. He wishes the beloved to be present to satisfy his desire in the case of love of desire. In the case of love of friendship, the person in love wants good for the beloved even when absent. This latter desire, Thomas adds, is not caused by something outside the person in love. Rather, it is caused by the pleasant feeling for the beloved rooted within the lover. Because of this inwardly rooted feeling, St. Thomas says, love is sometimes called "intimate," and sometimes people speak of the "heart of love."[10]

The person who loves is in the desire of the one loved because a person with a love of desire is not satisfied by:

> ...an extrinsic or superficial attainment or enjoyment of the beloved; but seeks to possess the beloved perfectly and, as it were, to reach the beloved's innermost feelings. But in a love of friendship the person in love is in the beloved inasmuch as he attends to his beloved's fortunes and misfortunes just as to his own, and he attends to his beloved's will just as to his own. For this reason, according to Aristotle, it is common for friends to like the same things, and to be made sad and to be delighted by the same things.[11]

So, inasmuch as a person in love considers his beloved's concerns to be his own, he is made one with the one he loves. And inasmuch as the person in love is acting on behalf of the beloved, just as he would on his own behalf, the beloved is in the lover as the lover is in himself.

Aside from "mutual inhesion" in mind and in desire, St. Thomas mentions one other way in which mutual inhesion can be understood to be an effect of love. In love of friendship love itself is reciprocal. Friends love each other, and they want, and do, good for each other. Hence, the love of each is returned to the other, or inheres in the other through return.[12]

The third effect of love discussed by St. Thomas is ecstasy. Ecstasy, he thinks, can happen to a person in mind or in appetite. Mentally, a person is in ecstasy when he is placed outside his normal mental activity, while, appetitively, a person is in ecstasy when his appetite reaches out towards an object of delight not possessed by the person.[13]

For St. Thomas mental ecstasy can happen in one of two ways. A person can be elevated to an understanding above the apprehension of reason and sensation to which he is naturally suited. Or he can be lowered to an understanding beneath the normal state of a human being, as happens, for instance, with people who are maniacs or who are out of their minds. Such ecstasy is caused by love through a kind of displacement because a person in love mentally dwells on the person loved. In so doing, he withdraws other thoughts from a place within his mind.[14]

With regard to appetites, St. Thomas thinks that ecstasy occurs to a person in love in a more direct way. For the appetite of a person in love reaches outside himself directly to the person loved, rather than to a thought of that person. For example, in love of friendship a person's desire cannot be put to rest by delighting in any good he possesses within himself. Instead, he seeks satisfaction in trying to bring some good to his friend. Love of desire does not cause as complete an ecstasy as that caused by love of friendship, but, at the very least, it shares with the latter, a reaching out to a good beyond itself. The way these two differ is that love of friendship causes a person's desire to be terminated when a good is achieved for his beloved, whereas love of desire causes a person's desire to be terminated when a good is achieved for himself.[15]

The fourth effect of love, for St. Thomas, is jealousy. The reason for this, as Thomas sees it, is that love causes a person to be strongly inclined towards something. And to be strongly inclined towards something a person must be strongly opposed to objects contrary to that thing.[16]

As St. Thomas sees it, there are two types of jealousy. There is jealousy of envy and there is jealousy on behalf of a friend. The first kind of jealousy is an effect of love of desire:

> For a person with an intense desire for something is repelled by anything which stands in the way of the attainment and peaceful enjoyment of that which is loved. And it is in this way that men are said to be jealous about their wives, that is, they fear that the uniqueness of the relationship which they seek with their wives might be impeded through their wives' association with others. And, similarly, those who seek success are repelled by those who seem to be successful, just as to impediments to their own success.[17]

Jealousy on behalf of a friend, or the second type of jealousy, is, on the other hand, an effect of love of friendship. As St. Thomas sees it, this kind of jealousy is of a more unselfish sort. For a person who is jealous in this way is repelled by anything which threatens a good for his friend.[18]

In addition to the four effects of love just discussed, St. Thomas cites four other effects: melting, enjoyment, langour, and fervor. And, he says, besides these appetitive effects there are bodily effects which correspond to the effects mentioned.[19]

With respect to melting, St. Thomas states that this is the opposite of freezing. A person in love readily receives what he loves. He is, therefore, like that which melts rather than like that which freezes. For what freezes is bound together and does not allow things easily to penetrate it. "Hence coldness or hardness of heart is a disposition repulsive to love. But melting suggests a certain softness of heart by which the heart easily conditions itself so that the beloved might enter into it."[20]

Enjoyment or delight accompanies love, St. Thomas says, if the cause of love is present to the person in love. If not, a sadness over its absence (langour) ensues and an intense desire for its possession (fervor).[21]

2. Hatred

Hatred, of course, is the contrary of love. Hence just as love is the wanting of good things for someone, so hatred is the wanting of bad things for someone. Just as "...love is a certain consonance of appetite in relation to that which it apprehends as suitable, hatred is a certain disconsonance of appetite in relation to that which it apprehends as repugnant and harmful."[22]

St. Thomas does not devote much space to an analysis of hatred. Love, for him, is the central human emotion. In fact, he thinks that love is the cause of every action involving the emotions, even of actions involving hatred. He holds this because, he says:

> ...love consists in a certain compatibility between the lover and the beloved, but hatred consists in a certain repugnance or disconsonance. Whatever the emotion, it is necessary

> first to consider what is compatible to it
> before considering what is repugnant to it;
> for what is repugnant to another is repugnant because it corrupts or impedes what is
> compatible for it. Hence it is necessary that
> love be prior to hatred; and nothing can be
> considered hateful except that which is contrary to something compatible which is loved.[23]

In light of what Thomas says, to understand different effects of hatred one need only consider the effects of love. For, by and large, hatred will produce contrary effects, or will, at any rate, negate in a person the presence of an effect produced by love.

3. Desire and Aversion

When examining the emotion called "love," we saw how this word applied to more than one kind of activity—to love of friendship and to love of desire, for instance. Well, this same flexibility of application is characteristic, also, of the word "desire." It applies to more than one kind of activity, but always in relation to some common feature.

The reason for this is that desire is an appetite within a power. Since powers differ in the acts they can exercise, so, too, do they differ in their appetites. For example, physical things have a receptivity for certain kinds of features but not for others. And when they receive certain features within themselves they tend to engage in similar kinds of activities. When heat is applied to water in a teapot, for instance, the water is "inclined to" boil. There is, in a wide way of speaking, then, a physical _desire_, that is, a movement towards a certain activity, within the water to exercise the activity of boiling when it is heated.

So, making the appropriate changes, the same kind of thing can happen within a sense power, or within an intellectual power. Given the presence within the power of a certain feature, there arises within a sense appetite or intellectual appetite an inclination towards or away from the exercise of some sort of activity. (Such desire "away from" is aversion.)[24]

When, for instance, our eyes are stimulated by color our power of sight is inclined, by nature (that is, instinctively _and_ without any knowledge) to exercise the activity of seeing. And when this same thing, say, which is stimulating our eyes through color, is apprehended through an image in our cogitative reason, or estimative sense, we are inclined to react with a judgment of sense suitability or unsuitability, and with the emotions of love or hatred, desire or aversion, and so on. Such a reaction is instinctive, or natural, but is is a natural reaction with sense knowledge. And the same thing can be said of reactions within our will. The power which brings the will into activity is reason, or intellect. Hence we always will things in conjunction with our minds.[25]

As we can see, then, there are at least 3 kinds of desire to which the word "desire" can be applied: physical desire, sense desire, and intellectual desire. So, when talking about desires, or wants, one has to be careful to indicate to which kind of desire one is referring.

This need to be careful is complicated by another problem regarding the word "desire." The problem is that, at times, we do not distinguish between desire and love. For we love the things we desire and we desire the things we love. And love, in turn, can mean liking, personal love, love of friendship, love of desire, or variations of these with effects of love, like ecstasy, langour and so on.

So, taking all these nuances of meaning into consideration, "desire," as we commonly use it to refer to an emotion, refers to an appetite, or movement towards, that which is pleasurable. It differs from love, or liking, in the sense that love suggests finding something compatible within a thing, while desire suggests not simply finding something compatible within a thing, but also pursuing what one loves. Desire, that is, presupposes love.[26]

4. Pleasure and Joy

As was the case with desire, pleasure, at times, is difficult to distinguish from love. At the same time, pleasure can be difficult to distinguish from desire. We love things which give us pleasure. We find pleasure in things we love. We desire what gives pleasure and find pleasure in things we desire.

Each of these emotions, as an emotion, is a movement, or reaction, within the sense appetite. The way they differ is in this. Love is a reaction to something attractive, suitable, or good caused by some object or thing. Desire is a reaching out towards, or striving for, the having of something loved. And pleasure is movement in an appetite caused by the perception that something suitable for a power exists within that power. So, in a sense, pleasure is a spontaneous reaction to something we love.[27]

As a spontaneous reaction within an appetite to something loved existing within a power, pleasure varies according to powers. There exists within a person, that is, a distinction between sensory and intellectual pleasures.[28]

    a. Sensory pleasure

Since pleasure demands a love within a person's appetite for an object, the more something is attractive to an appetite, the greater the pleasure realized upon satisfaction of the appetite. But what every appetite instinctively loves is the perfect operation of its power. Sensory appetites, therefore, have the greatest attraction by instinct, for the preservation of their subject. Now this means that sensory powers are sources of pleasure to a person to the extent that sense powers are capable of contributing to maintaining a person in existence under the direction of reason and will. And since the sense powers are able to contribute to the maintenance of a personal existence in the area of intellectual and physical life, the sense powers are sources of pleasure in relation both to intellectual and to physical life.

If we consider the senses in relation to physical life, St. Thomas says the pleasure of touch is the greatest. For touch connects all the senses. It is the one sense no animal can be without, and no sensation can occur without some touch or <u>contact</u> being involved in relation to a sense organ. Touch, as St. Thomas sees it, then, is most necessary for the preservation of the body. Hence he thinks that the bodily instincts or desires which are most strong are those which are directed towards touch. Consequently, pleasures of touch give rise to the greate<u>st</u> sense pleasures, namely, pleasures like food, sex, and so on.[29]

By saying that pleasures of touch give rise to the greatest sense pleasures we mean this only in reference to the intensity of the pleasure in relation to the body, not in relation to other parts of a person. For while the sense of touch is more delightful to the body, the sense of sight is more delightful to the mind. The reason for this is that, more than any other sense, the power of sight adds to our knowledge and to our ability to direct our actions through our reason and will. So, while more than any other sense touch gives us bodily pleasure, still we are inclined by instinct to take greater personal delight in sight. Hence, by instinct, we are inclined to prefer the loss of touch to sight in relation to leading self-directed lives, and to prefer the loss of sight to touch in relation to our bodily life.[30]

b. Intellectual pleasures

Just as there are physical pleasures, for St. Thomas, there are, also, intellectual ones. Pleasure, as we have seen, is an appetitive reaction to the presence within a power of something suitable. So pleasure can be within either the sensory appetite or within the intellectual appetite. The difference between the two is simply that intellectual delights require the use of the intellect. So whatever can be desired as a physical delight can be desired as an intellectual one as well.[31]

Still, St. Thomas thinks there is a special pleasure taken in intellectual delights which is absent from physical delights. And, for this reason, he gives a special name to intellectual pleasure, namely, "joy."[32]

Of course, a contention like this needs support. For most people seem to take a special delight in physical pleasures rather than in intellectual pleasures. In fact, St. Thomas himself makes note of this. He says that more people seek physical pleasures than seek intellectual pleasures. And he explains this in the following manner: "...more people," he says, "pursue physical pleasures because sensible goods are known better and more extensively. And, also, because men need pleasures as a remedy against multiple sorrows and sadnesses; and since many men are not able to attain spiritual pleasures, which are the special pleasures of the virtuous, the consequence is that they lean towards physical pleasures."[33]

But despite the fact that more people seek delight in physical pleasures, St. Thomas thinks that, for the person as a whole, intellectual pleasures are more intense. To demonstrate this point compare the pleasures of the mind to those of the body. Is it not the case that a person, in fact, gets more pleasure from knowing something through his intellect than from knowing it through his senses? How many people, for example, would prefer to have an intense sense awareness of pleasure if it meant that they had to be insane? And how many of us would take delight in physical pleasure if our minds were to have no awareness of this pleasure? or no awareness of the fact that we had sense powers in which pleasure could arise?[34]

Also, compare intellectual pleasures to bodily pleasures in relation to: 1) the thing pursued; 2) the power in which the pleasure is experienced; and 3) the union itself. In each of these areas St. Thomas thinks intellectual pleasure is, in fact, greater.[35]

In fact, people are inclined to, or bend in the direction of, enjoying intellectual goods over bodily goods. For few people enjoy even the most intense physical pleasure if it will cost them respect of a friend, the loss of a good reputation, or a position of honor among their peers. And who among us enjoys physical pleasure if it means one has to feel like a fool?[36]

It is clear, then, that mental goods tend to be preferred by us more than bodily goods. And the reason for this is that our mental powers are instinctively more valued by us than our sense powers. As St. Augustine says, there is no man who would prefer the loss of sanity to the loss of sight.[37]

In addition, the union between the intellect and its good is more intimate, complete, and firm than the union between a sense power and its good. Sense pleasures require movement within a sense organ. Hence sense pleasures are momentary and pass away quickly. Once candy is eaten, or the party is over, the sense pleasure disappears. But, for St. Thomas, intellectual pleasures do not require movement within a bodily organ. The things we think about are within us and do not soon disappear once they are possessed.[39]

Now, if all this be true, why is it that we spend so much of our time in pursuit of physical pleasure rather than in pursuit of intellectual pleasure? Well, as St. Thomas sees it, the reason for this is that the human body is more subject than is the mind to ailments which cause one sort of sadness or another. The body functions through a series of organs each of which can undergo some sort of damage. In addition, the body is always fighting off disintegration and decay.[40] The intellect, on the other hand, does not directly depend upon any organ.[41] And the intellect, for St. Thomas, is a power of the soul, which is not subject to physical decay.[42]

Still, if intellectual pleasures are, in fact, more intense than physical ones, why do many people not _feel_ them to be more intense? The answer seems to be that they do. They just do not _feel_ this in a sensory way. They feel them to be more intense in an intellectual way.

That is, intellectual pleasures cannot be sensed. We cannot feel them with our sense appetites like we feel the pleasure of a good meal or of a good drink. Sense pleasures feel more intense to some people because they are better known in a sensory way to these people. For things of sense are easy to know. So people who do not develop within themselves a knowledge of intellectual goods do not habitually delight in goods of the intellect. By instinct they are inclined to delight more in goods of the intellect than in goods of the body, but because they do not develop the habit of knowing intellectual goods, they are not in the habit of delighting in such goods.

c. The causes of pleasure

Pleasure, once again, for St. Thomas, is a kind of activity which results in an appetite through the presence of a suitable stimulus within a power. As he sees it, there are at least two prerequisites for the presence of pleasure within an appetite: 1) the attainment by the appetite of a fitting good; and 2) knowledge that such a fitting good has been attained. Now both 1 and 2 are activities. Hence St. Thomas concludes that activity is one of the causes of pleasure.

He adds that activity gives pleasure inasmuch as it is conducive to the receptive propensity of a power. Human powers, however (functioning, as most of them do, through organs), are limited in their operation by the conductive capacity of their organs. So, for human activity to be physically conducive, it has to respect the limited capacity of the body to function. For if we over-work our organs, pleasure becomes laborious and boring. It is for this reason, Thomas argues, that we take pleasure in activities like sports, leisure, and the like. They relieve us of the distress which comes from work.[43]

Aside from activity, another cause of pleasure is change, or variation. The reason for this, as St. Thomas sees it, is that both the person and the pleasurable object to which he is united are changeable. What suits a person at one time, then, does not suit him at another time. In winter we enjoy the heat from a fireplace, but in summer this is not what most of us would find delightful. And the more one thing acts on another, the more that agent's activity changes in intensity. The longer a fire burns, for example, the more wood it consumes. And the more a person is warmed by a fire the more intensely the fire heats him. So when the action of an object on a power becomes too intense, the removal of that object causes pleasure.

Beyond this, St. Thomas holds that people like to know something completely. But many of the things we know we experience piece-meal, one bit at a time. In this case, change is pleasurable, so that, by coming to know various features of the thing in question, a person can come to know it better.44

The third cause of pleasure cited by St. Thomas is hope and memory. The reason he holds this is that for one to feel pleasure he must have some pleasurable object, in some way, present to him. Now a thing can be present to a person either in existence or in knowledge. And in knowledge a thing can be present to a person either in the existing moment, in the past, or in the future.

If something be actually present to a person in existence, one's pleasure is in the existing moment, and so is one's knowledge of this and of one's pleasure. If, on the other hand, the object be not present in existence at the moment, the only kind of pleasure which can be derived is from a memory of union with it, or from hope for such union in the future.45

To activity, change, hope, and memory, St. Thomas adds five other causes of pleasure. They are: sadness, the actions of other people, good deeds, similarity, and wonder.46

Sadness, he argues, can cause pleasure in the present, or in memory. In the present, sadness can cause pleasure by recalling to mind something pleasurable whose absence at present is causing sorrow. That is, even though its absence causes sadness at present, the thought of the thing is a thought which causes pleasure.

In memory of some sadness, on the other hand, one can find pleasure in the present absence of the recalled sorrow. For escape from evil is itself a reason to rejoice.47

As far as the actions of others are concerned, one can obtain pleasure from these in three ways. First of all, one can derive benefit from being well-treated by others. Secondly, through the actions of others one can become aware of some good of his own. This is why, St. Thomas holds, people take pleasure in praise and honor from others, and even from flattery: namely, because this causes within them an estimation that there is something good about them. It gives people pleasure to be admired and loved by others because people love what is good and admire what is great. Hence by being admired and loved by others people estimate themselves to be, in some way, good and great. And this estimation causes pleasure. Of course, the pleasure is greater when the love and admiration come from people who are wise and good, but even flattery generates pleasure for it is a kind of praise--even when insincere.[48]

Just as the good actions of others towards us can cause us pleasure in three ways, so, too, can our own doing good to others cause us pleasure in three ways. First of all, consider the effect of doing good to others. "To the extent that we consider the good of another to be, as it were, our good because of a union of love, we delight in the good which is done to others, particularly to friends, through us just as we delight in our own good."[49]

Secondly, consider the terminating point of one's desire when doing to another. One may be hoping to get some good for himself from doing good. Since hope is a source of pleasure, so, too, is doing good to another.

Finally, consider the starting point of good deeds. From this perspective we find three possible sources of pleasure. First, by having a power to do good for another one might be made aware of an abundance of good existing within himself. Out of this abundance he might find something to share with others, and might take pleasure in this just as a man takes pleasure in his children or in something he makes. Second, if one's power be inclined to do good to others by habit, this can become a virtue for a man. To give to others is a pleasure for a man possessed of the virtue of liberality. Third, that which moves the power to action might be the love of doing good to another. Since love is the main cause of pleasure, whatever we do or suffer for love is pleasurable.[50]

Of course, one might, also, argue that while doing good deeds for another can be a source of pleasure, so can defeating, contradicting and punishing someone. Well, St. Thomas would readily admit this. But he would contend that doing good to others gives a person pleasure because of the good perceived in the act itself, while defeating, contradicting or punishing someone gives pleasure inasmuch as it seems to be related to one's own self. For example, by defeating someone one is made aware of one's own skill. Hence competitive games, games in which there can be a winner, produce the greatest delight for people. And by contradicting another one may derive pleasure from the feeling of knowledge or skill associated with intellectual superiority. (Of course, one might contradict someone in order to do him some good. In such a case contradiction would be good in itself.) The same holds for punishing someone.

If a person delights in punishing another through anger, for example, this is often because he feels belittled by some injury. By getting revenge a belittled person estimates himself to be superior and gains pleasure in this.[51]

In "evening the score," so to speak, a belittled person's behavior reveals another cause of pleasure, namely, being alike, or similar. Similarity, for St. Thomas, is a cause of pleasure because it is a cause of love, and because love is a cause of pleasure.

As St. Thomas pointed out with regard to love, anything a person likes about himself he can like about another. Hence anything a person enjoys about himself he can enjoy about another. What people find displeasing about other people, or other things, is not similarities but dissimilarities, or even similarities, which are harmful to one's self. For this reason the hungry man delights in food liking to his taste and appetite, but finds physical revulsion in over-eating. And for the same reason a merchant takes delight in his customer, with whom he shares a business relationship, but tends to dislike other merchants with whom he has to compete for business.[52]

The last cause of pleasure about which St. Thomas speaks is related more to knowledge than it is to love. Pleasure, it should be recalled, is caused, in general, by two things: the attainment of a suitable good and the knowledge of such an attainment. It is in relation to both of these, but more directly in relation to the latter, that wonder causes pleasure. For wonder causes pleasure when it is related to arousing a desire to find out how to get what one wants. Wonder, in short, arouses pleasure, because it suggests to the mind the possibility of attaining what one finds pleasant.[53]

d. The effects of pleasure

When considering the effects of pleasure many of us, today, might simply say that pleasure makes us "feel good." St. Thomas, however, lists four effects of pleasure: 1) spiritual dilation or enlargement; 2) thirst and desire; 3) alteration in reason; and 4) alteration in activity.[54]

Spiritual dilation occurs, for St. Thomas, as a result of some knowledge of union with a fitting good, and as a result of an ascension and acquiescence within an appetite as the appetite seeks to surround and to interiorize the known good. For a pleasurable good causes a person to expand his awareness and his desires in order readily to receive such a good. This kind of open receptivity may, as St. Thomas sees it, therefore, be metaphorically referred to as a "dilation" because this word suggests a dimension of magnitude, which is similarly suggested by openness for reception.[55]

Thirst and desire, St. Thomas contends, are produced by pleasure either directly or indirectly. These are not direct products of present pleasure, as St. Thomas sees it, for present pleasure itself puts desire to rest (at least it does if we understand "desire" to refer to a pursuit). But indirectly these can be caused by present pleasure inasmuch as one might be in a state of incomplete possession of a pleasurable good. For one might be delighting in something which can only be made present in a successive way, that is, in bits and pieces. Or one might be delighting in something which is completely present all at once, but which cannot be possessed all at once due to some weakness in the possessor.

Thirst and desire, however, must be products of pleasure when the pleasurable object is not present. Hence St. Thomas contends that remembered pleasures produce thirst and desire by returning a person to a disposition in which, at some prior time, he directly experienced pleasure. For unless a person's disposition to a past event has changed, the way he will apprehend this event will be with desire.[56]

Alteration in reason occurs as a result of pleasure insofar as the activity of reason is impeded or improved by pleasure. Reason, St. Thomas thinks, tends to be impeded by physical pleasures and improved by intellectual pleasures. The reason for this is that physical pleasures distract the mind from considering something solely according to reason. They, thereby, divide the attention of reason between the thing known and the pleasure associated with it. In addition, physical pleasures are accompanied by physiological changes which can hinder the use of imagination and sense powers. And these powers are needed by reason to exercise its proper activity. (For example, when a person is drunk or sick from over-eating his reasoning becomes impaired because his imagination and/or sense powers are disordered.) Beyond this, physical pleasures can impede reason by delighting in things in which reason finds no good reason to delight. In so doing they can weaken the estimations made by reason by encouraging an imprudent and untimely termination of the activity of reasoning. And this, according to St. Thomas, happens in the area of practical, or applied, knowledge rather than in the area of thinking as such. Physical pleasures interfere with practical judgment because practical judgments involve choices. And people are moved to choose in light of emotions and with emotions. That is, emotions play a direct part in practical knowledge by acting as a kind of go-between, relating the mind to an applied object. For example, in shooting a basketball or in hitting a golf-ball the amount and kind of emotion one puts into one's shot can impede the judgment of reason in relation to the best way to shoot. So, as an emotion, pleasure can directly impede the way the mind is exercised in practical application. And this is something which cannot happen when merely thinking about something for the sake of thinking.[57]

As regards alteration in activity St. Thomas thinks that pleasure can be both a help and a hindrance. It helps a power by putting its activity to rest in the thing it likes or loves. That is, it completes the activity of a sense or intellectual power by satisfying its appetite, and by causing an agent to be more eager and attentive about an action. The way that pleasure can hinder an activity is by dividing one's appetite in more than one direction, and by hindering the use of reason. For reason directs bodily activity through sense appetites. When these appetites are in conflict with one another, or in conflict with reason and will, one's concentration and eagerness to act becomes diffused and the efficiency of one's activity suffers.

Pleasure, one should recall, arises from a person's propelling appetite and from a person's will. What it does is to cause the appetite's activity to be more vigorous. In so doing it adds a further good to some attained good. For in satisfying one's appetite one fulfills a good beyond the good attained. And, beyond this, by causing an appetite to be more vigorous, pleasure causes a person to concentrate more attentively upon what he is doing (for he is enjoying what he is doing), and causes a person to perform his actions more diligently.

So, as St. Thomas sees it, by and large pleasure is an aid to an activity rather than a hindrance. The only case where he seems to take exception to this is the case of some physical pleasures. For some physical pleasures impede the use of reason. And human activities (that is, freely chosen activities) depend upon reason and upon its right use. Hence some physical pleasures, by impeding the use of reason, serve as a hindrance to human activity.[58]

e. Pleasure: Is it morally good or evil?

What St. Thomas has to say about pleasure might strike some contemporary readers as unusual. For Thomas seems to take a very receptive attitude towards pleasure. And contemporary critics of Christianity often contend that Christianity takes just the opposite view. As G.K. Chesterton points out:

> Nothing is more common, for instance, than to find such a modern critic writing something like this: 'Christianity was above all a movement of ascetics, a rush into the desert, a refuge in the cloister, a renunciation of all life and happiness; and this was a part of a gloomy and inhuman reaction against nature itself, a hatred of the body, a horror of the material universe, a sort of universal suicide of the senses and even of the self. It came from an eastern fanaticism like that of the fakirs and was ultimately founded on an eastern pessimism, which seems to feel existence itself as an evil'.[59]

Now how such a critic squares a view like this with Christianity's historic battles against Manicheeism and Albigensianism we do not know. Nor do we know how such a critic can account for the celebrations like Easter and Christmas, or for beliefs like that of the Incarnation and of the Resurrection of the dead. But what we find even more puzzling is how a critic like this can seriously not be embarrassed by the imprudence of such claims when faced with the teaching of Aquinas himself. For Aquinas is a major figure among Christian theologians. And while what he has to say might not be completely accepted by all Christians, we do not think that most Christians would find widespread disagreement with him on the living of a Christian life.

But to show how views like the above-cited one just do not square with the thinking of Aquinas, let us consider what St. Thomas has to say of the value of pleasure. What he has to say, however, about the value of pleasure resembles what he has already said about whether pleasure impedes or assists activity. For just as he holds that some pleasures assist activities and some pleasures impede activities, so, too, he holds that some pleasures are morally good and that some pleasures are morally bad.

What determines the moral value of a pleasure, for St. Thomas, is the point of rest of an appetite. If an appetite comes to rest in a good which does not agree with the good dictated by a rightly ordered reason and by the law of God, the pleasure of that appetite is morally bad. If, on the other hand, an appetite comes to rest in a good which does agree with the good dictated by rightly ordered reason and by the law of God, the pleasure of that appetite is, for St. Thomas, something morally good.[60]

The reason Thomas holds this is because things are judged morally good or morally bad according to their agreement with a rightly ordered reasoning power. Since pleasure is a feature of appetite or desire, for pleasure to be morally good desire must agree with rightly ordered reason. And for pleasure to be morally evil desire must run counter to correctly ordered reason.[61]

Now desire agrees with correctly ordered reason when desire is for something which is really good for a human being. Hence the pleasure derived from the satisfaction produced by virtue, for example, is unqualifiedly good. For virtues are, by definition, always good. To delight in virtue, then, is, for Thomas, something which is always good.[62]

Other goods, however, are not good without qualification. Certain goods we desire are only morally good because under certain circumstances and conditions they agree with rightly ordered reason.[63] So, for example, the use of drugs like morphine might be morally objectionable for a physically healthy person because they will cause debility in the body. But these same drugs might have just the opposite result in a physically sick person. And in such a case they would be morally good.

So, as St. Thomas sees it, physical pleasure is not evil. In fact, he thinks that no one can live without it, and, consequently, people will ignore those who teach that it is. For those very people who teach that pleasure is evil will more likely than not be discovered by others delighting in some pleasure or other. And this discovery will cause people to ignore such teaching. For people are moved, he says, "... more by example than by words."[64]

f. Are some pleasures unnatural or abnormal?

A question like the one just posed directly above might, at first sight, look prudish and out of place. For, after all,

98

many of us, today, seem to use physical pleasure as the measure of a thing's moral goodness. And, beyond this, many of us just do not see how, today, anyone could be so unsophisticated and out of step as to call something "unnatural" or "abnormal." Well, because of the general difficulty we think many readers might have in understanding how such a view can make sense, we had better make clear how we are using the words, "unnatural" and "abnormal."

Obviously, these words can be understood in a variety of senses. For they can be said of all kinds of things, situations, feelings, relations and so on. So, while something might be considered unnatural or abnormal when we understand these words in one sense, that very same thing might not be considered unnatural and abnormal when these words are understood in another sense. At the very least, however, these words do seem to have some vaguely discernable common element to which each constantly refers. "Unnatural" suggests something which disagrees with nature and "abnormal" suggests something which disagrees with a norm.

Of course, by saying this we do not think we have pointed out anything to a reader which will cause him to pat himself on the back for having bought this book. For what we said seems self-evident. We understand the meaning of "unnatural" and "abnormal" by relating these words to "natural" and "normal." What, then, is meant by "natural" and "normal"?

Well, "natural" means that which agrees with a nature, and "normal" means that which agrees with a norm. The words "nature," and "norm," however, are just as vague as the words "natural" and "normal." So what might be called a "nature" or "norm" in one sense of the word might not be a nature or norm in another sense.

"Nature," as St. Thomas understands it, is primarily used to refer to a distinguishing power which exists within a thing, and which is the source of movement which originates within a thing.[65] And "norm," for St. Thomas, is something in comparison to which another thing is measured.[66]

When talking about a <u>human nature</u>, St. Thomas thinks the word "nature" can be taken in two senses. It can refer to man's intellect and will because it is by virtue of these powers that a person engages in activities not found in other kinds of things. Or it can refer to what a person shares in common with other things. That is, it can refer to non-rational and to non-volitional features of a person.[67]

Hence, when St. Thomas says that some pleasures are unnatural, what he means is that they do not agree either with man's rational or non-rational movements. That is, pleasures are unnatural for a <u>human</u> being to the extent that they do not agree with <u>human</u> nature. A <u>human</u> nature, however, is a nature which has a rational power and a sense power. And each of these kinds of power seeks, by instinct, to exercise its own activity in perfect operation, and to adhere to an order of subordination through which a person gains complete control over the direction followed by a person through his powers.

A pleasure, therefore, is an unnatural human pleasure to the extent that it does not agree with reason, or with the instinctive order of subordination which exists within the human person. For it is through reason that a person maintains control over the direction followed by his powers.

An unnatural human pleasure is, therefore, an emotion which, in some way, weakens a power or weakens a power's disposition to be directed by reason. It is a pleasure which takes delight in something which is destructive to a person's life, faculties or direction by reason. For example, to delight in destroying one's eyes for the sole purpose of getting rid of one's sight is perverse because the movement of nature is towards preserving sight. For such an instinctive movement or "push" is a norm of natural activity. That is, it is the instinctive push of a power, or nature, to move its actions in one direction rather than in another which is employed as the measure of normalcy for the actions of a power or nature. And anything which goes against this sort of push is both unnatural and abnormal.[68]

Now, granted, it is not always clear, at times, just when pleasures are normal and abnormal. For circumstances can create exceptions to what is most often the case. Yet we think few people would call "normal" a person who delights in rape, or in having abortions, or in fornicating with porcupines.

And we think this is so because we think Aquinas is right here. But we realize that what he says is not taken as the norm by many people today. Rather, many people, today, would consider nothing unnatural and only a few things, perhaps, abnormal. And what they would use as a norm of action would not be the inclination or push of a thing's nature, but the custom of a culture.

Why is this so? What makes it so difficult for contemporaries to recognize that things have ways of putting themselves together and of taking themselves apart? What makes it so difficult to see that there are ways in which things push towards and away from one another, ways which are independent of the human mind and human will? What makes it so hard to admit that there exist sources of movement within things which give them a way of acting towards which they are inclined?

Well, we think that two things make all this difficult. The first is the habit of observation which contemporaries have adopted from the physical sciences. And the second is the ineptness with which traditional moral teachings, like those of Aquinas, have been explained to contemporary students.

Contemporary thinkers do not tend to use human nature as a norm of human activity because they try to observe human nature the way physical scientists observe things. They look for it with their senses. And not finding it by means of their senses they conclude that it does not exist at all.

Having concluded that human nature does not exist, such contemporary thinkers are at a total loss to account for any movement being internal to anything. For the nature of a thing causes movement to arise within a thing. Hence, for them, whatever movement is attributed to a thing must actually be external to that thing. And when the thing which is moving is a human being, and when this human being is moving in a repetitive fashion, the only conclusion they seem able to draw is that human activity is caused by some sort of identical external relation which they name "custom," or something similar to this.

Now, given this way of looking at things, it is quite natural to expect that contemporary thinkers will be unable to consider the action of anything to be unnatural or intrinsically abnormal. For in such a view nothing is unnatural or intrinsically abnormal. And given these presuppositions, people who argue that some actions are unnatural and intrinsically abnormal cannot help but look like fools.

So, when we say that some actions are "unnatural," and intrinsically "abnormal," we must be understood as using these words within the context of a power ontology and psychology of the sort adopted by Aquinas. Certainly no actions are unnatural or intrinsically abnormal in the contemporary sense which we have just described.

But in saying this we do not wish to suggest that this divergence in meaning between Aquinas and some of our contemporaries is just a word game. No, what we wish to suggest is that Aquinas is right and our contemporaries are wrong. And the reason we hold this is simply that if we deny to things internal sources of movement and activity, or "natures," we can never attribute to things any movements or actions of their own. That is, without natures, things can never cause actions to occur. And if things can never cause actions to occur, things can never do anything.

When we extend such reasoning to the area of distinctively human behavior, what we are faced with is this. No human being can ever be held responsible for his or her behavior because no human being can ever be the source of his or her own actions.

Now surely such a view of human beings and of things in general is absurd, and ought finally be put to an end. For not only does this view make moral activity a farce, it also makes the act of knowing impossible. That is, by denying internal sources of activity to things it makes it impossible ever to attribute actions to things. And this means we can never say that anything ever _does_ anything. But if nothing ever does anything how can we ever know anything?

Of course, in criticizing this contemporary attitude regarding natures, we do not want our readers to think that the prevalence of this view, today, is due solely to the dominance of a philosophical attitude influenced by the habit of observation proper to the physical sciences. Rather, we think that a main reason this view has become prevalent is due to an inability on the part of more traditionally-oriented philosophers to articulate their own views in an intelligible and interesting way.

Whatever the case may be, however, we have spent enough time on this issue to get our point across. So let us get back to St. Thomas's treatment of the emotions. We have just discussed pleasure. So let us now consider its contrary--pain.

5. Pain and Sorrow

The same two factors which St. Thomas considers necessary for pleasure he considers necessary for pain--namely, union with some good and perception of this union. St. Thomas thinks that the both of these are necessary because, as he sees it, unless something is apprehended as good or evil for someone, a person finds neither pleasure nor pain in that object. And unless someone is united to some object, in some way, a person cannot find pleasure or pain in an object either.[69]

Pain, like pleasure, can, for St. Thomas, be attributed to either the sensory appetite or to the will. When attributed to the sensory appetite, we call an apprehended evil a "pain," but when attributed to the will we call an apprehended evil a "sorrow." Sorrow, therefore, is the contrary of joy just as pain is the contrary of pleasure.[70]

According to St. Thomas there are four kinds of sorrow: pity, envy, anxiety, and torpor. St. Thomas divides sorrow up in this way on the basis of various objects to which one's own sorrow can be related. That is, as St. Thomas sees it, the proper object of sorrow is a subject in whom some evil is present. But one can, in a way, feel sorrow even when there is no direct evil present to one's self. In this way one feels pity for another person when some evil befalls him. For one pities another by taking sorrow in another's misfortune and by estimating it to be one's own. Or one feels envy for another by taking sorrow in some good-fortune which happens to another. And one does this by judging this good fortune, in some way, to be evil for one's self.

One feels anxiety and torpor, on the other hand, by adding a sorrow to one already possessed. It is characteristic of a person in sorrow to avoid the evil which is causing one's sorrow. When this is prevented a person feels anxiety, that is, a kind of confusion and immobilization of mental and spiritual direction. Another name Thomas gives to such a feeling is angst. This state can be aggravated to such an extent that one can even lose movement in one's limbs and can be made speechless. Such a state is what St. Thomas refers to as torpor.[71]

a. The causes of pain and sorrow

St. Thomas lists several causes of pain and sorrow. These are: 1) union with evil; 2) desire for good; 3) and an irresistible power.[72] We have already mentioned union as a necessary factor involved in pain. And the reason this factor is a cause of pain seems obvious. Pain is an emotion which arises from the perception of the presence of some evil, in some way, within a human power. Now such a perception is not possible unless some evil be joined to a person in some way, either in bodily organs, in sense powers, in imagination, memory, appetite or reason. Hence union with evil is required for the existence of pain.[73]

The reason St. Thomas holds desire for good to be a cause of sorrow lies in the relation of an appetite towards good. As

St. Thomas sees it, to be inclined to avoid evil one must first be inclined to possess good. One's inclination towards good gives rise to sorrow when the satisfaction of this inclination becomes frustrated. That is, inasmuch as one has hope of obtaining what one desires one has pleasure. But to the extent that one's hope is diminished to that extent is one's pain increased.[74]

Since a person is inclined by nature to avoid evil, and since pain is related to a resistance of the appetite to evil, pain is caused by an action stronger than one's power of resistance. St. Thomas contends, in addition, therefore, that to the extent that an inclination to resist some stronger agent is changed to an inclination towards receptivity for that agent, the result is not pain but pleasure.[75]

This close connection which St. Thomas sees between pleasure, pain and the inclination of an appetite is so intimate that Thomas considers interior pain to be stronger than exterior pain. As St. Thomas sees it, the cause of exterior pain is some evil repugnant to the body, but the cause of interior pain is some evil repugnant to the appetite as perceived through imagination or reason. Now unless exterior pain is repugnant to an interior appetite, not only does one not feel pain; one actually experiences joy. But when exterior pain is accompanied by interior pain, the pain is increased. For not only does the body sense evil, but this evil is perceived by one's imagination and reason, and is thereby intensified. For objects of imagination extend beyond those which are experienceable by the body.[76]

b. Effects of pain or sorrow

St. Thomas lists four effects of pain and sorrow. These are: 1) a lessening of one's ability to learn; 2) depression of the spirit; 3) a weakening of all one's activities; and 4) physical harm.[77]

One's ability to learn is decreased because pain divides one's attention. As St. Thomas sees it, all of a person's psychic powers arise from the same source. In a sense, they all feed off the same nature as the origin and continuation of their activities. Or, to put it in another way, all of a person's psychic powers are capable of acting because they are energized by one and the same nature. A person's intention, or desire, however, directs the flow of activity from his nature through his powers. And when a person's intention is concentrated in a vigorous way on one object, the flow of activity throughout other powers is necessarily lessened. Just such a concentration happens in relation to physical pain because a person's body is weak and its preservation demands great attention. Intense pain, therefore, is an obstacle to learning because it prevents the focusing of concentration required by learning. And unless a person is a great lover of learning he can become so totally absorbed by physical pain that not only can he become prevented from learning anything, but he can even become incapable of giving his attention to things he already knows.[78]

Beyond lessening one's ability to learn, physical pain can cause psychic depression. Now, in saying this, St. Thomas points out that he is speaking metaphorically. That is, he holds that emotional effects are often described by use of metaphors because there is a likeness between movements of psychic appetites and movements of bodily tendencies. For example, pleasure is uplifting, at times, because it is experienced after the removal of some painful obstacle. And physical bodies are, at times, uplifted in order to avoid a physical obstacle. So, St. Thomas says:

> It is clear from what has been said that sorrow arises from the presence of evil. And it is also clear from this that the presence of evil which repels the movement of the will depresses the soul insofar as it prevents one from getting what one wants. And if the sorrow-producing evil be not so strong as to drive away all hope of avoiding it, although the soul might be depressed insofar as it does not possess in the present that which it wants, there remains within it the movement to repel this evil. If, however, the strength of the evil looms so high that it excludes hope of evasion, then absolutely the interior motion of the soul in anguish is so impeded that it is able to turn neither one way nor another. And, at times, the exterior motion of the soul is so impeded that a man is struck dumb.[79]

The depression of one's spirit which St. Thomas relates to sorrow does not always completely impede a person's actions. In fact, as St. Thomas sees it, some actions are actually caused by sorrow. Such actions, he thinks, are augmented by sorrow so long as hope of overcoming the sorrow remains. For the more a thing causes a person sorrow, the more he tries to overcome it. But other actions (actions which <u>cause</u> sorrow rather than actions which result from sorrow) are weakened by sorrow because sorrow weakens our will to act. And the will is the cause of distinctively human actions.[80]

Of course, sorrow takes a toll on the body just as it does on the soul. All emotions, in some way, affect the body, particularly the heart, but, according to St. Thomas, sorrow more than any other emotion causes bodily harm. The reason he gives for this is that "...human life consists in a certain motion which is diffused from the heart into the other bodily parts." But this motion is suitable for human nature only within certain limits. Otherwise it causes damage to bodily organs. And whatever impedes the flow of this life motion is harmful to human life by nature. Sorrow, in particular, impedes the flow of life through the body because the appetitive reaction of aversion or flight which is characteristic to sorrow causes a disruption in the orderly conduction of life throughout the parts of the body. That is, sorrow acts in a fashion different from emotions like joy, pleasure and desire. The latter emotions cause the movement of one's appetite to seek what is not harmful to the motion of life throughout the body. So, when kept within certain boundaries, these are good for bodily health. But sorrow directly disrupts the conduction of life through the body by contravening the natural order of operation instinctively sought by the human body.[81]

c. Remedies for sorrow or pain

As St. Thomas sees it, the best remedy for sorrow is pleasure, no matter what the cause of sorrow. For sorrow is to one's appetite what fatigue is to the body. And since any sort of physical rest brings relief from physical fatigue, so any sort of pleasure brings relief from sorrow.[82] In particular, however, St. Thomas posits the following actions as remedies for sorrow: 1) crying; 2) the compassion of friends; 3) contemplation of truth; and 4) sleeping and bathing.[83]

St. Thomas gives two reasons to explain why crying helps to alleviate sorrow. One reason is that pleasure is caused by the performance of suitable actions. Crying, however, is suitable to a person in pain or sorrow (presumably because it is an instinctive reaction in such cases). So, in consequence, crying alleviates pain and sorrow through the pleasure derived from the very suitableness of crying when in pain and sorrow.

The second reason crying alleviates pain and sorrow is that everything harmful is more greatly afflictive to one's appetite when it is closed up inside the appetite. For this causes an increase in the intensity of one's concentration within the appetite. To release the affliction from one's appetite one must displace the affliction with some pleasure. This is what happens in crying. The unpleasantness experienced within the appetite is displaced from the appetite through the pleasure derived from crying.[84]

The second remedy for sorrow, namely, the compassion of friends, works in a fashion similar to crying. That is, it displaces one's sorrow through external assistance and pleasure. Just as crying helps a person's appetite to release some of the attention fixed on its sorrow, so the compassion of friends helps it to lighten its burden. For the knowledge that others are helping him bear his sorrow lessens the depression the sorrow makes on a person.

Furthermore, when a person's friends share his sorrow a person perceives that they love him. This causes pleasure, and pleasure lessens sorrow. Hence compassion of friends lessens sorrow.[85]

Since pleasure lessens pain and sorrow, St. Thomas considers contemplation of truth to lessen pain and sorrow. The reason for this is that just as the mind can overcome dispositions of the body and can influence mental and bodily movements regarding things it wants done, so delights of the mind can overcome mental sorrow and bodily pain. "Contemplation" suggests not simply awareness of something, but concentration of attention on an object. Now the experience of pain presupposes knowledge of pain. To the extent, then, that a person increases his knowledge or "consciousness" of pain, to that extent the pain increases for that person. So if a person can fix his knowledge on a pleasure, he divides his attention on the pain and, thereby, reduces it. Truth, however, is a pleasure for the mind because pleasure satisfies a power, and truth satisfies the mind. And as the power in a person whereby a person is most internally self-directing and self-initiating in his actions, the human mind, or intellect, is the highest human power. For one power is higher than another on the basis of its ability to initiate and to control its own activities. Contemplation of truth, then, is, for St. Thomas, the highest human pleasure pursued by human instinct. And, for him, the more a person develops the habit of loving wisdom, the more a person is able to control pain and to lessen its influence. For a person who is in the habit of loving wisdom more than anyone else has control over what influences the direction pursued by his mind.[86]

The last of the remedies for pain and sorrow which St. Thomas posits is to sleep and to bathe. He proposes these remedies because of the special harm which sorrow and pain inflict upon the body. As he sees it, sleeping and bathing help to restore to the body the tempo of movement which instinctively is generated through the heart. Sorrow, and pain, that is, disrupt the regular movement produced through one's normal heartbeat. And sleeping and bathing work to restore this regular movement. In achieving this these produce pleasure. For the natural order to which the body tends automatically produces pleasure.[87]

d. Pain: Is it morally good or evil?

To some people the above question might seem easy to answer. After all, what person would hold that pain is morally good? Well, we think a number of people would. For, just as with pleasure, the moral goodness and evil of pain is determined by the point of rest of an appetite. That is, if an appetite comes to rest in something which does not agree with rightly ordered reason, the pain experienced by that appetite is morally good.

The reason for this, according to St. Thomas, is that it is good for a person to recognize evil and to consider it unwelcome. This, however, is precisely what happens when a person feels sorrow upon the presence of evil within his appetite. He feels evil as evil and rejects it as such. Now moral good is a good which is measured by correct reasoning about individual actions to be chosen. Consequently sorrow and pain are morally good when these are felt to result from choices which willingly do not agree with correct reasoning about right actions to be done. And, in addition, these are useful because they provide people with an additional motive for avoiding evil. For sorrow and pain cause people to be more attentive than usual to the avoidance of evil.[88]

The Contending Emotions

Having completed our examination of the propelling emotions, it remains for us to consider the contending emotions. These are hope and despair, fear and daring, and anger.

1. Hope and Despair

Hope, in a way, resembles love, desire and pleasure. Hope, that is, is attracted towards good. But the good towards which hope is attracted is blocked by some difficult obstacle. So the object of hope is a good one desires to have in the future and is a good which is possible to attain. For no one hopes to get what is either already possessed or is impossible to attain. Hope, in short, "...is a movement of the appetitive power resulting from the apprehension of a good which is future, arduous and possible to attain...."[89]

St. Thomas contends that hope can be caused by a number of different things: wealth, courage, instruction, persuasion, experience, stupidity, or any other thing which can augment the possibility, or the suspicion of the possibility, that some good is attainable.[90] In particular, St. Thomas refers to young people, drunkards, and fools as instances of hopeful individuals. As he puts it:

> The youth possess much of the future and not enough of the past. Consequently, because memory is of the past, but hope is of the future, they are too short on memory, and live much on hope.
> Again, because of a warmth of nature the young have a lot of spirit, and so they are big-hearted. From this big-heartedness arises that which inclines them towards that which is arduous. And so the young are full of life and are of good hope.
> Similarly, those who have not suffered defeat, nor experienced obstacles in their pursuits, readily estimate something to be possible. Hence the young, because of a lack of experience with obstacles and failures, readily estimate something to be possible. And so the young are of good hope.
> Two of these characteristics are also present in drunkards, namely warmth and high spirits (due to wine), and the lack of consideration of danger or of defeat. And for the same reason all those who are fools, and do not employ deliberation, will try everything and are of good hope.[91]

Inasmuch as hope causes a person to estimate that an obstacle might be overcome, St. Thomas thinks that hope is an aid to action. Unlike despair, hope does not turn away from an obstacle as impossible to overcome. It excites attention and increases effort. For it recognizes a formidable obstacle to demand attention, but, also, to be conquerable.[92]

2. Fear

The cause of fear, like the cause of hope, is something complex. Hope is caused by some good which is future, arduous and possible of attainment. Fear is caused by some evil which is future, difficult and irresistible. Hence fear is not simply a subjective attitude. It is a reaction to a particular kind of stimulus, namely, to a formidable one which one desires to avoid. A person who is afraid is a person, therefore, who is, in some way, weak, and who is confronted by some potentially overwhelming strength.[93]

As St. Thomas sees it, fear is caused both by elements outside the person and by elements inside the person. External to the person one has to deal with a strong evil which is imminent. Internal to the person one has to deal with the image of this evil and one's estimation of one's own strength. Hence St. Thomas says that "...riches and strength and a multitude of friends and power drive out fear...."[94] In addition, internally one has to confront one's own fear of being afraid. For this can immobilize activity. And one has to confront the power of one's will to face the impending evil.[95]

There is, also, a time element involved in one's experience of fear. Future evils which are a long way off tend to appear less fearsome, while imminent evils, especially of a sudden nature, increase a person's fear. This is so because "...the painfulness of a present evil is lessened by the passage of time...," and because fear of evil is lessened by premeditation. Sudden evils tend to distract a person from remedies which might be used to repel these evils.[96]

According to St. Thomas there are six kinds of fear: laziness, embarrassment, shame, amazement, stupor, and agony.[97] And he gives the following argument to support this division:

> ...fear is related to a future evil
> which exceeds the power of a person
> in fear, so that he is unable to re-
> sist it. However, what is good for

a man and what is evil for him can be considered either in his activity or in exterior things. In a man's activity a twofold evil can be feared. First, there is the labor which burdens his nature. This causes laziness when someone refuses to act because of a fear of excessive labor. Second, there is disgrace which damages his reputation. If one fears disgrace in the action one is beginning, one is embarrassed; if, however, one fears disgrace about what is already done, one is ashamed.

An evil which consists in exterior things can exceed the power of a man to resist in three ways. First of all, by reason of its magnitude--namely, when someone considers something to be so great an evil that its exit does not diffuse fear. This is amazement. Second, by reason of its strangeness--namely, because some unfamiliar evil offers itself to our consideration and is mystifying by our estimation. In this way fear is stupor, which is caused by a strange object in one's imagination. Third, by reason of lack of provision-- namely, because it cannot be provided for. In this way future misfortunes are feared. And such fear is called agony.[98]

As far as the effects of fear are concerned, St. Thomas reduces these to four: 1) contraction; 2) trembling; 3) deliberation; and 4) alteration of action. The former two are primarily physiological reactions. The latter two are primarily psychological.[99]

According to St. Thomas there occur within the human body reactions to emotions which resemble, in a proportionate way, the reactions which occur within a person's appetite. That is, bodily movements result from psychic movements and, reproduce in a bodily way, movements similar to those found on the psychic level.

As an example of this St. Thomas points out how fear is caused in one's appetite by the apprehension of an image of something which one estimates to be an imminent evil and difficult to repel. Such a thing is judged fearsome not simply because it is evil, but because one cannot overcome it. Not all evils produce fear, then. Only formidable ones, and ones which cause a person to suspect his own weakness. Hence the awareness of one's own weakness causes a mental withdrawal and appetitive withdrawal from the evil. That is, one shrinks back, or contracts one's mind and appetite from facing the evil. This mental attitude not only contracts a person's appetite, it contracts his body. For the contraction of the sense appetite disrupts the movement of life throughout the body and causes a concentration of this movement and of heat, by means of which life is conveyed, to transfer from exterior to interior bodily organs.

St. Thomas says that, as a result of this withdrawal of heat and activity from the external organs, a frightened person becomes cold. That is, the sense appetite withdraws its motive activity from the body, and in withdrawing this activity decreases the amount of heat around the heart through which motor activity is conducted. Thus people in fear withdraw rather than press forward like people in anger or daring. The latter press forward because the sense appetite conveys movement to the body through an increase in heat and energy around the heart, which enable a vigorous transfer of movement to the external parts of the body. The same kind of physiological reaction occurs to men who have been injured or who are in pain. And this concentration of extra activity within them causes them to cry out. For they seek to direct outside of themselves the excess of motive energy being concentrated within.[100]

People in fear do just the opposite, however. In fear motive activity withdraws from the external regions of the body; a person becomes prevented from speaking and starts to tremble. As St. Thomas says:

> ...in fear heat deserts the heart, inclining from top to bottom, so that the heart of those in fear trembles most of all, and so do the bodily members which have some connection to the chest area where the heart is located. From this, fearful people tremble especially in speech, because of the closeness of the vocal artery to the heart. Indeed the lower lip and the whole lower jaw tremble because of their connection to the heart, and from this chattering of the teeth follows. And for the same reason arms and

hands tremble. But it might also be that these members are more mobile. For this reason the knees of fearful men shake, according to the verse of <u>Isaiah</u>, <u>Strengthen the weak hands and make firm the trembling knees</u>.[101]

Regarding the effect of fear upon deliberation, St. Thomas thinks that fear can promote deliberation and can detract from it. Because the evils which cause fear are formidable and imminent St. Thomas thinks that fearful men are most anxious to deliberate. But the state of fear itself is a handicap to wise deliberation. So while fear causes deliberation in the sense that it makes one willing to seek counsel, it does not cause deliberation in the sense that it creates a climate conducive to the exercise of prudent judgments.[102]

Fear affects action in a fashion similar to its affect upon deliberation. It can help it or hinder it. Fear of something can paralyze action because fear disrupts bodily functions. But fear can cancel out the ill-effects produced in the body by causing a man to be more careful and attentive to what he is doing, unless the fear is so great that it even disrupts reasoning. And in this way fear can help a person to action by causing him to deliberate about the means of escaping what is feared.[103]

3. Daring

When referring to daring St. Thomas first prefaces his explanation of this emotion by recounting how all the emotions pertain to an appetite, and how every movement of an appetite is either an advance or a retreat, which can be either primary or secondary. That is, primarily a person is attracted towards what is good and is repelled by what is evil. In a secondary way, however, a person can be attracted to what is evil and repelled by what is good. For we might be attracted to something evil because of some good to which it is related, or we might be repelled by what is good because of some evil to which it is related. The pursuit of evil, however, is directly a pursuit of good and only indirectly a pursuit of evil (because it is related to good). And the avoidance of good is directly an avoidance of evil and only indirectly an avoidance of good (because it is related to evil).[104] So, as St. Thomas says:

> ...the pursuit of evil follows the pursuit
> of good, just as the avoidance of good fol-
> lows the avoidance of evil. These four re-
> actions, however, pertain to four emotions:
> for the pursuit of good pertains to hope,
> avoidance of evil to fear, the pursuit of
> terrible evil to daring, and avoidance of
> good pertains to despair.[105]

Following this summation of the relation between appetitive reactions and emotions, St. Thomas draws his conclusion about daring. Daring is an effect of hope, he declares, and it is the contrary of fear. Its cause can be either something which promotes hope or something which excludes fear, and can be related either to one's appetite or to one's body. For daring results from hope and fear.[106]

In relation to appetitive reaction St. Thomas contends that what promotes hope, and, therefore, also, daring, is that which causes a person to estimate that he can achieve success. The success need not be achievable through his own power, through his own physical strength, experience with danger, wealth, and so on. It can be achievable through outside help, like that given by friends or by God. For a person can estimate success to occur in a variety of ways independent of his own power. And daring is a reaction to the estimation of success.[107]

In addition, what dispels fear is the elimination of approaching evils. Fear arises when a person, aware of some weakness on his part, estimates himself to be imminently exposed to an evil which can exploit that weakness. Very often we notice that these sorts of estimations are aroused in us by other people rather than by things. For very often we injure other people and this causes us to expect injury in return. So St. Thomas says that a person who has injured no one is not aware of imminent danger. "For to those who injure others dangers seem especially imminent."[108]

In the body the arousal of hope and the supression of fear cause heat to arise around the region of the heart. This warming of the heart, as St. Thomas sees it, causes the heart to dilate and to expand. And this acts to promote daring by creating bodily conditions which allow the parts of the body to be conducive to quick and forceful reaction.[109]

So a person who has daring need not be experienced with danger or sound of mind. He can be young, or drunk, or a fool.

For daring is a reaction to a sense estimation of danger. Such an estimation is spontaneous, and is likely to overlook something therefore. Hence, as St. Thomas sees it, unless a person tempers daring with reason, which can discover difficulties overlooked by spontaneous estimation, daring cannot be sustained in the face of unexpected complications.[110]

4. Anger

Anger is the last of the contending emotions discussed by St. Thomas. And as Thomas sees it, anger is, to some extent, a composite of other emotions. It contains elements of love and hatred, desire and aversion, hope, pleasure, and sorrow. For anger has two objects, one good and the other evil, namely revenge, and a person by whom one has been injured and against whom one seeks revenge. The revenge one loves, desires, hopes for and delights in, but the person against whom the revenge is sought one hates, and one finds to be repugnant, unpleasant and a source of sorrow.[111]

As a contending emotion, anger involves some obstacle or difficulty. Hence St. Thomas claims that unless there be some major obstacle related both to revenge and to the person against whom revenge is sought there is no anger. Unless some obstacle stands in the way of revenge, or unless some obstacle obstructs a person's dislike or aversion for another, there is no angry reaction. For this reason, we tend not to become angry about things which are of little importance to us.[112]

As a desire for revenge, anger involves reasoning. For a vengeful person has to consider some manner of inflicting punishment in return for an injury to himself. So, say, for example, a person is slightly drunk, yet capable of reasoning. Such a person, as St. Thomas sees it, is susceptible to anger because he can reason. But when he gets so drunk that he loses the capacity to reason he loses his anger.[113]

In addition to reasoning, according to St. Thomas, anger involves justice. He says this because he thinks an angry person desires evil to happen to another person to a certain degree. Unlike hatred, which wills unlimited evil to befall another, anger seeks retributive evil. That is, "...anger seeks evil under the aspect of just revenge. So when the inflicted evil exceeds the measure of justice in accord with the estimation of the one in anger, then he laments."[114] And the angry man wants the one suffering to be made aware that the reason for his suffering is retribution for an evil.[115] This is unlike the hateful man who wants to inflict punishment simply because he wishes evil to befall someone else.[116] Since he is not motivated by justice, he has no concern about informing his enemy about some just retribution as the cause for his action.[117]

a. Types of anger

Anger is divided by St. Thomas into three kinds: 1) bitterness; 2) mania; and 3) furor. And the basis for this division lies in something which increases anger, either by facilitating this reaction, by causing it to endure, or by being the object towards which it is directed.[118]

For St. Thomas bitterness is a kind of anger based upon ease of reaction. A person is "bitter" when he easily responds in anger to someone. Mania, in turn, is a kind of anger which is caused to remain (manere) for a long time in one's memory. (The root of the word in Latin suggests that which abides or lasts.) So a person is a "maniac" when he broods over his anger for a long time and becomes saddened by his inability to achieve revenge. Finally, furor is a kind of anger which is not quieted until punishment is exacted. A "furious" person will not rest until he has gotten his revenge.[119]

b. The causes of anger

St. Thomas reduces all the possible causes of anger to one: belittlement.[120] As St. Thomas sees it, anger is always caused by an injury done to a person. So, strictly speaking, inanimate objects cannot arouse anger. This is not to say that a person cannot, at times, feel anger towards a stone or towards a dead man. But this is not anger in a precise sense. For anger requires reason and seeks to have the one being punished made aware of the retributive nature of the punishment being exacted. So anger towards inanimate objects is more of a spontaneous sensory response than it is an act of reason. For it is irrational to try to punish what can feel no punishment. Just revenge demands a person against whom it can be directed.[121] And this is what anger seeks: to punish a person as a means of obtaining just revenge.[122]

According to St. Thomas there are three kinds of belittlement: 1) rudeness; 2) spite; and 3) contempt. By analyzing these St. Thomas explains why belittlement includes all causes of anger.

Anger, he argues, seeks just revenge. And this means that anger reacts to some injury regarded as unjust. Injury, however, can be caused in three ways by a person: out of ignorance, out of emotion, and out of deliberate choice. Injury out of rudeness is injury out of ignorance. Injury out of emotion is spite. And injury out of deliberate choice is contempt.

Of these three types of belittlement St. Thomas thinks that belittlement out of contempt is most likely to cause intense anger. For to be unjustly injured by another when such injury is done out of ignorance or out of lack of rational control of the emotions reduces the amount of injustice involved. But to be unjustly injured through a deliberate choice intensifies the injustice and, with it, the anger.[123]

St. Thomas thinks that anger can, also, be intensified in particular when the injured party is either superior in some way to the injuring party or has some defect, or when the injuring party has some defect.[124] With respect to the injured party, being superior to the injuring party gives the injured party a greater motive for being easily angered. For anger is motivated by unjust belittlement. And the more talented and skilled, or superior, a person is, the more unjust is any belittlement of his talent, skill, or superiority. Furthermore, when an injured party has a defect, he is already sensitive to further injury. For a defect is a kind of injury. Since anger is motivated to inflict painful injury, people with defects are particularly vulnerable, and are, consequently, more readily angered.[125]

With respect to the injuring party, when such a person has a defect this may cause an injured party to be more or less angered. As St. Thomas puts it:

> A defect or shortcoming in the one against whom we are angry causes anger to increase inasmuch as it increases the undeservedness of the belittlement. For just as one who is superior is more unworthy of belittlement, so one who is inferior is less deserving to belittle. And, therefore, nobles are angered if they are belittled by peasants, or wise men by fools, or masters by servants.
> If, however, a shortcoming or a defect softens the undeserved belittlement, such a shortcoming does not increase, but decreases, anger. And in this way those who are sorry for wrongs they have done admit themselves

to have made a mistake, and who humble themselves and ask forgiveness mitigate anger...inasmuch as such people seem not to belittle but more to hold in high regard those before whom they humble themselves.[126]

c. The effects of anger

As far as the effects produced by anger are concerned, St. Thomas considers appetitive, mental and physical alterations.[127] Appetitively, he thinks anger produces pleasure, and fervor.[128] Mentally, anger both causes a person to reason and interferes with the formulation of rational judgment.[129] And physically anger causes diverse internal and external alterations to the heart, face, eyes and tongue, and, when extreme, interferes with speech.[130]

Appetitively, pleasure is related to anger inasmuch as anger is caused by pain and pleasure is a remedy for pain. Anger is a reaction to a painful injury which seeks revenge as a remedy for the pain. When revenge is achieved so too is pleasure, and the pleasure is greater as the pain is greater. In eliminating the pain of anger vengeance is enjoyed and puts anger to rest. Before eliminating the pain revenge is pleasant as something hoped for. And without the presence of hope for revenge anger is not possible. For it is the desire for the pleasure of revenge which causes anger. In addition, prior to eliminating the pain of anger, revenge is pleasant as something continually considered. Even the images and dreams about revenge are pleasant.[131]

Fervor is related to one's appetite for anger inasmuch as pain is a present evil destructive to the appetite. Every appetite, however, strongly reacts to present evils which are destructive to its operation. Hence intense desire is generated by anger to repel the injury and to achieve revenge. This intense desire is fervor.[132]

With regard to mental activity anger stimulates reasoning as an essential element of anger itself. One becomes angry after reasoning that one has been unjustly belittled. But anger impedes reasoning which occurs subsequent to one's becoming angry by not obeying its reasoning. For anger agitates the body to move swiftly and this agitation hinders reasoning.[133]

The bodily agitation just referred to is one of the effects produced by anger on the body. As St. Thomas sees it, anger produces a fervor in the heart analogous to the appetitive fervor it causes. This "fervor" is an intense heat in the blood and activity surrounding the heart which act as the conductors for emotional activity throughout the body. Fervor, aside from inflaming the heart, increases the heartbeat, causes the body to tremble and the tongue to falter. It warms the face, fires the eyes, causes one not to recognize familiar things, causes the mouth to form sound, and makes the person who speaks unaware of what he is saying.[134]

Of course, not all anger reaches this extreme. The point St. Thomas wishes to make is that anger greatly influences the movement of the heart. And action which disturbs coronary activity causes disruptive movements, particularly in the eyes, face and tongue. So, while anger will always tend to warm the face, cause irregularity in breathing, and unusual motion in the eyes, at times it will cause a person to speak, and, at other times, it will make a person speechless. In fact, St. Thomas says anger can be so strong that a person will be unable to move a hand or foot, or might even die. For agitation of the heart can be so intense that it immobilizes bodily activity, even of the heart.[135]

CHAPTER 5

LAW AND GRACE

The final ingredients which, for St. Thomas, cause an action to take on the form of a human action are law and grace. A moral life is, once again, for St. Thomas, a distinctively human life. A distinctively human life, however, is a self-mastered life. And a self-mastered life is a life in which a person is in the habit of making right choices under direction of rightly ordered appetites and reason. Thus far, we have stressed powers, appetites, emotions, dispositions, habits and virtues as elements of a self-mastered, or moral, life because human beings incline, or bend, their actions into shape, under the influence of all these elements. But, in addition to these elements, St. Thomas adds law and grace to this list because he thinks human action is, also, shaped to completion by means of these.

St. Thomas's reasoning here is that law is a kind of directive (regula) and measure of human action by which someone is induced or is turned back from acting.[1] That is, law is a directive whereby human beings are commanded to order their choices in the direction of one mode of action or another. For human acts are freely chosen acts of human beings. Law directs human action because law is a directive of reason and because reason commands human action through its directives to act, or through what St. Thomas calls an "executive order."[2]

Law, then, as St. Thomas sees it, presupposes reasoning. Law is an executive order to act which results from a person reasoning about the ways of achieving some desired operation. The most desired operation of human action, however, is, for St. Thomas, man's ultimate end.[3] This operation above all else gives direction to acts of human choice. Hence law, more than anything else, is concerned with and gets direction from man's ultimate end, that is, from human happiness.[4]

Human happiness, for St. Thomas, however, comes down to perfection in being human—that is, to perfection in living the life of a material being endowed with reason. And for such a being to thrive in existence through the exercise of his powers, St. Thomas thinks an ordered community life is necessary. Consequently, St. Thomas holds that law, in the most exact sense, is concerned with ordering individual human actions in relation to common human happiness.[5]

Or, to put it in another way, since law, for St. Thomas, is a directive of human action, and since a person is directed to happiness by living in co-operation with other people, "law," in the most precise sense, is directed to co-operative human life—to that ordering of human choices called the "common good."[6] Law, that is, is not a directive of just anyone's reason. It is the product of a people or of their representative.[7] As St. Thomas says, "Law is nothing other than a directive (ordinatio) to the common good promulgated (that is, instituted and written down) by someone in charge of a community."[8]

In the case of the human person several diverse kinds of law are necessary because, simultaneously, one and the same individual belongs to several different communities.[9] A human being seeks perfection in being human not only in relation to other people but, as St. Thomas sees it, also in relation to God. A human being is not only a member of an earthly political community. He is, also, a member of a species with its own characteristics, and a member of a created community which receives its directives from its creator. Hence, for St. Thomas, there are, in general, six types of law: 1) Eternal law; 2) natural law; 3) human law; 4) the Old Law; 5) the New Law; and 6) the law of lust.[10]

General Consideration of Law

Eternal law (lex aeterna), as St. Thomas understands it, is a law by which God governs the whole community of the universe. Eternal law, in other words, is the eternal idea behind God's creation. It is the idea by which He governs.[11]

The second type of law mentioned by St. Thomas, that is, natural law, is not, properly speaking, a rule or measure in God, as is Eternal law. Rather, it is a rule or measure in certain of God's creatures lying in an order of tendencies within them caused by the impression of Eternal law upon them. The creatures of which we speak St. Thomas calls "rational creatures," whom, he says, share in Eternal law by a natural inclination to provide for themselves and for others.[12]

Natural law, for St. Thomas, provides human beings with common and indemonstrable principles which act as the starting points of practical knowing, just as theoretical reason is provided by God with indemonstrable principles of speculative knowing. These natural principles, however, are only general directives, and, as such, are insufficient for determining just what to do in the individual circumstance. Hence St. Thomas holds that, "...from these common and indemonstrable principles it is necessary for human reason to proceed to more particular arrangements." These particular arrangements St. Thomas calls "human laws."[13]

Besides Eternal law, natural law, and human law, St. Thomas holds that the direction of human life requires another law, what he calls divine law (<u>lex</u> <u>divina</u>). He gives four reasons for this. First, because, he says, the ultimate end of human life toward which all human beings are directed is beyond the power of attainment of natural human faculties; yet law directs man to acts which are suited to the achievement of his ultimate end.

Second, because, Thomas says, the uncertainty of human judgment, especially about contingent and particular issues, results in the passage of diverse and contrary laws. To preclude any doubt about how to act and how to live in order to achieve eternal life, a divinely given law is necessary.

Third, because, he argues, while men can make laws about exterior actions, which they can observe and judge, they cannot make pronouncements about interior acts. But complete virtue requires a man to be correct in both areas. Since human law cannot grasp and sufficiently direct interior acts, a divine law has to supervene.

Fourth, because, Thomas holds, with St. Augustine, that human law cannot forbid and punish every evil because human law aims at mutual co-operation among many people of different degrees of virtue. Since to attempt to forbid and to punish every evil would go beyond the capacity of human law, such an attempt would actually do away with much good and would be an obstacle to human concord. But since man's eternal happiness requires that no evil go unforbidden or unpunished, a divine law had to be added to human law.[14]

For St. Thomas this divine law is one in kind, but has two parts related to one another as undeveloped to developed. That is, it consists of the Old Testament and the New Testament. St. Thomas says this because of three elements he has already noted which pertain to law—namely, that law is a directive of human action toward man's ultimate end; that law directs human action in a manner suited to the achievement of this ultimate end; and that law leads men to observe commands. He looks at the Old Testament as undeveloped divine law, then, first, because man's ultimate end is twofold; one is a material and earthly good, and the other is a spiritual and heavenly good. "To the first," he says, "the Old Law was directly ordered...." From its very institution this law, Thomas states, "...invited its people to the earthly kingdom of Chanaan." To the second, the New Law is ordered. So, "...from the beginning of His preaching Christ invited people to the kingdom of heaven."

Second, St. Thomas looks at the Old Testament as undeveloped law because he thinks a law which governs not only exterior acts, but also interior ones, is more fully law. The Old Law, he says, "restrains the hand," but the New Law, by governing inner acts of the soul, "restrains the spirit."

Finally, he says that the Old Testament is undeveloped because it leads men to keep commands through fear of penalty. The New Law, on the other hand, leads men to obey commandments by flooding "...into our hearts through the grace of Christ." This grace of Christ "...is conferred by the New Law, but it is prefigured in the Old."[15]

Or to put all this in another way, for St. Thomas, man's complete final good cannot be achieved except through the grace of Christ. "Natural law," he says, "directs men according to certain general precepts in which the undeveloped share as much as the developed. And so it is one for all."[16] That is, natural law does not direct a person in the fine details of right action. It only sets him on his way with general guidelines, and these same guidelines are given to all people whether they be virtuous or not.

Divine law, on the other hand, is a guide to particular acts, to acts to which the undeveloped and developed are not similarly related. It is for this reason, Thomas holds, that divine law is twofold—that is, because at different stages of human history different kinds of actions are demanded of people to advance the development of the human race towards complete virtue, two laws were necessary. The purpose of the Old Law, as he sees it, was not to bring all men to eternal happiness, but to prepare people for the New Law which would achieve this. Hence the Old Law had to be fulfilled through the advent of Christ.[17]

The sixth law which St. Thomas discusses is what he calls the law of lust (*lex fomes*), and it is not so much a law as it is a penal consequence for the violation of a law. But because penal consequences fall within the realm of a legal order, he holds that mankind's impulse towards sensuality has, in this sense, the character of law. That is, as a penal consequence of law, this impulse has the quality of law, but since the rightful condition of man is to act under the direction of reason, rather than under the direction of sensuality, man's impulse to sensuality is, for St. Thomas, more properly a deviation from law.[18]

Particular Consideration of Law

1. Eternal Law

Considering law from a more detailed perspective, St. Thomas makes six points about Eternal law. First, he argues that Eternal law is nothing other than the idea of divine wisdom whereby God directs the movements and actions of everything.[19] Second, he contends that this law is, in some way, known by all, at least with respect to general principles of natural law.[20] Third, he holds that no one of us comprehends this law because we only know it through God's effects, but each of us knows it, in some way, according to his own capacity.[21] Fourth, he says that every law is derived from this law insofar as a law agrees with it because the governing ideas of lower rulers are derived from the governing ideas of higher rulers, and because the force of all law comes from God.[22] Fifth, he shows that both necessary and contingent matters are subject to Eternal law because all contingent matters and all necessary matters, other than God Himself, are subject to Eternal law.[23] And, sixth, he argues that all human affairs are subject to Eternal law either by being in complete agreement with it or by suffering as a result of incomplete fulfillment of God's intention.[24]

2. Natural Law

In his consideration of the particular details of natural law, St. Thomas, also, makes six points. First, he holds that, in a precise sense, natural law is not a habit because a habit is a settled disposition or quality of appetite, or mind, whereby one acts.[25] That is, a habit is not an inborn, or innate, tendency to act. It is a tendency which is, in some way, derived either by practice, in the case of intellectual and acquired moral virtues, or by infusion, in the case of theological virtues. But since a habit is what is possessed by holding, natural law can, in an extended sense of the term, be called a "habit."

Second, regarding the principles of natural law, St. Thomas argues that there are several of these just as there are several first principles of knowledge by demonstration. That is, for St. Thomas, just as the ability to link judgments together in such an arrangement, or order, as to form a demonstrative argument presupposes some kind of pre-demonstrative knowing about how to form and to order judgments, in a similar way, he thinks the ability to direct human choices in a practical order presupposes a knowledge of how to form and to order human choices. How to form and to order these we know by the first overriding directive, or principle, of natural law: to pursue and to do good and to avoid evil. This directive determines and measures all other commands related to free human choice.

All other commands of natural law are based upon this first instinctive command, and are derived from it according to an order, or set of priorities, instinctively adhered to within the nature of a person. This order runs from more general instincts to more particular ones, and starts with what a person shares in common with all substances. Thus, inasmuch as the first principle of natural law is a directive governing a substantial being, this directive instinctively presents itself as a directive for a substance, namely, to pursue and to do good, and to avoid evil, in a manner befitting a substance. A substance, however, is, for St. Thomas, a power, and the good instinctively sought by any power is perfect operation. Hence the first command which issues from the first principle of natural law, and which human beings share in common with other substances, is to seek perfect operation of one's substance and to avoid whatever obstructs such operation.

A human being, however, is a composite substance. So in seeking a perfect operation befitting a substance, a human being instinctively pursues a perfect operation which befits a composite substance. That is, in seeking to operate well as a composite substance, a human being instinctively seeks to use all of the powers at his disposal in a natural order of subordination most appropriate for maintaining the perfect operation of a human substance.

The second directive which issues from the first principle of natural law is to seek good and to avoid evil in a manner appropriate to an animal substance. To St. Thomas this means that in the pursuit of perfect human operation a person is instinctively directed to preserve and to foster in existence elementary goods specific to animals, like mating and educating the young.

The final directive which St. Thomas considers to issue from the first principle of natural law is related to what is proper only to reasoning beings. By this directive a person instinctively seeks to preserve and to foster in existence such actions like living in society, avoiding ignorance and knowing God.[27]

These directives of natural law are, in short, commands which issue from a rational tendency within the human being. They are commands which direct the manner in which human choices are to be formed and to be measured. That is, natural law is an instinct, but it is an instinct which exists in a person because of a distinctively human power called "human reason." It is an instinct which commands adherence to direction by human reason in determining right human choices and right human action. And, finally, it is a directive which requires that human reason measure the rightness of human choices and human actions by means of an inborn set of priorities or order of instincts found within each and every human person.[28]

The third point which St. Thomas makes regarding natural law deals with the question "whether every act of virtue is from natural law." Thomas says, as he so often does, in one way, "Yes," and in another way, "No." That is, when talking in general, all acts of virtue are subjectified in man's natural instinct to act according to the direction of reason. But by nature not all of us are immediately inclined to the same virtues. Some of us might, for instance, tend instinctively to be mild mannered, while others might not. Hence some virtues have to be prompted by reasoning and investigation.[29]

St. Thomas's fourth point regarding natural law deals with the question "whether natural law is the same for all." Once again, St. Thomas says, in one way, "Yes," and, in another way, "No." Since natural law pertains to human instincts, it is the same for all people. That is, all people possess an instinct to direct their lives according to the decisions of correct reasoning. But, as St. Thomas sees it, since direction of one's life according to correctly ordered reason involves the making of practical decisions about contingent matters, natural law is the same for all only with respect to general commands. With respect to the particular decisions and conclusions based upon these general directives, however, these are not the same for all. As St. Thomas puts it, "In actions practical truth or rightness is not the same for all with respect to particulars, but only with respect to common principles, and the practical truth of particulars which exists among these people is not recognized in exactly the same way by all."[30]

The fifth point deals with "whether natural law can be changed." Here St. Thomas holds that particular conclusions, which are closely derived from natural law, can be changed on rare occasion. The first principles of natural law, however, are unalterable.[31]

And a similar conclusion is derived by St. Thomas regarding his sixth point, that is, regarding the possibility of obliterating the natural law from man's heart. The principal commands or directives are known in an instinctive way and cannot be effaced. The application of a general directive to a particular situation, however, can be frustrated, and conclusions closely derived from principle directives of natural law can be obliterated by things like bad habits and customs.[32]

3. Human Law

As a principle of moral activity St. Thomas considers natural law to be of major import. Still, he does not identify moral activity with natural law. Natural law is one principle among several whereby moral activity originates. In itself it is insufficient for the performance of complete moral action. In fact, it is the very insufficiency which exists within natural law which, for St. Thomas, gives rise to human law. Man cannot realize the living of a completely moral life through natural law alone, so human law is needed to be added to natural law.

Human law, then, is a derivative and supplement of natural law. And it gets its binding force from natural law. For by instinct human beings seek happiness through co-operative living with others. Hence, as St. Thomas sees it, the end of human law is to maintain peace and just order within a community.[33] For this reason he thinks legislators frame laws to fit the majority of cases. For a human community is composed of many people differing in their degree of virtue.[34] Hence laws should not try to restrain all vices, but only those which are obstacles to peaceful and just living. "Human law," he says, "is posited for the multitude of men, the major part of whom are not perfect in virtue. So human law does not prohibit all vices from which the virtuous abstain, but only the more serious ones from which it is possible for the major part of the multitude to abstain, and principally those vices which do harm to others, without the prohibition of which human society cannot be preserved, like homicide, theft and so on."[35] Indeed, St. Thomas thinks that human law is incapable of preventing all vices, and that, were it to attempt to do so, those not thoroughly possessed of virtue, not being able to bear the strain of such laws, might break out into worse evils.[36] Hence he also holds that there is a need for flexibility in human law,[37] and that it must always be changed to meet the situation when an evident gain from its change can be realized.[38]

4. The Old Law

As a Christian, of course, St. Thomas does not think that human, or civil, law can thoroughly achieve man's ultimate goal any more than can natural law. And the reason for this is the obvious one that man's ultimate end is supernatural and eternal, while the end serviced by natural law and human law is principally natural and temporal. Hence St. Thomas uses the very insufficiency he finds within both these types of law, when coupled with the instinctive quest he finds all humans to have for an everlasting and unrestricted happiness, as the foundation upon which he builds his argument for the need of a divine law.[39]

Moral activity, it should be recalled, is an <u>inclination</u> to agree with nature in one's actions. Since, for St. Thomas, man's nature directs him to an end which surpasses his nature, an inclination to follow his nature in a moral way suggests to St. Thomas that man be directed in a supernatural way by a divine law.

Now whether the happiness sought by humans be a temporal and finite one, or an eternal and infinite one, it should be noted that it is something which people have to work at achieving. But, as St. Thomas sees it, when a human being seeks after something in a human way, he has to have some sense of where he is headed. When a human being pursues something which, in some way, he wants, he is inclined by nature to direct his choices by comparing alternatives like parts to a whole. A person will tend to move himself to action by carrying on an internal argument about the various alternatives open to him. He will weigh the comparative contributive fitness of one way of acting over another. He will tend to sit down, or to walk around, and to plot out the most fitting strategy or plan for getting what he wants.

As St. Thomas sees it, however, what all people want more than anything else is to be perfect people. They wish instinctively to live perfect personal lives both temporally on earth and eternally with God. With respect to earthly existence, being a perfect person entails developing the habit of thoroughly virtuous living under the guidance of natural law and just human law. And with respect to life with God, being a perfect person entails possessing the habit of thorough-going charity under the guidance of divine law and grace.

Or to put it in another way, for St. Thomas, what all people seek more than anything else is complete moral activity. This, for St. Thomas, is the activity which human beings were created by God to manifest. And this activity, for St. Thomas, lies within the power of man's reason, in possession of truth, so impressing itself upon the human will and the human appetites, that the choices one makes are, by habit, not only in perfect harmony with the instinctive order of natural subordination of powers and appetites which exist within the person, but are, also, in perfect harmony with man's natural environment and with the intellect and will of man's God. In short, perfect moral activity, for St. Thomas, is the life of perfect virtue. Towards this activity St. Thomas thinks all people are directed by natural law, human law and divine law.[40]

Of course, having said this, we find ourselves somewhat perplexed. For it seems that what St. Thomas considers to be the most instinctively desired of all human activities is the same one which human beings are most strikingly incapable of achieving. Yet, at the same time, we think that this very perplexity can serve as a means for clarifying the moral teaching of St. Thomas.

The moral teaching of St. Thomas is the moral teaching of a Christian theologian. As such, it cannot be completely understood apart from St. Thomas's view of human history. For, as a Christian, St. Thomas considers God actively to have intervened in human history by establishing a covenant with the people of Israel and by becoming man through the Incarnation. That is, as St. Thomas sees it, mankind's moral history involves three periods of moral development: the period of the law of nature, the period of the Old Law, and the period of the New Law.[41]

The first stage of mankind's moral education was, for St. Thomas, a stage in which man took pride in his knowledge and thought that he could achieve eternal happiness through his own natural reason. To overcome man's pride, and to enable man to discover the weakness of his reason, St. Thomas thinks God left man without the support of a written law. Then, around the time of Abraham, God gave man the Old Law. For, at this time, St. Thomas argues, man had debased himself in idolatry and in the worst of vices. As he says:

> It must be said that it was most suitable for the Old Law to have been given during the time of Moses. The reason for this can be arrived at from two factors, inasmuch as there are two kinds of men upon whom any kind of law is imposed. For it is imposed upon some who are stubborn and proud, who are restrained and subdued by law. And it is imposed upon good people who are instructed by the law, and who are thereby helped to bring about what they intend. It was fitting therefore that the Old Law should have been given at that time in order to overcome the pride of men. For there were two things about which man was proud: namely knowledge and power. He took pride in his knowledge just as though his natural reason could suffice for his salvation. And so that this pride of his might be overcome man was left to the guidance of his own reason without the support of written law. And by this experiment man was able to discover that the weakness of his reason was evident. For around the time of Abraham men had debased themselves in both idolatry and in the most disgusting vices. And so from this time on a written law had to be given as a remedy for human ignorance...But as soon as man had been instructed by the Law his pride was convicted of weakness during the time he was not able to put into practice what he knew....
>
> As far as good men are concerned, the law was given to help them. For it was most necessary for the people living at that time when the natural law was beginning to be obscured by the superabundance of sins. Still it was necessary for help of this kind to be given in a certain order so that imperfect men might be nursed through imperfection to perfection. So it was necessary that the Old Law be given between the law of nature and the 'law of grace.'[42]

The purpose of the Old Law, as St. Thomas sees it, then, was to add something to natural law. And what it added was an aid not only to eternal happiness, but to temporal happiness. That is, it seems to us that, for St. Thomas, a moral activity based solely upon natural law is insufficient not only for achieving eternal happiness, but also for achieving temporal happiness. The directives of natural law are general in character. Yet they need to be applied to particular situations. Particular conclusions need to be deduced from the general principles of natural law. And it is precisely here that the Old Law is an aid to human conduct. For in deducing appropriate human behavior from general directives, mankind, at times, judges to be lawful actions which are morally wrong. So with respect to natural law and human law the Old Law acts as a means to overcome such deficiencies. It helps a person to draw right conclusions in more particular situations regarding moral behavior. And, in so doing, it improves upon the character of natural law and of human law, and assists mankind to achieve a level of natural and supernatural happiness which could not be reached without it.[43]

5. The New Law

But, as St. Thomas sees it, the Old Law is likewise insufficient for the living of a complete moral life. He reasons that the Old Law was not given primarily to prepare mankind for eternal happiness. For eternal happiness demands the performance of completely virtuous activity, and the Old Law, Thomas thinks, does not enable one to achieve this. The reason for this is that it inclines people to perform virtuous activity through fear of various punishments and through the promise of temporal good. For St. Thomas, however, those who are fully developed in virtue are inclined to perform works of virtue because of a love of virtue and not because of some extrinsic punishment or reward. Hence, for him, the Old Law was intended to prepare the human race for a New Law whereby mankind would be directed to perform fully developed acts of virtue. This New Law inclines men to do good not through fear and punishment, but through a transformation of the will through love of good. As St. Thomas says:

> ...all the differences which are assigned between the New Law and the Old are taken from the difference between the developed and the undeveloped. For the precepts of any law whatsoever are given with a view towards the exercise of virtues. For in order to perform

acts of virtue the undeveloped, who do not yet have the habit of virtue, are inclined to act in one way, while those who are developed in virtue are inclined to act in another way. Those who do not yet have the habit of virtue are inclined to exercise an act of virtue through some cause extrinsic to them, for example, the threat of punishment, or the promise of some extrinsic reward, like honor or riches, or something like this. And so the Old Law, which was given to the undeveloped, that is to those who have not yet obtained sanctifying grace, was called 'the law of fear,' inasmuch as it induced one to observe precepts through fear of various punishments; and it is said to hold certain temporal promises. However those who have virtue are inclined to perform works of virtue because of a love of virtue, not because of some extrinsic punishment or reward. And so the New Law, which principally consists in sanctifying grace, itself implanted in the hearts of men, is called the 'law of love'; and it is said to hold spiritual and eternal promises, which are the objects of virtue, especially charity. And so men are inclined to these intrinsically not through something extrinsic, but, as it were, through something proper to them. And it is for this reason that the Old Law is said to 'restrain the hand, not the soul,' because whoever abstains from some sin because of fear of punishment does not absolutely withdraw his will from sin. And for this reason the New Law, which is the 'law of love,' is said 'to restrain the soul.'[44]

Yet, surprisingly enough, St. Thomas does not even think the New Law to be sufficient to enable man to achieve completely virtuous living; at least not if by the New Law one means testimonies of faith and directives which order human actions and human emotions. For St. Thomas, that is, the New Law can be understood in two senses. Principally, it refers:

...to the grace of the Holy Spirit given within, and, in this sense, the New Law justifies. Whence Augustine says, 'There'—that is, in the Old Testament—'law is posited without, by which

the unjust are threatened; here'—that
is, in the New Testament—'the law by
which one is justified is given within.'
Secondarily, it refers to the Law of the
Gospel, that is, to testimonies of faith
and to precepts which order human emotions
and human acts; and, in this sense, the New
Law does not justify. Whence St. Paul says
in II 'Corinthians,' 'The letter kills, but
the spirit gives life,' and Augustine explains
that by 'letter' is understood writings existing
outside men, even of moral precepts such as
those contained in the Gospel. Whence even
the Gospel letter kills if the healing grace
of faith be not present within.[45]

What is primary to the New Law, for St. Thomas, is not moral works or sacramental works. What is primary, for him, is the grace of the Holy Spirit given inwardly to those who believe. For this, as he sees it, restores the human will to a condition of goodness whereby it can perform good acts through a love of goodness and not through external compulsion.[46]

Thus, he contends that the New Law did not abolish observance of the Old Law except with respect to ceremonial practices. For these practices, while more sufficient than natural law for making man morally fit, cannot provide man with the supernatural virtues of faith, hope and charity whereby, for Thomas, man becomes spiritually attached to God through love.[47]

The grace of the Holy Spirit has, for St. Thomas, been around for a long time. In fact, he holds that there have been men at all times who have received this grace and have been men of good will.[48] Hence what St. Thomas is objecting to in the Old Law is not the absence of goodness within it. What he is objecting to is the notion that man can achieve perfectly good will through the performance of ceremonial practices. This, for him, is true neither in the Old Law nor in the New Law. He thinks, that is, that the spiritual message of the New Law is the spiritual message of the Old Law. But in the New Law this message is made explicit, whereas in the Old Law it is implicit.[49]

For example, as St. Thomas sees it, all the precepts of the Ten Commandments are related to charity, to love of God and to love of neighbor.[50] However, he thinks that these precepts were misinterpreted by the Scribes and Pharisees. It was not until the coming of Christ that the application of these precepts could be fittingly made. For, according to St. Thomas, the Sermon on the Mount contains all the information needed for the perfect regulation of man's reason and will, and for the leading of a Christian life. For through the practice of the precepts given by Christ in the Sermon on the Mount a person's interior movements of mind, will and emotion become perfectly regulated in relation to God, neighbor and self.[51]

Grace and Moral Activity

The point which St. Thomas makes regarding the relationship of the New Law to the Old Law is, we think, very important for understanding St. Thomas's moral teaching as a whole. Very often we find students of St. Thomas speaking of the moral theology and the moral philosophy of St. Thomas as if St. Thomas made some sort of rigid division between the two. Frankly, after examining St. Thomas's treatment of law, we do not see how such a division can be made, except as an artificial accretion to the doctrine of St. Thomas. That is, while there might be a moral philosophy which can be derived from the writings of St. Thomas, we do not think St. Thomas himself ever constructed a moral philosophy outside the context of his theology. And, given what St. Thomas says about the matter in the <u>Summa theologiae</u>, and elsewhere, we do not see why such an independent moral philosophy would be present in St. Thomas.

Of course, we realize that some Thomists might disagree with us here, and we might be wrong in what we are saying. So let us see whether we can articulate the reasons why we think that St. Thomas did not develop a moral philosophy outside the context of his theology.[52]

One reason we have for saying this is because, for St. Thomas, man has one ultimate end.[53] This end is to know God, and it influences not just some moral actions, but all moral actions. Being the end of the human intellect, which is the most self-directed of all human powers, this end directs all actions which come under direction of the human intellect. Hence all acts of will, and acts of sensory appetite come under direction of man's ultimate end. The ultimate end of the human intellect is, therefore, the end of all human, or moral, actions. As St. Thomas says:

> ...in all agents and movers arranged in order, it is necessary that the end of the first agent and mover be the end of all,

just as the end of the commander of an
army is the end of all his subordinates.
Among all the parts of man, however, the
intellect is found to be the superior mover;
for the intellect moves the appetite by placing
before it its object. The intellectual appetite, on the other hand, which is the will,
moves the sensory appetites, which are the
contending and propelling; and for this reason
we do not obey the propelling appetite unless
there be present a command from the will. The
sensory appetite, moreover, with the advent
of consent from the will, now moves the body.
The end, therefore, of the intellect is the
end of all human actions. The end and good
of the intellect, however, is truth. Consequently, the ultimate end of the whole man
and of all his operations and desires is to
know the first truth, which is God.[54]

The point we wish to make here about man's ultimate end
is that, while it orders all moral actions, it cannot be
achieved through philosophical knowledge, or through any sort
of human activity unaided by supernatural assistance. Thus
St. Thomas states:

If, then, ultimate human felicity does not
consist in the knowledge of God by which
he is generally known by all or most men,
according to a kind of confused estimation;
and yet if it does not consist in the knowledge of God by which he is known by way of
demonstration in speculative sciences; and
also not in the knowledge of God by which he
is known through faith, as has been seen in
the foregoing; and if it is not possible in
this life to arrive at a higher knowledge of
God so that he might be known through his
essence, or at least in the way that, when
the other separate substances are understood,
God might be known through them as if from
something closer, as has been shown; and if
it is necessary, however, that human felicity
be located in some sort of knowledge of God,
as has been shown above; then it is impossible
that ultimate human happiness be in this life.[55]

Since man's ultimate happiness cannot be in this life, this happiness cannot be achieved through any of man's natural powers or instincts. For St. Thomas creatures below man are directed to their natural ends by God according to a kind of general providence suitable to members common to a species. These creatures, however, have no awareness of the providence which guides them, and this distinguishes their governance by God from man's. As St. Thomas sees it, man, too, is subject to a kind of general providence as a member of a species, but, by virtue of his power of reason man is aware of the providential nature of his governance, and, so, he says that the direction of man's actions as a member of a species takes on the status of natural law:

> ...the rational creature submits to divine providence in a more excellent way insofar as it is itself a partner in providence by providing for itself and for others. Whence it participates in the eternal reason through which it has a natural inclination towards its due act and end. And such a participation in a rational creature of the eternal law is called 'natural law.'[56]

This awareness which man has through natural law, however, is directed to man as a member of a species. Hence it is insufficient to provide each individual man with the particular guidance needed for him to see God in His essence. So, for St. Thomas:

> ...beyond natural law and human law it was necessary to have divine law for the direction of human life...because through law man is directed towards actions in line with his ultimate end. If man were ordered towards an end which did not exceed the proportion of natural human faculty, it would not be necessary for man to have any directive of reason beyond natural law and human positive law, which is derived from natural law. But because man is ordered towards an end of eternal beatitude, which exceeds the proportion of natural human faculty, as we maintained above, therefore it was necessary that beyond natural law and human law he be directed by a divinely given law.[57]

Now, if man is directed towards an end which exceeds the proportion of his natural human faculty, does not this end simultaneously have to exceed the proportion of philosophical speculation unaided by revelation? Clearly it seems to us that it does. And in so doing man's ultimate end exceeds any moral philosophy unaided by divine assistance.

But perhaps we are wrong here. After all, the moral teaching we have been examining is developed within a theological work. One would be inclined to expect St. Thomas to show the dependence of man's natural reason upon revelation and upon faith in such a work. But what about the possibility of a purely philosophical ethics, one not dependent upon revelation or faith? Could not such an ethics be possible for St. Thomas to adopt in relation to man's natural end? For, after all, natural reason is proportioned to achieve man's natural end. So why could not St. Thomas have, separate from his theology, an independent moral philosophy directed to the living of the good human life on earth? Why could he not advocate a purely philosophical teaching whereby human beings could learn to live a life of virtue and of right action in relation to others and to themselves?[58]

Well, as we see it, the reason St. Thomas could not, and does not, have a moral philosophy independent of his theology is several-fold. First of all, even if man does have a natural end in addition to an eternal end, man's natural end is subordinated to his eternal end. That is, man's eternal end is, for St. Thomas, man's ultimate end. And he thinks that unless a person has his reason firmly attached to his ultimate end, he cannot for long completely adhere to the right order of action appropriate to his eternal end or to his natural end. As he puts it:

> ...just as the inferior appetite ought to be subject to reason, so also reason ought to be subject to God, and to fix in him the end of its will. Moreover, it is necessary that all human actions be directed through their end, just as the motions of the inferior appetite must be directed through the judgment of reason. Therefore, just as there cannot help but be disordered motions in a sensory appetite not totally subjected to reason, so also many disorders result in the acts of reasoning in the reason of a man not living subjected to God. For when a man does not have his heart attached to God, so

> that he does not wish to be separated
> from him for the sake of obtaining any
> good or avoiding any evil, many goods to
> be obtained and evils to be avoided arise
> for the sake of which a man recedes from
> God, by rejecting his precepts. And so he
> sins mortally, especially because 'in un-
> expected situations a man operates according
> to a preconceived end, and according to a
> pre-existing habit,' as the Philosopher says,
> although through prior reflection of reason
> a man can do something outside the order of a
> preconceived end, and outside the inclination
> of habit. But because a man cannot always
> be in such prior reflection, it cannot happen
> that he remain for long without acting in a
> manner consistent with a will turned away from
> God, unless he be restored quickly through
> grace to his due order.[59]

Now, if St. Thomas thinks that a reasoning faculty not firmly fixed on God as its ultimate end cannot help but give rise to disordered human activity, why would he construct a moral philosophy independent of his theology? Furthermore, according to St. Thomas, "...in the state of fallen nature man falls short of what he is capable according to his nature so that he cannot fulfill the whole of this good through his natural endowments." If such be the case, then "...he cannot perform the whole good connatural to himself so that it is defective in no respect."[60] Hence to achieve even his complete natural good man, for St. Thomas, must be aided by divine law. And if this be so, why would St. Thomas construct a moral philosophy independent of his theology? For if man is inclined by nature towards perfect human operation, and if, in the state of fallen nature, man cannot achieve perfect human operation without the aid of divine law and of grace, then is not man, by nature, inclined in some respect, towards acting under the benefit of revelation?[61]

Beyond this, consider the context within which St. Thomas develops his views on natural law. By and large it appears to be an historical one in which St. Thomas is pointing to superiority of the New Law over the Old Law and the natural law. Why would St. Thomas construct his teaching on natural law in this way if he were developing some sort of moral teaching independent of his theology? And if he did develop a moral teaching based solely upon philosophy and natural law, why would he say what he does in his commentary On the Trinity?

In Article 1 of Question 3 in that work St. Thomas considers the problem of the necessity of faith for mankind. And within the context of that article St. Thomas tells us that faith is "supremely necessary for man" because without faith man "can neither do nor have anything good."[62] In addition, he states that without faith human society cannot be preserved. For the preservation of human society requires that one believe in the promises, testimonies, and other such things made by one person to another. And, finally, he points out the danger of attempting to discover the purpose of human life through reason unaided by faith! Thus, as Thomas says:

> ...for anyone striving for happiness it is necessary to know in what he ought to seek happiness, and in what way. But this cannot be done more easily than through faith, since the inquiry of reason cannot attain to such an object except through a previous knowledge of much which is not easy to know. And one cannot do this with little danger, since human inquiry comes easily to error because of the weakness of our intellect; and this is clearly demonstrated from those philosophers, who searching for the end of human life by way of reason and seeking within themselves the method of arriving at this end, fell into many and most disgraceful errors; disagreeing to such an extent back and forth among themselves, that scarcely two or three of them all accepted one concordant opinion. Through faith, on the other hand, we see that many people are brought together in one way of thinking.[63]

Why, we ask, would St. Thomas criticize those who attempt to discover the end of human life by way of reason alone, and then go out and join their ranks? As we see it, he would not do this, nor did he do it. That is, as we understand the view of St. Thomas, he recognizes the possibility of there being an ethics based solely upon reason unaided by revelation. But while he recognizes the possibility of such an ethics, he does not advocate its development. For St. Thomas thinks that natural reason ought to give assent to things which are said by God. And he thinks that in man's present state of fallen nature, human reason can rightly guide human behavior only to the extent that it adheres to God as its ultimate end. Hence to live in accord with reason in his present state man ought not to attempt to guide his life by reason unaided by revelation, but he ought to seek to direct natural reason in light of revelation. So, as St. Thomas says:

> ...to live in accord with reason is the good of man inasmuch as he is a man; to live apart from reason can in one way mean a shortcoming, just as it is in those who live according to sense, and this is bad for man. In another way, it can mean a surpassing of reason, as when by means of divine grace a man is led to that which exceeds reason; and to live apart from reason in this way is not bad for man, but a superhuman good. And such is the cognition of those things which are of faith, although faith itself is not in all ways apart from reason; for natural reason holds this, that assent ought to be given to those things which are said by God.[64]

Of course, simply because we contend that, for St. Thomas, moral philosophy should not exist outside the context of theology, this does not mean it cannot so exist. The only point we wish to make here is that while contemporary philosophers do moral philosophy without considering revelation, and while some contemporary Thomists attempt to construct a moral philosophy based upon moral principles adopted from St. Thomas, but apart from the influence of revelation, we do not think one should confuse the approaches taken by these contemporary thinkers to ethics with that taken by St. Thomas. For we think that when such confusions arise one loses the key theme of the moral teaching of St. Thomas. More than anything else the moral teaching of St. Thomas is an "ethics of good-will," or a "Christian ethics of faith and love." This is the ethical teaching adhered to by St. Thomas, and this is the ethical teaching he advocated others to adopt. To do good one has to be good. And to be good one has to have a good will. But to have a good will one has to love God. Not very complex, is it? Yet this, in a nutshell, is, we think, the main message which St. Thomas wished to convey in his ethics. Hence we find the following to be an excellent summation of the moral teaching of St. Thomas:

> ...the end of every law, and particularly of divine law, is to make men good. A man, however, is called good because he has a good will, through which he may reduce to

action whatever good is in him. The will, however, is good because it wills that which is good, and principally the greatest good, which is the end; so the more the will desires such a good, the more a man is good. But a man has more desire for what he desires because of love than for what he desires because of fear only; for what he desires because of fear only is said to be an object of mixed involuntariness, just as someone who wants to throw his merchandise into the sea because of fear. Therefore, love of the highest good, namely of God, more than anything else makes men good and is more than anything else the intent behind divine law.[65]

CHAPTER 6
THE PERFORMANCE OF MORAL ACTION

Having examined the starting points of moral activity, it remains for us now to consider what is involved in the actual performance of a moral action. Since moral activity is activity which involves the practical application of a person's mind and will to the choice of the right action to perform in light of one's distinctively human end, moral activity involves factors both internal to a person's mind and will, and factors external to these. Hence we will first examine the mental and volitional factors involved in moral activity, and then we will examine factors external to these.

Mental and Volitional Factors of Moral Acts

According to St. Thomas, the human will is an appetite located within human reason. The will is an inclination by which human reason pursues or avoids what reason apprehends as fitting for itself or, in some way, fitting for the person.[1] As a _rational_ appetite, the will is inclined to listen to the directives of reason. It is inclined, that is, to take orders from reason as to the means whereby reason can reach its ultimate end. In addition, because it is an appetite of reason, the will achieves its own perfect operation when it adheres to the commands of reason. For without conformity to reason perfect operation of the will is impossible.

In addition to human reason, the will can be set in motion by the sensory appetite, and by causes outside the person. The reason for this lies in the fact that the will is moved to act by that which is presented to it through reason and through sense perception. Through reason and sense perception, however, one apprehends things external to the person, and reactions produced within the sensory appetite. Hence both of these can move the will to act.[3]

Since the human will can be moved by elements aside from human reason, human choice can be influenced by elements aside from human reason. To understand moral activity one should understand the ways in which human choice is influenced by reason, sense appetite, and by causes outside the person.

The question of importance here, of course, is how factors external to the will can cause the will to move without destroying human freedom. For St. Thomas the human will is not wholly free nor is it, for that matter, wholly necessitated. As an inclination within the human mind, the will necessarily wills whatever is instinctively pursued by the human mind. Hence its appropriate and fitting object is complex. For it embraces wanting what is good for a person as a whole and what is good for each of the individual powers of a person.[4] In addition, the human will can be caused to move by the human mind, by the sensory appetite, by environmental and physiological changes and by God. Yet, for St. Thomas, in none of these cases does the cause of the will's movement cause the will to be completely necessitated.[5]

The reason for this is that, for the will to exercise its activity, it has to be presented with an object by the human mind. Now whatever a person thinks about he always has the power not to think about. For nothing about which a person thinks is so unrestrictedly good that he cannot think of something better. But only that which is unrestrictedly good, or good in all respects, can totally necessitate the will to desire it. Since the human mind cannot perfectly comprehend that which is good in all respects, and since the will only desires that which it apprehends through the mind, the will is not totally necessitated by anything with respect to willing or not willing. The will, that is, is always free to will or not to will by directing the mind to think or not to think about something.[6]

Of course, this does not mean the will is not influenced or, in some way, limited by things external to it. People are products of their heredity and environment, as the social scientists are fond of telling us. But that is not all that people are. People are not lumps of plastic or pieces of silly-putty just waiting placidly to be molded into shape by external agents. For St. Thomas people have powers and sources of internal activity which arise within themselves, and which have ways of going together and of taking themselves apart. Reason can cause the will to move, and so, too, can the sensory appetite, and external influences which stimulate bodily organs. In addition, bodily makeup can dispose people to be prone to respond to organic stimuli with one emotion over another. So some people are more easily angered than others, or are more mild-tempered than others.[7] And, for Thomas, God causes the will to move. But the sensory appetite does not necessitate that the will move,[8] and external influences which stimulate bodily organs do not necessitate it to move either.[9] As for God, He moves the will in a way which agrees with the way it is inclined to move by nature. Hence, for St. Thomas, God moves the will in a way which does not cause it to lose its power to make choices, nor compel it to act in only one way. Rather, He moves the will in a way which makes it to exist in act as a will.[10]

Moral acts, for St. Thomas, are acts which involve the will and the mind. They are what St. Thomas calls "voluntary acts," that is, acts which agree with the will and the mind. To put it in another way, voluntary acts are acts which arise from human reason and will, and which are brought to fulfillment under the natural direction and control of human reason and will.[11]

St. Thomas distinguishes voluntary activity from compelled (or violent) activity. As an inclination within the intellectual power, the will has a direction in which it pushes itself to act, and it has the ability to direct other powers which come under control of the intellect. In relation to the former, St. Thomas thinks that no compulsion can touch the will. For nothing can compel the will to act. But in relation to the latter St. Thomas thinks compulsion can affect the will. For in relation to the way it directs other powers an external agency can frustrate commands of reason and will and can cause an activity to be compelled. Such acts are, to the mind of St. Thomas, totally involuntary. Consequently, they cannot be evaluated as to their moral worth. For, strictly speaking, they have none.[12]

Other kinds of acts, on the other hand, can influence the decision of the will without completely negating the voluntariness of its activity. For example, when acting under compulsion the contribution of the act of the will is replaced by some externally injected activity, but when acting through fear or through sensuality the act of the will does contribute, in some way, to the action performed. In the case of fear, the act is not completely voluntary because there is some evil involved in the act which repels the will. What makes an act of fear voluntary, however, is the fact that the will consents to act, whereas, in an act of compulsion, the will withdraws its consent, or power of agreements, to act.[13] In fear, on the other hand, a person consents to move in order to escape from an evil, and so his action is voluntary, but insofar as he moves to avoid some externally impending evil, the act is involuntary. Hence to St. Thomas deeds done through fear are a mixture of voluntary and involuntary, but are more voluntary than involuntary. For they originate within the will and contribute to the kind of action performed.[14] Actions done through sensuality are, likewise, mostly voluntary. In fact, in most cases St. Thomas thinks sensuality increases, rather than decreases, the voluntariness of an action because it increases the willingness to act. For sensuality is a reaction to a sense good. Hence a man acting out of sensuality is not inclined to act otherwise if given the opportunity at the moment of sensual desire, while a man in fear or acting under compulsion would act otherwise if his present difficulty could be removed. The only cases he finds exceptions to this are those in which sensuality totally overwhelms knowledge and drives it out, or impedes knowledge by swaying one's judgment in relation to a particular action.[15]

Aside from violence (or compulsion), fear and sensuality, St. Thomas thinks that ignorance can alter the voluntariness of an action. For voluntary acts are acts of both intellect and will. Hence any ignorance which deprives an action of the knowledge required to make that action voluntary makes it involuntary.

When dealing with the question of the influence of ignorance upon voluntary activity, St. Thomas considers the relation of ignorance to the will in a threefold way: as antecedent, as conjoined, and as consequent. He describes antecedent ignorance as a kind of ignorance of the type involved in the act of a reasonably cautious man who, while in the process of shooting an arrow, has some unexpected passerby cross in front of his line of fire, and kills him. The archer's ignorance precedes his act of willingness to shoot, and it causes him to will what he would not otherwise have willed. For he is ignorant of some circumstance of his act which he has no way of anticipating, and which, if he were to know it, would alter his subsequent action. Hence, for St. Thomas, the acts caused by such ignorance are, in all respects, involuntary.

The case of the archer above would be different, to St. Thomas, if the man killed happened to be someone the archer wanted to kill anyway, but just happened to shoot by accident. When a person wants to kill someone, and succeeds in doing so even though he is unaware of this fact, his action is not involuntary because he does not act _against_ his will, but it is non-voluntary because it is done _without_ the will consenting to the action which ensues. That is, an _involuntary_ action goes against the movement of the will, whereas a _non-voluntary_ action is one in which the will is not directing or consenting to performance of an action. An action, it should be recalled, involves both the subject which initiates movement and the terminating point of the movement initiated. Hence a <u>voluntary</u> action is an action which a will directs to be performed. And in the case just cited the person who acts is not directing his action to killing the person who winds up dying. So his action is not of his will, but, once again, not <u>against</u> it either. And the type of ignorance involved in his action St. Thomas considers to be conjoined rather than antecedent or consequent.

As far as consequent ignorance is concerned, St. Thomas considers all acts which result from it to be voluntary acts rather than involuntary or non-voluntary. For this is an ignorance which is either directly willed or involves something which we can and should know. It is directly willed when a person chooses not to know something either to excuse himself for the wrong he does, or to excuse himself for not avoiding what he is doing. St. Thomas calls this "affected ignorance." It involves something which we can and should know when a person, either as a result of emotions or settled habit, does not take into consideration what he can and should take into consideration; or when a person takes no care to acquire the guiding principles of right conduct which he ought to have. The former St. Thomas calls "ignorance of bad choice," and the latter he refers to as "ignorance of the right principles."[16]

Aside from being an act of will and a voluntary act, a moral or human act is, for St. Thomas, distinguished by the following features: intention, counsel or deliberation, consent, choice, command, employment, and delight.[17] Let us consider each of these in its turn and see what it contributes to determining an act as moral.

For Thomas the very sound of the word "intention" suggests tending into something. As he understands it, intention is an act of the will rather than an act of the mind. And it is an act directly related to the terminating point of human desire rather than to the means of reaching this terminating point. Hence when we intend to do something we not only want to do it, but our will stretches out towards what is desired so strongly that we are moved to perform the appropriate acts which will put our desire to rest. This, of course, means that intention involves not only things which terminate, or end, desire but means whereby these things are attained. And it also means that, while intention is an act of the will, in some way it involves reason. For intention refers to an act of the will which presupposes reason directing and ordering actions so as to achieve a desired end.[18]

Given something one intends to do, the next step involved in human activity is some sort of questioning about how to obtain what one wants. As St. Thomas says:

> Much uncertainty, however, is found in matters involving action because actions are concerned with the singular and the contingent, which, being variable, are uncertain. Reason, however, does not pronounce judgments without preceding inquiry in dubious and uncertain matters; and the investigation of reason is necessary therefore before a judgment of choice. And this inquiry is called 'counsel.'[19]

The word "counsel" is commonly used to refer to a discussion involving several people, and might cause one to think about a bunch of people sitting down together in a conference. The reason for this is that one consults with others about contingent and dubious matters when many conditions and circumstances have to be considered. For this complicates the problem and makes it possible for something to escape the attention of one person acting alone. But, for Thomas, what is distinctive about counsel is not a multiplicity of people, but thinking about singular and contingent events. Hence even one person can engage in counsel or consultation when questioning himself about something to be done.[20]

Today, instead of talking about counsel, we might use the word "deliberation." But, no matter what word we use, for St. Thomas, what we are talking about is some inquiry regarding means to a desired end. The desired end, therefore, is the background against which we measure the rightness or wrongness of means. And it is from the desired end that we derive reasons whereby we measure means. The desired end, that is, is taken for granted in deliberation, and it is in light of this end that we determine whether or not a reason given for selecting a means is a good reason or is any reason at all.[21] Deliberation, therefore, cannot go on endlessly. For deliberation is about something we actually intend to do, and the object of our intention limits the actual means we can pursue to obtain what we want.[22]

Following after deliberation what occurs is consent. Consent, for St. Thomas, is "...the application of an appetitive movement to something existing within one's power." That is, con-sent is a joining together of an appetite with something it likes. By applying an appetite to the getting or doing of something we, thus, consent to what we are doing or getting. We unite our appetite with an action or a thing, and appetitively agree to what we are doing or to what we are getting. In so doing, we put to rest any uncertainty as to whether or not we should resist something and we make a decision in favor of one thing or another.[23]

After consent the next feature distinctive to a human act is choice. To St. Thomas choice combines together two sorts of acts, one mental and the other volitional. It is neither wholly mental nor wholly volitional. And it is quite complex, presupposing consent, deliberation, voluntariness and volition. The Latin word which St. Thomas uses to express what, today, we call "choice" is the word <u>electio</u>. But this Latin term seems to us to signify more than "choice" as we use this word in common parlance today. For by choice we seem, today, simply to mean taking something. For St. Thomas, however, choice, or perhaps better, elective choice, suggests selecting something by a kind of vote. That is, a person chooses by comparing alternate options in light of the proximity or distance these options have to the acquisition of a desired good. As St. Thomas sees it, reasoning comes before election, or deliberate choice. The mind presents to the will several means from among which the will can take one. The will compares these means to the good primarily wanted by the will, and approximates the relative contributive fitness of the alternative means to the acquisition of the desired good. Then, as a result of its comparison, the will wants, or prefers, one means over another.

As a result of the procedure involved in choice, St. Thomas concludes that all choice, in the sense of "election," involves only what is possible and is free. As he sees it, the only reason for choosing something is that it attains or leads to what one desires. Choices, that is, are always related to actions. For actions obtain for us what we desire. Actions, however, are always possible because, by the fact that they are actions, they <u>are</u>. Hence choices, since they involve actions, always involve what is possible. In addition, choice presupposes reasoning. Indeed, it concludes a process of reasoning. But it can conclude a process of reasoning only if it involves possible courses of action. For no conclusion of reasoning can be derived from impossible courses of action.[24]

The fact that choice, or election, involves the use of reason is used by St. Thomas not only to show that choice involves possible courses of action, but also to show that choice involves freedom. The will, he contends, operates in conjunction

with the power of reason. Whatever reason can apprehend as good
the will can desire. But reason can apprehend as good both
willing and acting, and not willing and not acting. No matter
what particular good it thinks about, reason can apprehend in
it some defect. And this allows the will not to be totally
determined to choose any particular thing presented to it by
reason. In fact, choice demands that things presented to the
will as alternative courses of action have some defect attached
to them. For choice involves comparison of two things in relation to one being better than another in relation to some
good we want. Were a thing to be apprehended by reason as
being perfect in all respects, or good without restriction, the
mind would be unable to compare it to some other good as being
closer to what the will wants than another good. For such a
good would have to be what the will wants more than anything
else, not an approximation of it or a means to it. The will,
that is, is incapable of not wanting what has no defect attached to it. Hence in the presence of such an object the
question of elective decision, choice or comparison becomes
meaningless.25

Having made a choice, the next step which follows in the
line of moral activity is that of commanding the employment of
one's choice in action. That is, to employ choice in action
requires some directive of reason to do so. Hence between
choice and the actual employment of choice comes command.26

Once a command to employ a choice in action is made the
actual employment of choice can ensue. Such employment of
choice is, as St. Thomas sees it, analogous to consent.27 For
by consent a person unites his intention to act with an action,
and by employment of choice a person unites his choice with an
action. The latter is done by reason directing a power to do
what has been chosen by the will, and it can relate to any
power which can come under the command of reason.28

But what powers come under the command of reason? According to St. Thomas, these powers are those of will, reason,
sensory appetite, and some bodily organs.29

To command is an act of reason, St. Thomas tells us, whereby reason arranges the parts of an action through some movement.
Commanding, that is, reflects a personal preference. It puts
one activity in the place of priority over another within the
power of reason. Whatever power, therefore, can be moved by
reason can be commanded by reason. The will, however, can be
moved by reason for the will only moves towards or away from
something to the extent that that thing is known by reason.
Hence the will can be commanded to will by reason.30

Indeed, reason itself can, as St. Thomas sees it, be commanded to reason. As examples of this he cites how reason can command itself to think about something, to pay attention, and to use reason in one's thinking. In addition, he points out how some things we accept as true are accepted by the conviction of immediate evidence, while other things are accepted as true through a command of reason. Hence to accept that a triangle has three sides is commanded by the evidence for it is impossible to think about a triangle without simultaneously thinking about three sides. But to assent to matters left open to doubt, or to matters not commanded by immediate evidence, requires a command of reason.[31]

Aside from being able to move the will and to move itself, reason, according to St. Thomas, is able to move the sensory appetite. And through the sensory appetite it is able to move the sensory emotions. But the way in which reason can command the sensory appetite and the emotions is, as St. Thomas sees it, limited by the disposition of the human body. For, according to him, the sensory appetite is a power conducted by bodily organs. And every power which exercises its function through a bodily organ is limited in its exercise by the condition of its bodily organ. As a power, the sensory appetite works through the imagination and through the estimative sense, both of which are subject to respond to the command of reason. Hence both the sensory appetite and the human emotions are, in this respect, subject to reason.[33]

However, for St. Thomas, bodily dispositions can impede the exercise of rational commands made upon the appetites and the emotions. Some people, that is, are born with a physical disposition to be more or less prone to certain emotional and appetitive responses. Hence some people are more easily prone to be angered than are others, and some people have a bodily disposition towards being mild-mannered while others do not. Such bodily dispositions make the emotions and the appetites not completely responsive to reason. And this is especially so when emotional and appetitive dispositions like these are suddenly stimulated. For under such a situation movements arising from these dispositions can get beyond the control of reason.[34]

The last feature distinctive to human activity is delight. This is a feature which, like the rest of the features we have been discussing within this chapter, is not, as St. Thomas sees it, found in animals. People experience delight, just as people deliberate, command, intend, consent, and so on. Animals, he thinks, experience none of these. For delight resides in reaching a desired good and in understanding the meaning of the good one has attained. Since animals do not comprehend the meaning of good, delight is an experience not open to them.[35]

Measuring a Moral Act and a Good Moral Act

Now that we have distinguished those features distinctive to a moral act, we will be able to measure to what extent an act is or is not moral. For now we have some standard features to which we can compare acts, and size them up so to speak. That is to say, all measurement involves comparison of one thing to another. Things are measured insofar as they have a certain amount of something. In other words, the something they have is what is used to measure the things.[36] Thus a thing is said to have so much size, or so much weight, or so much speed, to the extent that size, or weight, or speed is recognized to be present within that thing. Well, a moral, or human, act is measured by being voluntary, intended, deliberate, consented to, chosen, commanded, and employed, and by being related to man's ultimate end. Hence the more an act has these features present within it, and is an act directed towards man's ultimate end, the more completely is an act a moral act.[37]

But to say that an act is a "moral act" is not the same, for St. Thomas, as to say that it is a "good moral act." That is, the way we measure the morality of an act is different from the way we measure the goodness of a moral act. For we measure the goodness of a moral act by the extent to which a moral act is directed by reason towards fulfilling the ultimate end of the human person. Thus to the extent that a person's action is voluntary, deliberate, intended, commanded, chosen and consented to, in relation to the ultimate end of the human person, his action is a _moral_ action. But to the extent that the act employed is freely conformed to the directives of a rightly ordered reason, the employed act is a _morally good_ act.[38]

To make our point here somewhat more clear let us take an example. Suppose, for instance, that we consider a baseball player. How are we to measure the goodness of such a person's activities as regards playing baseball? That is, how do we distinguish a good baseball player from a bad one? Well, we do so in two ways. First, we have to know what the activity of playing baseball aims at achieving. Then we have to measure a person's baseball playing activity by the extent to which it is directed towards fulfilling the end of the activity of playing baseball. A person is a good baseball player to the extent that he voluntarily consents to employ those deliberately chosen and intended activities which, in their exercise, actually promote winning a game in accordance with the rules of baseball. Thus measuring a good baseball player requires that one consider both subjective and physical aspects of a person. From the standpoint of the subject who acts, a good baseball player is a player who intends to win according to the rules and who chooses to command the employment of those activities which promote this goal. Such a psychological condition makes a person the complete author of the activities which he employs. And it is from this perspective that we are saying that the actions of such a person are those of a "good ballplayer." That is, as an acting subject, a ballplayer is good to the extent that he is master of the actions which come from him. And he is master and author of those actions insofar as he can command his body to respond to the directive to perform actions which promote the winning of a game.

A completely good ballplayer, however, is not simply a ballplayer who is in control of the acts which his body performs. He is a ballplayer who, in addition, performs acts which in fact promote the winning of games. Hence when either a ballplayer's mind and will are not directed to the right end, or the acts he performs do not serve to promote that which is right and willed, then what we have is a somewhat lousy ballplayer.

Well, the same is true, mutatis mutandis, regarding moral activity. Completely good moral acts include both acts internal to the subject (like consent and deliberation) and acts external to the subject (like killing or healing).[39]

From the standpoint of internal acts, good moral character comes chiefly from the human will directing itself towards that which is the ultimate good of human life. Human reason, however, is that which directs the will towards its ultimate good. For as the appetite of the faculty of reason, the good of the will is the good of the intellect. Thus the will can reach this good only through the apprehension of reason. And acts of the will, therefore, are dependent upon reason, just as they are dependent upon the ultimate good of human life, for their goodness.[40]

What this means is that not only is a good moral act measured by its suitability for fulfilling the ultimate good of human life, it is also measured by human reason inasmuch as human reason is directed in accord with Eternal law.[41]

Yet this seems to present a problem. For, on the one hand, Thomas says that an act of the will is good when directed by a reason which agrees with Eternal law. And, on the other hand, he says that every will at discord with reason, whether reason be right or wrong, is always bad.[42] How can this be?

Well, in order to understand how both these views can be reconciled, we have to understand what is a reasoning power which agrees with Eternal law, and what is a will at discord with reason. A reason which agrees with Eternal law and divine will pursues truth and avoids error. It commands that the will desire what is really good and that it avoid what is really evil. Such a reason, however, is a <u>human</u> reason. It is finite and is subject to make mistakes. Yet this is how it was created by God, and this is how it is to be followed.[43] The only time the will can be morally excused from following the directives of reason occurs when reason itself is not adhering to direction by Eternal law. That is, when reason is mistaken because of voluntary ignorance, or through an ignorance which is due to neglect of one's knowing what one can and should know, a will at discord with such a reason is not bad. For such a reason is itself at discord with Eternal law and divine will.[44]

As St. Thomas sees it, therefore, an act of the will is made bad either when a person wills something bad by mentally considering it to be in some way good, or when a person wills something good by mentally considering it to be in some way bad. In order for a will to be good, he says, it must will "...a good from the mental perspective of being good, that is, it must will the good because it is good."[45]

External Factors of Moral Acts and Good Moral Acts

From the stress which St. Thomas places on the role played by the will in moral activity, one might get the impression that, for St. Thomas, the entire worth of human acts depends upon the will. For St. Thomas, however, this is not the case. For him the internal voluntary act and the external act constitute one single moral act. And the outward deed, therefore, adds some good or bad to the inward act of will.[46]

As St. Thomas sees it, when determining the worth of a moral act one has to consider both the activity which goes on inside a person's mind and will, and the activity which results from the employment of human choice. When judging the goodness of the activity going on within a person one has to measure that activity against the good most instinctively sought after by human beings. This end, for Thomas, is twofold. It consists of an earthly good of directing one's choices according to reason, and it consists of a heavenly good which lies in what Christians call "the beatific vision of God." Hence, for Thomas, goodness of reason and will is determined by reason and will being correctly headed in the direction of man's earthly and heavenly ends. What heads man in the direction of these ends is, for St. Thomas, divine reason and will as manifested in Eternal law, divine law and natural law. Hence, for him, for reason to be good and right it must be in conformity with these laws. This, in turn, means that goodness of the will is determined by its agreement with a rightly directed reason. For the will is good when it wills the ultimate human good presented to it by a rightly directed reason.[47]

But how does one determine the moral goodness of the moral act which one chooses to perform? How does one measure the moral goodness of the act which results from one's voluntary choice? Well, if moral acts are human acts, and if human acts are deliberately chosen acts, do not moral acts get their character of goodness from something which they possess from their agents? For example, are not comical acts acts, in some way, of comical beings, or military acts acts, in some way, of military beings? And do not these acts get their character from some organization or direction given to them by their agents? So, is not the same thing to be said of moral acts? That is, in measuring a deliberately chosen act as morally good or morally bad, are we not measuring the extent to which an act is organized and directed by a reasoning faculty which is correctly headed in the direction of the ultimate end of human life?

It appears to us that this is precisely what we are doing. When we are considering the moral goodness of a chosen act what we are considering is the positional location, or place, an act occupies in relation to the right direction to an end. What we want to know about the act is whether or not it is "out of place" given the right direction to get somewhere or something. What we judge about the chosen act is whether or not it agrees with, or fits together with, this direction. Thus we measure the chosen act by its relation to an arrangement of actions being positionally constructed to obtain a desired goal. If it heads in the same direction as the right direction, it is fitting and is good, and if it deviates from this direction it is unfitting and bad.[48]

Morally chosen acts, however, get their direction from reason. Hence acts performed by deliberate choice are measured by their conformity to rightly directed reason. To the extent that they conform to this sort of reason they are morally good, and to the extent that they deviate from this reason they are bad.[49]

But what, one might wonder, could make a chosen act deviate from the direction of reason? The answer, as St. Thomas sees it, is one's own emotions and will. Choices are made regarding particular acts under varying circumstances, places, times, and conditions.[50] What reason commands to be done within the context of some situation can be thwarted by changes in the situation, or by obstacles presented to reason by emotions and will. Impediments to the rational direction of chosen acts which are beyond control of one's reason and will, however, do not enter into the moral worth of a deliberately chosen act.[51] But impediments which are voluntarily thrown in the way of a rightly ordered reason in its attempt to control and to direct deliberately chosen acts, make such acts morally bad. Thus when, through voluntary ignorance of what one should know, through voluntary neglect of developing right principles and habits of conduct, or through viciousness of will, or of emotion, one prevents a rightly directed reason from imposing its directives upon human acts, one acts in a way which is morally corrupt.[52]

A deliberately chosen act is morally good or bad, then, to the extent that it is an act which is being directed by a rightly ordered reason through rationally directed emotions and will. Morally good acts of choice are deliberate acts directed by right reason. And morally bad acts of choice are acts of choice which are rationally disordered as a result of obstacles thrown in the way of reason by one's will or one's sensory appetites and emotions.

Reasoning About Making Good Moral Choices

Having explained how, for St. Thomas, moral acts are to be measured, we think it would be helpful at this point to consider how a person is supposed to figure out the right thing to do in a particular circumstance. How does one go about distinguishing right moral choices from wrong moral choices?

Well, as St. Thomas sees it, making a right moral choice always involves referring a chosen act to man's ultimate good.[53] Given a knowledge of this, one can know the directives to use to measure one's choices as right or wrong, good or bad. For St. Thomas, however, man, once again, has a twofold end. Man's eternal end is the intellectual apprehension of God's essence in the beatific vision. Man's temporal end lies in the direction of human life by rightly ordered reason. In addition, man's temporal end is subordinate to man's ultimate end. Hence for the former to be completely achieved a person must consider the former to be directed towards the latter.

Alright, then, granting this to be man's twofold end, let us consider how one applies good moral reasoning in relation to this end. What is good reasoning about the intellectual apprehension of God's essence? And what is good reasoning about directing human life by rightly ordered reason?

Well, good reasoning in both instances is reasoning about choices which lead us to the acquisition of these desired goods. St. Thomas thinks that man instinctively wants to see God in His essence, and that man seeks to live a reasonable life in peace and co-operation with others. Good moral reasoning, therefore, involves choices to be made in light of directives which achieve these goods. If one wants to see God one has to measure the choices which one makes by directives which promote the vision of God. And if one wants to live a reasonable life in peace and co-operation with others, one has to measure the choices which one makes by directives which promote rationally directed social life.[54]

The directives which govern both these desired goods are laws. By Eternal law and divine law a person measures the reason which makes choices whereby he is led to a vision of God. And by natural law and human law a person measures the reason which makes choices whereby he is led to live in peace and cooperation with others. Thus, for example, a well-reasoned moral choice for a Christian wishing to achieve the beatific vision is measured by the directives given in the Ten Commandments, and in the New Testament directives of love of God and of neighbor. And a well-reasoned moral choice for a person wishing to live a reasonable life among other people is measured, at the very least, by directives instinctively present in all human beings through natural law. In addition, in difficult cases measurement by human law and divine law are, also, necessary.

Hence suppose, for example, a person be confronted by the choice of whether or not to take something which belongs to another person. How is one to measure such a choice? Well, if a person judges that the taking of something from another be unjust, and if he be a Jew, or a Christian, or a morally good person, he knows he may not take the object in question. The Jewish person knows this because he knows it is forbidden by the Old Testament. The Christian knows it because it is forbidden by the New Testament. And the person of natural moral goodness knows it because it is out of place in relation to his instinctive drive to live in peace and co-operation with others.

The conclusion of moral reasoning is a choice to do or not to do something.[55] How we measure that choice differs in light of the end for which the choice is being made, and in light of the directives governed by the end in view. Thus the conclusion, "Do not do this!", can be measured by diverse directives. One might reason, for example: "Avoid choosing acts which break your covenant with God. Stealing breaks your covenant with God. This act is stealing. Do not choose this act." Or one might reason: "Avoid choosing acts which are unjust. Stealing is unjust. This act is stealing. Do not choose this act."

From the standpoint of a Jew or a Christian both forms of reasoning make good sense, while from the standpoint of a non-theist only the latter form of reasoning would be cogent. And, of course, even a non-theist would not find such reasoning cogent unless he thought unjust acts deviated from some end, either natural or conventional.

St. Thomas would reject the notion that good moral reasoning could be ultimately determined by a conventional end because, for him, moral reasoning is about moral acts, and moral acts are human acts. That is, moral acts are the products of distinctively human powers inclined towards definite operations in which they find their end and fulfillment. Since convention cannot give to human powers instinctive tendencies whereby they act, convention cannot determine distinctively human ends. Convention, that is, cannot determine how people <u>should</u> behave because people act through powers which have tendencies to behave which in no way depend upon convention or upon majority vote. In short, if moral acts be human acts, and if human acts be choices made through human powers having inborn tendencies of their own, the ends of moral acts are to be found within the direction of these tendencies, not within external conventions.

But, aside from this, another problem arises here regarding moral reasoning. The problem is how does one recognize the appropriate moral act in the appropriate circumstance? For, after all, one might well know that one should avoid choosing acts which are unjust, and that stealing is unjust, but how is he to know that this act is one of stealing?

The answer to this question seems to be, "Through the habit of directing one's individual choices by means of rightly ordered reason." Just by the very fact that they are human, that is, people are able to distinguish right choices from wrong choices under simple circumstances. Thus few people have trouble determing whether they made a wrong choice regarding eating a certain kind or amount of food, or taking drugs, or speeding in their automobiles. For actions like these very often cause consequences which can readily be recognized as being deviations from the happiness which we seek as human beings. Where most of us seem to have a problem, however, is in more complex circumstances, or in circumstances where our will or our emotions are at odds with our reason as to what action to choose. It is in situations such as these that it becomes necessary to be in the habit of directing our choices by means of rightly ordered reason. For only such a reason can recognize the nature of a right moral action under such conditions.

Thus by the practice of doing good acts one becomes better able to recognize a good act when presented to his choice. By developing the habit of making right choices in simple circumstances, and mildly emotional and volitional situations, a person develops the habit of making right choices in more complex circumstances, and in more strongly emotional and volitional situations.

Of course, one might counter what we say here by arguing that no matter how much we attempt to develop the habit of making choices under the direction of rightly ordered reason, we are going to make mistakes. Certainly such an objection has some truth to it. For no matter how much we try not to, we will wind up, nonetheless, making some rotten choices. But, as St. Thomas sees it, from a moral standpoint we need feel no guilt about such mistakes for we are morally excused from culpability when acting with a good will under the direction of rightly ordered reason. And, in addition, when so acting we are much less likely to make bad moral choices than are people who do not develop good habits of choice.

So, for St. Thomas, the person who desires to make good moral choices must develop the habit of directing his choices by a reasoning faculty which is acting in conformity with natural law. Beyond this, however, a person must measure his choices against just human law, against divine law, and against Eternal law. For, as St. Thomas sees it, natural law alone does not provide a person with directives which are particular enough to measure right behavior in complex individual circumstances. Just human law, in a sense, taps the wisdom of all ages. For human law which is just endures the passage of time and provides a person with the benefit of the practical experience and advice of just people who have faced similar choices in the past. And yet, while just human law is a help to our better judgment in individual circumstances, it, too, cannot cover all the details of a particular situation. In the particular situation a person very often does not have time for prolonged deliberation, and, at times, the surrounding circumstances and emotional influences are too difficult for right choices to be made. Hence to recognize the right thing to do in the individual circumstance a person, for St. Thomas, needs the benefit of divine law and of as much moral virtue as he can achieve. For divine law goes into more detail than human law, and in individual circumstances actions are chosen through moral virtues, civic virtues, and theological virtues which enable a person to implement the directives of natural law, human law and divine law in individual circumstances.[56]

Of all the virtues at the disposal of a human being, however, the one which, for St. Thomas, a person needs beyond all others is charity, or friendship with God.[57] The virtues which a person needs in order to live a good human life are enormous in number. Surely most of us can, through practice, become somewhat just, temperate, courageous and so on. But, according to St. Thomas, none of us can ever become completely virtuous through practice, and none of us can, through practice, develop those virtues which lead us to union with God in friendship.[58] People who are friends of God in charity, however, develop all the virtues necessary for living a good human life.[59] For God transforms the wills of such people and, through the grace of the Holy Spirit, helps them to make right choices about how to live.[60] Hence, as we see it, the whole of the moral teaching of St. Thomas can be summarized in the judgment that the complete moral good of man can only be achieved through charity. As St. Thomas says:

>...charity is called the end of the other
>virtues because it directs all the other

virtues to its end. And because a mother is one who conceives in herself from another, for this reason charity is called the mother of the other virtues, because from the appetite for the ultimate end it conceives the acts of the other virtues by ordering them to be done.[61]

CHAPTER 7

HUMAN HAPPINESS AND

THE EXISTENCE OF GOD

Throughout different parts of this work we have mentioned that, for St. Thomas, human happiness is twofold. It consists in an earthly happiness which resides in the living of a life of perfect virtue, and in a heavenly happiness which lies in the beatific vision of God. In addition, we have mentioned that, for St. Thomas, earthly happiness is subordinated to heavenly happiness, and that the former cannot be perfectly achieved without the latter. Indeed, for him, the life of perfect virtue requires that man know God as much as possible in this life. Thus, for St. Thomas, the life of perfect virtue is impossible without the virtue of religion.[1]

That such a view should be held by St. Thomas Aquinas, the Dominican friar, should not really surprise anyone. The reasonableness of St. Thomas's moral teaching, taken as a whole, stands or falls with the reality of God.

One should note, however, how this complex view of human happiness differentiates the moral teaching of St. Thomas from that of the great Greek philosophers of the ancient world. Many of these extolled life of virtue as the ultimate end of human life, and, by and large, all of them eschewed riches, honor, power, fame, and sensory pleasure as goods most worth pursuing. But no ancient Greek philosopher understood by human happiness what St. Thomas understood by it. With St. Thomas, as with St. Augustine before him, one finds an emphasis placed upon human happiness as putting to rest all human desire and as something which is unachievable without a good will.[2] But, for the Greeks, human happiness was not seen as that which terminates all further desire. And the Greeks seem to us to have had little, or no, sense of what St. Thomas meant by a will, or of the role played by the will in moral activity.

So much for the distinctive character of St. Thomas's moral teaching. What about its reasonableness? This, as we just mentioned, stands or falls with the reality of God. If God does not exist the moral teaching of St. Thomas might have some value, but this is questionable. And even if it does have value this would be in light of some ultimate end other than the one envisioned by Aquinas.

Because of the importance of the existence of God to the moral teaching of St. Thomas, we should try to give some argument here as to just why St. Thomas is convinced God exists. We could do this by presenting the celebrated "Five Ways" given by Aquinas in his Summa theologiae, but we have already examined these elsewhere.[3] Besides, St. Thomas himself recognized that there are other ways of knowing God exists aside from philosophical arguments from effect to cause.[4] Hence, instead of concentrating here on St. Thomas's more well-known arguments for God's existence, we would like to consider how, for St. Thomas, man has a natural knowledge of God's existence through the human pursuit of happiness.

In saying this we do not mean to suggest that, in some way, all human beings have an obscure awareness that the God of Christianity exists. No, what we mean to suggest here is this. St. Thomas, as did other medieval thinkers, thought that man had a natural appetite for an infinite good. And he thought that this natural appetite could not be in vain.[5] That is, he thought that the possession of such an appetite entailed the existence of some unrestrictedly good being. Understandably enough, as a Christian, he identified this being with God, but he realized that other people might identify it with something else.

What intrigues us about this thinking is the conviction that natural appetites cannot be in vain, and that man has an appetite for an infinite good. We do not think many philosophers would readily accept either conviction, today, and we have wondered for some time about the reasoning which led the medieval thinkers so readily to adopt such positions. While we do not claim completely to understand the reasoning involved, we think we have some understanding of the medievalists' attitude about these matters. And we think the medievalists' attitude merits more serious consideration than most philosophers would give it today.

The crux of the difficulty, as we see it, is that medieval thinkers considered physical things to have natures, or distinguishing powers, which had within them forces of attraction and repulsion which they called "appetites." Such appetites meant, for them, something akin to what magnetism or gravitation means to many of us today. Just as for us, today, magnetism and gravitation demand agents of attraction or repulsion, so, too, for many medieval thinkers natural appetites demanded agents of attraction or repulsion. Appetites were, for many of them, reactions to stimuli, much like a tropism in a plant is for us. Hence, to them, if a thing had an innate or instinctive appetite for something, this could only be because, in some way, it was being stimulated by something. And, therefore, if man had a natural appetite for infinite good this could only be because, in some respect, man was being stimulated to pursue that which is infinitely good.

The question, however, here becomes, "How does one know one has a desire for that which is infinitely good?" Well, for St. Thomas, one seems to us to know this in at least two ways. One is the way people pursue what they consider to be that which makes them happy. And the other is the disproportion a person recognizes to exist between what he knows to be good and what he desires as his happiness.

With regard to what most people pursue as their ultimate end, St. Thomas notes, how, no matter what it be—it could be wealth, or power, or fame, or something else—if it be recognized as an ultimate end, people are not satisfied with just a little bit of it; they tend to want as much of it as they can get. To Thomas this suggests that the ultimate end of human desire is an infinite good.[6]

In and of itself, however, such a conclusion does not appear to follow of necessity from the evidence. It takes on added strength only when joined to another feature of man's pursuit of happiness. For St. Thomas no one can be completely content so long as there remains for him something to desire or to seek.[7] What human beings desire and seek, however, is something which is presented to the human will by the human mind. And no matter what the human mind thinks about, it can never be so good that the mind cannot think of something better. For the proper object of human knowledge resides in features of material things. And, insofar as these are material features, they always have some defect attached to them. Hence whatever the human mind presents by itself to the human will can never be apprehended by the will as completely satisfying.[8] Consequently, for Thomas, there is a fundamental disproportion which exists between what man desires as his happiness and what his mind can discover by itself unaided by God. It seems to us that it is man's knowledge of this disproportion between the quest of his will and the power of his mind which reveals to St. Thomas that human happiness resides in an infinite good. And this same disproportion, we think, suggests to St. Thomas that human happiness can be achieved only through an elevation of the human mind by divine grace to a condition in which it apprehends the essence of God and, thereby, brings perfection to the soul.

Could it suggest anything else to a theologian like St. Thomas? For above all else, is not his moral teaching a Christian ethics grounded on charity, or friendship with God? And is not any description of his moral teaching which fails to include this dimension to its view an incomplete and perhaps misleading representation of his teaching?

CONCLUSION

We have written this work on the moral teaching of St. Thomas not simply to provide readers with an awareness of moral activity as St. Thomas understood it, but also to provide our contemporaries with a practical guide to the living of a reasonable life. We hope, by this time, that most of our readers are as convinced as we are that St. Thomas was a profoundly wise human being who had an understanding of the human condition which was not simply "creative," "inventive," "imaginative," and so on, but which was, more importantly, by and large correct.

We do not think that what St. Thomas says is true because he says it, but we think that he says a number of things which are true, and which far transcend anything which is being offered to us by our contemporaries, or which has been offered to us by previous thinkers in the history of the West. Our presentation of St. Thomas's moral teaching has been sketchy at best. What he says in the original text is so much better than this report of ours that we are almost embarrassed to present it as a representation of his teaching. But even from what one can glean from what we have said, can anyone, in all seriousness, find a philosopher or psychologist who gives a more thorough and exact explanation of human behavior in all its complexity than does St. Thomas? To whom are we to compare him? To Skinner? Dewey? Descartes? Kant? Hegel? Hume? Marcus Aurelius? Plato? Aristotle? Sartre? Heidegger?

In all honesty, we think that whatever truth one finds in each of these thinkers, one also finds in St. Thomas. But one finds, in addition, within St. Thomas truths which escape the notice of these same thinkers. For us the moral teaching of St. Thomas strikes a middle ground between exaggerated rationalism and voluntarism, between complete determinism and libertinism, between moral relativism and abstract absolutism. There is room within the moral teaching of St. Thomas for reason and emotion, for freedom and for determinism, for objective principles and for subjective application of these principles, for grace and for nature. Of what other thinker can all this be said?

Of course, the mere fact that we are making these claims about the moral teaching of St. Thomas is no guarantee of their truth. With respect to the truth of what St. Thomas says, "The proof of the pudding is in the eating." That is, if what he says be true, an application of his principles to the living of one's life should prove to promote one's happiness. And if, through the application of his moral principles to one's life, one finds that one is becoming increasingly wretched, well, then, we would have to admit that "there is something rotten in Aquino." We have found in the living of our own life that, when we listen to Thomas, the kind of self-mastery and satisfaction which he describes does come to us, and that when we deviate from his principles the roof tends to fall in on us, and we tend to make a mess of things. We are convinced, therefore, that if there is something rotten to be found in ethics, one is not likely to find it in the ethical teaching of St. Thomas. But the best way for someone to discover this to be so is by practice. So do not take our word for it. Apply his moral teaching to your everyday life and we think you will find that not only was St. Thomas an "Angelic Doctor," but he was a thoroughly human one as well.

ENDNOTES

INTRODUCTION

[1] Vernon J. Bourke, "Is Thomas Aquinas A Natural Law Ethicist?" The Monist 58, no. 1 (January, 1974), p. 52.

[2] James A. Weisheipl, O.P., Friar Thomas D'Aquino: His Life, Thought and Work (New York: Doubleday and Co., Inc., 1974), p. 260.

[3] Armand A. Maurer, C.S.B., "Introduction," to his translation of Questions V and VI of St. Thomas's Commentary on the de Trinitate of Boethius entitled, The Division and Methods of the Sciences (Toronto: The Pontifical Institute of Mediaeval Studies, 1963), p. VIII.

[4] See our treatment of different kinds of knowing in Peter A. Redpath, A Simplified Introduction to the Wisdom of St. Thomas (Washington, D.C.: University Press of America, Inc., 1980), 21-32. See St. Thomas's Quaestio disputata de veritate, q. 11, a. 1, and The Division and Methods of the Sciences, q. V.

[5] Mortimer J. Adler, How to Think About God (New York: Macmillan Publishing Co., Inc., and London: Collier Macmillan Publishers, 1980), pp. 60-68.

[6] Mortimer J. Adler, St. Thomas and the Gentiles (Milwaukee: Marquette University Press, 1948), p. 5.

CHAPTER 1

[1] S. Thomae Aquinatis, Summa theologiae (Ottawa: Institutum Studiorum Medievalium, 1941-45), I, qq. 1-119. Hereafter we will refer to this work as S.t.

[2] Ibidem.

[3] Ibid., I, qq. 65-72.

[4] Ibid., I, q. 115, a. 2, Respondeo; I, q. 47, a. 2, Respondeo; and I-II, q. 10, a. 1, Respondeo.

[5] Ibid., I, q. 76, a. 1, Respondeo; I, q. 77, a. 2, Respondeo; and I, q. 65, a. 4, Respondeo.

[6] Ibidem.

[7] Ibid., I, q. 91, a. 3, ad 3.

[8] Ibid., I, q. 78, a. 2, Respondeo.

[9] Ibid., I, q. 78, a. 4, Respondeo.

[10] Our reasoning here is influenced by Henry Veatch's works, For an Ontology of Morals (Evanston: Northwestern University Press, 1971), especially pp. 3-36, and Two Logics, especially pp. 242-253; and S.t., I, q. 76, a. 1, Respondeo.

[11] S.t., I-II, q. 57, a. 2, Respondeo.

[12] See above pp. 4-9.

[13] S.t., I, q. 9, a. 2, Respondeo.

[14] Ibidem.

[15] Ibid., I, q. 103, a. 8, Respondeo; and I, q. 80, a. 1, Respondeo.

[16] Ibid., I, q. 78, a. 1, ad 3.

[17] Ibid., I, q. 78, a. 3, Respondeo.

[18] Ibid., I, q. 119, a. 2, ad 4; and I, q. 78, a. 4, Respondeo.

[19] Ibid., I, q. 77, a. 4, Respondeo; and II-II, a. 26, a. 2, Respondeo.

[20] Ibid., I, q. 47, a. 1, Respondeo; and I, q. 47, a. 2, Respondeo.

[21] Ibidem.

[22] Ibid., I, q. 4, a. 2, Respondeo.

[23] Ibid., I, q. 3, a. 4, Respondeo.

[24] Ibid., I, q. 104, a. 1, Respondeo.

[25] Ibid., I, q. 50, a. 2, ad 3.

[26] Ibid., I, q. 50, a. 5, ad 3.

[27] Ibid., I, q. 75, a. 7, ad 3.

[28] Ibid., I, q. 76, a. 1, ad 5; and I, q. 75.

[29] Ibidem.

[30] Ibid., q. 75, a. 6, Respondeo.

[31] S.t., I, q. 76, a. 1, Respondeo.

[32] Ibidem.

[33] Ibid., I, q. 76, a. 2, ad 2.

[34] Ibid., I, q. 84, a. 4, Respondeo.

[35] Ibid., I, q. 50, a. 2, Respondeo.

[36] Ibid., I, q. 76, a. 1, Respondeo.

[37] Ibidem.

[38] Ibid., I, q. 84, a. 3, Respondeo; and I, q. 55, a. 2, Respondeo.

[39] Ibid., I, q. 77, a. 2, Respondeo.

[40] Ibid., I, q. 77, a. 4, Respondeo.

[41] Ibid., I, q. 78.

[42] Ibid., I, q. 78, a. 2, Respondeo.

[43] Ibid., I, q. 78, a. 3 and a. 4.

[44] Ibid., I, q. 79.

[45] Ibid., I, q. 78, a. 3, Respondeo; and I, q. 77, a. 4, Respondeo.

[46] Ibid., I, q. 77, a. 4, Respondeo.

[47] Ibidem.

[48] Ibid., I, q. 78, a. 4, Respondeo.

[49] Ibid., I-II, q. 1, Prol.; and I, 91, a. 3, Respondeo.

[50] S.t., I, q. 82, a. 3 and a. 4; and I, q. 83, a. 1, Respondeo.

CHAPTER 2

[1] S.t., I-II, q. 58, a. 1, Respondeo.

[2] Ibid., I-II, q. 31, a. 7, Respondeo; I-II, q. 10, a. 1, Respondeo; and I-II, q. 6, a. 5, ad 2.

[3] Ibid., I-II, q. 1, a. 2, Respondeo.

[4] Ibid., I-II, q. 6, a. 1, Respondeo; and a. 2, Respondeo.

[5] Ibid., I-II, q. 58, a. 1, Respondeo.

[6] Ibid., I-II, q. 1, a. 3, Respondeo.

[7] Ibid., I-II, q. 6, a. 1, Respondeo.

[8] Ibid., I-II, q. 1, a. 1, Respondeo.

[9] Ibid., I-II, q. 6, a. 1, Respondeo, and a. 2, Respondeo.

[10] Ibidem.

[11] Ibid., I, q. 13, a. 5, Respondeo.

[12] Ibid., I-II, q. 1, a. 3, Respondeo.

[13] Ibid., I-II, q. 1, a. 1, Respondeo.

[14] Ibidem.

[15] Ibid., I-II, q. 1, a. 1, Prol.

[16] Ibid., I-II, q. 1, a. 1, Respondeo.

[17] Ibid., I-II, q. 1, a. 2, Respondeo.

[18] Ibid., I, q. 78, a. 4, Respondeo.

[19] Ibidem.

[20] Ibid., I, q. 85, a. 5, Respondeo.

[21] Ibid., I-II, q. 13, a. 1, Respondeo.

[22] Ibid., I-II, q. 1, a. 5, Respondeo.

[23] Ibid., I, q. 76, a. 5, ad 4.

[24] See above p. 32.

[25] Joseph Owens, An Elementary Christian Metaphysics (Milwaukee: The Bruce Publishing Co., 1963), pp. 204-06.

[26] Ibidem.

[27] S.t., I-II, q. 18, a. 1, Respondeo, and a. 2, Respondeo; and I-II, q. 19, a. 10, Respondeo. See Henry Veatch, For an Ontology of Morals, op.cit., pp. 110-124.

[28] St. Thomas Aquinas, Quaestio disputata de veritate, q. 11, a. 1.

[29] See above p. 24.

[30] S.t., I-II, q. 31, a. 6, Respondeo.

[31] Ibid., I-II, q. 31, a. 5, Respondeo. St. Thomas is citing St. Augustine, De Trinitate, XIV, 14.

[32] S.t., I-II, q. 6, a. 5, Respondeo.

CHAPTER 3

[1] S.t., I-II, qq. 49-114.

[2] Ibid., I-II, q. 9.

[3] Ibid., I-II, q. 6, Prol.

[4] Ibid., I, q. 78, a. 3, Respondeo; and a. 4, Respondeo.

[5] Ibid., I, q. 78, a. 4, Respondeo.

[6] Ibidem.

[7] Ibid., I, q. 79, a. 8, Respondeo.

[8] Ibid., I, q. 76, a. 5, Respondeo; and I, q. 78, a. 4 Respondeo.

[9] Ibid., I, q. 78, a. 4, Respondeo.

[10] Ibid., I, q. 80, a. 1, ad 3; and I, q. 81, a. 2 Respondeo.

[11] Ibidem.

[12] Ibid., I, q. 78, a. 4, Respondeo.

[13] Ibid., I, q. 81, a. 3, Respondeo.

[14] Ibid., I, q. 81, a. 3, Respondeo; and I-II, q. 17, a. 1.

[15] Ibid., I, q. 82.

[16] Ibid., I, q. 81, a. 3.

[17] Ibid., I, q. 13.

[18] Ibid., I-II, q. 13, a. 1, ad 2.

[19] Ibid., I-II, q. 13, a. 2, Respondeo.

[20] Ibid., I-II, q. 13, a. 6, Respondeo.

[21] Ibid., I-II, q. 23, a. 4, Respondeo.

[22] Ibid., I-II, q. 22, a. 2, ad 3.

[23] Ibid., I-II, q. 22, a. 1, Respondeo.

[24] Ibid., I-II, q. 23, a. 4, Respondeo.

[25] Ibid., I-II, q. 23, a. 2, Respondeo.

[26] Ibid., I-II, q. 25, a. 4, Respondeo.

[27] Ibid., I-II, q. 23, a. 2, Respondeo; and I-II, q. 23, a. 3, Respondeo.

[28] Ibid., I-II, q. 23, a. 2, Respondeo.

[29] Ibid., I-II, q. 23, a. 3, Respondeo.

[30] Ibid., I-II, q. 25, a. 3, Respondeo.

[31] Ibid., I-II, q. 24.

[32] David Hume, *An Inquiry Concerning Human Understanding*, ed. Charles W. Hendel (Indianapolis and New York: The Bobbs Merrill Co., Inc., 1955), pp. 74-75.

[33] *S.t.*, I, q. 81, a. 3, Respondeo.

[34] See above pp. 18-19.

[35] *S.t.*, I-II, q. 49, a. 4, Respondeo.

[36] Ibid., I-II, q. 49, a. 1, ad 3.

[37] *S.t.*, I-II, q. 50, a. 3, Respondeo, and a. 6, ad 1.

[38] Ibid., I-II, q. 49, a. 2, ad 3. As we understand St. Thomas, a disposition does not grow into a habit, but it conditions a power to a point of becoming capable of exercising a habit.

[39] Ibid., I-II, q. 51, a. 3, Respondeo.

[40] Ibid., I-II, q. 49, a. 4, Respondeo.

[41] Ibid., I-II, q. 50, a. 2, Respondeo.

[42] Ibidem. For St. Thomas a habit may, also, belong to the soul itself, rather than to powers or faculties of the soul, but this is a special kind of habit.

[43] *S.t.*, I-II, q. 50, a. 3, Respondeo.

[44] Ibid., I-II, q. 5, a. 3, ad 3.

[45] Ibid., I, q. 81, a. 3, Respondeo.

[46] Ibid., I, q. 50, a. 4, Respondeo.

[47] Ibidem.

[48] Ibid., I-II, q. 50, a.5, Respondeo.

[49] Ibid., I-II, q. 61, a. 2, Respondeo.

[50] Ibid., I-II, q. 50, a. 5, Respondeo.

[51] Ibid., I-II, q. 55, a. 2, Respondeo.

[52] Ibid., I-II, q. 56, a. 1, Respondeo.

[53] Ibid., I-II, qq. 57-62.

[54] Ibid., I-II, q. 57, a. 1, a. 2 and a. 3.

[55] Ibidem.

[56] Ibid., I-II, q. 57, a. 2, Respondeo.

[57] See footnote 54.

[58] S.t., I-II, q. 58, a. 2, Respondeo.

[59] Ibid., I-II, q. 58, a. 4, Respondeo.

[60] Ibid., I-II, q. 61, a. 1 and a. 2.

[61] Ibid., I-II, q. 61, a. 1, Respondeo.

[62] Ibidem.

[63] Ibid., I-II, q. 58, a. 3, ad 1.

[64] Ibid., I-II, q. 57, a. 4, Respondeo.

[65] Ibid., I-II, q. 63, a. 4, Respondeo.

[66] Ibid., I-II, q. 60, a. 5, Respondeo.

[67] Ibid., I-II, q. 61, a. 3, Respondeo.

[68] Ibidem.

[69] See above pp. 58-59.

[70] S.t., I, q. 83, a. 3, Respondeo.

[71] Ibid., I-II, q. 62, a. 1, Respondeo.

[72] Ibid., I-II, q. 62, a.3, Respondeo.

[73] Ibid., I-II, q. 62, a. 1, Respondeo.

[74] Ibid., I-II, q. 62, a. 2, ad 1.

[75] Ibid., I-II, q. 62, a. 3, Respondeo.

[76] *Ibid.*, I-II, q. 58, a. 2, Respondeo.

[77] *Ibid.*, I-II, q. 62, a. 3, Respondeo.

[78] *Ibidem.*

[79] *Ibid.*, I-II, q. 63, a. 2, Respondeo.

[80] *Ibid.*, I-II, q. 63, a. 3, Respondeo.

[81] *Ibid.*, I-II, q. 63, a. 4, Respondeo.

[82] *Ibid.*, I-II, q. 63, a. 2, Respondeo.

[83] *Ibid.*, I-II, q. 63, a. 4, Respondeo.

[84] *Ibid.*, I-II, q. 65, a. 3, Respondeo.

[85] *Ibid.*, I-II, q. 63, a. 4, Respondeo.

[86] *Ibid.*, I-II, q. 68, a. 4, Respondeo.

[87] *Ibid.*, I-II, q. 70, a. 1, Respondeo.

[88] *Ibid.*, I-II, q. 69, a. 1, Respondeo.

[89] *Ibid.*, I-II, q. 68, a. 1, Respondeo.

[90] *Ibidem.*

[91] *Ibid.*, I-II, q. 68, a. 4, Respondeo.

[92] *Ibid.*, I-II, q. 10, a. 4, Respondeo.

[93] *Ibid.*, I-II, q. 70, a. 3, Respondeo.

[94] *Ibid.*, I-II, q. 69, a. 4, Respondeo.

[95] *Ibid.*, I-II, q. 65, a. 2, Respondeo.

[96] *Ibid.*, I-II, q. 65, a. 4, Respondeo.

[97] *Ibid.*, I-II, q. 69, a. 3, Respondeo.

[98] *Ibid.*, I-II, q. 69, a. 4, Respondeo.

[99] *Ibid.*, I-II, q. 69, a. 3, Respondeo.

[100] *Ibid.*, I-II, q. 69, a. 4, Respondeo.

[101] Ibid., I-II, q. 69, a. 3, Respondeo.

[102] Ibid., I-II, q. 69, a. 4, Respondeo.

[103] Ibid., I-II, q. 69, a. 3, Respondeo.

[104] Ibid., I-II, q. 69, a. 4, Respondeo.

[105] Ibid., I-II, q. 90, a. 2, Respondeo.

[106] Ibid., I-II, q. 91.

CHAPTER 4

[1] Aristotle, Nichomachean Ethics, trans. by Martin Ostwald (Indianapolis and New York: The Bobbs-Merrill Co., Inc., 1962), Book II, Ch. 2, 1103b 25-30.

[2] S.t., I-II, q. 13, a. 1, Respondeo.

[3] Ibid., I-II, q. 26, a. 4, Respondeo.

[4] Ibid., I-II, q. 27, a. 1 and a. 2.

[5] Ibid., I-II, q. 27, a. 3, Respondeo.

[6] Ibidem.

[7] Ibidem.

[8] Ibid., I-II, q. 28, a.1, Respondeo. The quote in Augustine is from De Trinitate VIII, 10.

[9] Ibid., I-II, q. 28, a. 2, Respondeo.

[10] Ibidem.

[11] Ibidem.

[12] Ibidem.

[13] Ibid., I-II, q. 28, a. 3, Respondeo.

[14] Ibidem.

[15] Ibidem.

[16] Ibid., I-II, q. 28, a. 4, Respondeo.

[17] Ibid., I-II, q. 28, a. 4, Respondeo.

[18] Ibidem.

[19] Ibid., I-II, q. 28, a. 5, Respondeo.

[20] Ibidem.

[21] Ibidem.

[22] Ibid., I-II, q. 29, a. 1, Respondeo.

[23] Ibid., I-II, q. 29, a. 2, Respondeo.

[24] Ibid., I-II, q. 30, a. 3, Respondeo.

[25] Ibid., I-II, q. 9, a. 1, Respondeo.

[26] Ibid., I-II, q. 3, a. 2, ad 2.

[27] Ibid., I-II, q. 31, a.1, Respondeo.

[28] Ibid., I-II, q. 31, a. 3, Respondeo.

[29] Ibid., I-II, q. 31, a. 6, Respondeo.

[30] Ibidem.

[31] Ibid., I-II, q. 31, a. 3, Respondeo.

[32] Ibidem.

[33] Ibid., I-II, q. 31, a.5, ad 1.

[34] Ibid., I-II, q. 31, a. 5, Respondeo. cf. Henry Veatch, Rational Man (Bloomington and London: Indiana University Press, 1962), pp. 55-58.

[35] S.t., I-II, q. 31, a. 5, Respondeo.

[36] Ibidem.

[37] Ibidem. The quote from Augustine is from De Trinitate XIV, 14.

[38] Ibidem.

[39] Ibidem.

[40] Ibidem.

[41] Ibid., I, q. 84, a. 6, Respondeo.

[42] Ibid., I, q. 90, a. 2, ad 1.

[43] Ibid., I, q. 32, a. 1, Respondeo.

[44] Ibid., I, q. 32, a. 2, Respondeo.

[45] Ibid., I, q. 32, a. 3, Respondeo.

[46] Ibid., I, q. 32, a. 4-8.

[47] Ibid., I, q. 32, a. 4, Respondeo.

[48] Ibid., I, q. 32, a. 5, Respondeo.

[49] Ibid., I, q. 32, a. 6, Respondeo.

[50] Ibidem.

[51] Ibidem.

[52] Ibid., q. 32, a. 7, Respondeo.

[53] Ibid., q. 32, a. 8, Respondeo.

[54] Ibid., q. 33.

[55] Ibid., q. 33, a. 1, Respondeo.

[56] Ibid., q. 33, a. 2, Respondeo.

[57] Ibid., q. 33, a. 3, Respondeo.

[58] Ibid., q. 33, a. 4, Respondeo.

[59] G.K. Chesterton, *The Everlasting Man* (New York: Doubleday and Co., Inc., 1955), p. 226.

[60] Ibid., I-II, q. 34, a. 1, Respondeo.

[61] Ibidem.

[62] Ibid., I-II, q. 34, a. 3 and a. 5.

[63] Ibid., I-II, q. 34, a. 5, Respondeo.

[64] Ibid., I-II, q. 34, a. 1, Respondeo.

[65] Ibid., I-II, q. 10, a. 1, Respondeo.

[66] Ibid., I-II, q. 90, a. 1, Respondeo.

[67] Ibid., I-II, q. 31, a. 7, Respondeo.

[68] Ibidem.

[69] Ibid., I-II, q. 35, a. 1, Respondeo.

[70] Ibid., I-II, q. 35, a. 2, Respondeo. This is not always the case, however. To rejoice in good is not contrary to taking sorrow in evil. See I-II, q. 35, a. 5, Respondeo.

[71] Ibid., I-II, q. 35, a. 8, Respondeo.

[72] Ibid., I-II, q. 36.

[73] Ibid., I-II, q. 36, a. 1, Respondeo.

[74] Ibid., I-II, q. 36, a. 2, Respondeo, and ad 3.

[75] Ibid., I-II, q. 36, a. 4, Respondeo.

[76] Ibid., I-II, q. 35, a. 7, Respondeo.

[77] Ibid., I-II, q. 37.

[78] Ibid., I-II, q. 37, a. 1, Respondeo.

[79] Ibid., I-II, q. 37, a. 2, Respondeo.

[80] Ibid., I-II, q. 37, a. 3, Respondeo.

[81] Ibid., I-II, q. 37, a. 4, Respondeo.

[82] Ibid., I-II, q. 38, a. 1, Respondeo.

[83] Ibid., I-II, q. 38.

[84] Ibid., I-II, q. 38, a. 2, Respondeo.

[85] Ibid., I-II, q. 38, a. 3, Respondeo.

[86] Ibid., I-II, q. 38, a. 4, Respondeo.

[87] Ibid., I-II, q. 38, a. 5, Respondeo.

[88] Ibid., I-II, q. 39, a. 2, Respondeo.

[89] Ibid., I-II, q. 40, a. 2, Respondeo.

[90] Ibid., I-II, q. 40, a. 5, Respondeo.

[91] Ibid., I-II, q. 40, a. 6, Respondeo.

[92] Ibid., I-II, q. 40, a. 6, Respondeo.

[93] Ibid., I-II, q. 42, a. 4; and I-II, q. 43, a. 2.

[94] Ibid., I-II, q. 43, a. 2, Respondeo. St. Thomas is quoting Aristotle's *Rhetoric* II, 5, 1383b1.

[95] Ibid., I-II, q. 42, a. 4, Respondeo.

[96] Ibid., I-II, q. 42, a. 5, Respondeo. St. Thomas is quoting Cicero *De Tusculanis Quaest.* III, 30, DD IV, 20.

[97] Ibid., I-II, q. 41, a. 4, Respondeo.

[98] Ibidem.

[99] Ibid., I-II, q. 44.

[100] Ibid., I-II, q. 44, a. 1, Respondeo, ad 1 and ad 2.

[101] Ibid., I-II, q. 44, a. 4, Respondeo.

[102] Ibid., I-II, q. 44, a. 2, Respondeo.

[103] Ibid., I-II, q. 44, a. 4, Respondeo.

[104] Ibid., I-II, q. 45, a. 2, Respondeo.

[105] Ibidem.

[106] Ibid., I-II, q. 45, a. 3, Respondeo.

[107] Ibidem.

[108] *Ibidem.*

[109] *Ibidem.*

[110] *Ibid.*, I-II, q. 45, a. 4, Respondeo.

[111] *Ibid.*, I-II, q. 46, a. 3, Respondeo.

[112] *Ibid.*, I-II, q. 46, a. 1, Respondeo.

[113] *Ibid.*, I-II, q. 46, a. 4, Respondeo, and ad 2.

[114] *Ibid.*, I-II, q. 46, a. 6, ad 1.

[115] *Ibid.*, I-II, q. 46, a. 6, ad 2.

[116] *Ibidem.*

[117] *Ibid.*, I-II, q. 46, a. 6, Respondeo.

[118] *Ibid.*, I-II, q. 46, a. 8, Respondeo.

[119] *Ibidem.*

[120] *Ibid.*, I-II, q. 47, a. 2, Respondeo.

[121] *Ibid.*, I-II, q. 47, a. 8, ad 1.

[122] *Ibid.*, I-II, q. 47, a. 1, Respondeo.

[123] *Ibid.*, I-II, q. 47, a. 2, Respondeo.

[124] *Ibid.*, I-II, q. 47, a. 3 and a. 4.

[125] *Ibid.*, I-II, q. 47, a. 3, Respondeo.

[126] *Ibid.*, I-II, q. 47, a. 4, Respondeo.

[127] *Ibid.*, I-II, q. 48.

[128] *Ibid.*, I-II, q. 48, a. 1 and a. 2.

[129] *Ibid.*, I-II, q. 48, a. 3, Respondeo.

[130] *Ibid.*, I-II, q. 48, a. 4, Respondeo.

[131] *Ibid.*, I-II, q. 48, a. 1, Respondeo.

[132] *Ibid.*, I-II, q. 48, a. 2, Respondeo.

[133] *Ibid.*, I-II, q. 48, a. 3, Respondeo.

[134] *Ibid.*, I-II, q. 48, a. 2, ad 1.

[135] *Ibid.*, I-II, q. 48, a. 4, ad 1 and ad 3.

CHAPTER 5

[1] *S.t.*, I-II, q. 90, a. 1, Respondeo.

[2] *Ibid.*, I-II, q. 9, a. 1, Respondeo.

[3] *Ibid.*, I-II, q. 90, a. 2, Respondeo.

[4] *Ibidem.*

[5] *Ibid.*, I-II, q. 3, a. 2, Respondeo; I-II, q. 3, a. 4, Respondeo; and I-II, q. 90, a. 2, Respondeo.

[6] *Ibid.*, I-II, q. 90, a. 2, Respondeo.

[7] *Ibid.*, I-II, q. 90, a. 3, Respondeo.

[8] *Ibid.*, I-II, q. 90, a. 4, Respondeo.

[9] *Ibid.*, I-II, q. 91.

[10] *Ibidem.*

[11] *Ibid.*, I-II, q. 91, a. 1, Respondeo.

[12] *Ibid.*, I-II, q. 91, a. 2, Respondeo.

[13] *Ibid.*, I-II, q. 91, a. 3, Respondeo.

[14] *Ibid.*, I-II, q. 91, a. 4, Respondeo.

[15] *Ibid.*, I-II, q. 91, a. 5, Respondeo.

[16] *Ibid.*, I-II, q. 91, a. 5, ad 3.

[17] *Ibid.*, I-II, q. 91, a. 5, ad 2.

[18] *Ibid.*, I-II, q. 91, a. 6, Respondeo.

[19] *Ibid.*, I-II, q. 93, a. 1, Respondeo.

[20] *Ibid.*, I-II, q. 93, a. 2, Respondeo.

[21] *Ibid.*, I-II, q. 93, a. 2, ad 2.

[22] *Ibid.*, I-II, q. 93, a. 3, Respondeo.

[23] *Ibid.*, I-II, q. 93, a. 4 and a. 5.

[24] *Ibid.*, I-II, q. 93, a. 6, Respondeo.

[25] *Ibid.*, I-II, q. 94, a. 1, Respondeo.

[26] *Ibidem.*

[27] *Ibid.*, I-II, q. 94, a. 2, Respondeo.

[28] *Ibid.*, I-II, q. 94, a. 2, Respondeo.

[29] *Ibid.*, I-II, q. 94, a. 3, Respondeo.

[30] *Ibid.*, I-II, q. 94, a. 4, Respondeo.

[31] *Ibid.*, I-II, q. 94, a. 5, Respondeo.

[32] *Ibid.*, I-II, q. 94, a. 6, Respondeo.

[33] *Ibid.*, I-II, q. 96, a. 3, Respondeo.

[34] *Ibid.*, I-II, q. 96, a. 2, Respondeo, and a. 6, Respondeo.

[35] *Ibid.*, I-II, q. 96, a. 2, Respondeo.

[36] *Ibid.*, I-II, q. 96, a. 2, ad 2.

[37] *Ibid.*, I-II, q. 97, a. 1, Respondeo.

[38] *Ibid.*, I-II, q. 97, a. 2, Respondeo.

[39] St. Thomas, in fact, uses man's inability perfectly to adhere to natural law as an argument for the need for man's guardianship by angels! See *S.t.*, I, q. 113, a. 1, ad 1.

[40] *S.t.*, I-II, q. 3, a. 1.

[41] *Ibid.*, I-II, q. 98, a. 6, Respondeo.

[42] Ibidem.

[43] Ibid., I-II, q. 99, a. 2, ad 1 and ad 2.

[44] Ibid., I-II, q. 107, a. 1, ad 2.

[45] Ibid., I-II, q. 106, a. 2, Respondeo.

[46] Ibid., I-II, q. 107, a. 1, Respondeo.

[47] Ibid., I-II, q. 107, a. 2, Respondeo.

[48] Ibid., I-II, q. 107, a. 1, ad 2.

[49] Ibid., I-II, q. 107, a. 2, Respondeo.

[50] Ibid., I-II, q. 100, a. 5, Respondeo, and ad 1.

[51] Ibid., I-II, q. 107, a. 2, Respondeo.

[52] While this view might appear strange to some, Etienne Gilson makes the same point in his, The Christian Philosophy of St. Thomas Aquinas (New York: Random House, 1956), pp. 303-304. Contrasting the moral teaching of St. Thomas to that of Aristotle, Gilson says: "What an enlarging of the perspectives which so limited Aristotle's moral teaching! We should see this much better if St. Thomas had himself believed it necessary to take the trouble to expound his own moral doctrine in purely philosophical terms. This is what we are making him do today, but he never actually did it himself. Why construct a completely self-sustaining moral philosophy as if there were no Christian revelation or as if it were not true? Christian revelation does exist, and it is true. This at least is St. Thomas's point of view." Gilson, it should be noted, is no minor figure in the history of Thomism.

[53] S.t., I-II, q. 1, a. 5, Respondeo.

[54] St. Thomas Aquinas, Summa contra gentiles, editio manualis Leonina (Rome: Marietti, 1946), III, Ch. 25.

[55] Ibid., III, Ch. 48.

[56] S.t., I-II, q. 91, a. 2, Respondeo.

[57] Ibid., I-II, q. 91, a. 4, Respondeo.

[58] See above footnote 52.

[59] S.t., I-II, q. 109, a. 8, Respondeo.

[60] Ibid., I-II, q. 109, a. 2, Respondeo.

[61] See below footnote 64.

[62] St. Thomas Aquinas, Expositio super librum Boethii de Trinitate, ed. Bruno Decker (Leiden: E.J. Brill, 1955), q. 3, a. 1.

[63] Ibidem.

[64] Ibidem.

[65] Summa contra gentiles, III, Ch. 116.

CHAPTER 6

[1] S.t., I-II, q. 8, a. 1, Respondeo.

[2] Ibid., I-II, q. 17, a. 1, Respondeo; and I-II, q. 17, a. 5, ad 2.

[3] Ibid., I-II, q. 9.

[4] Ibid., I-II, q. 10, a.1, Respondeo.

[5] Ibid., I-II, q. 9.

[6] Ibid., I-II, q. 13, a. 6, Respondeo; and I, q. 83, a. 1, Respondeo.

[7] Ibid., I-II, q. 9, a. 2, Respondeo.

[8] Ibid., I-II, q. 10, a. 3, Respondeo.

[9] Ibid., I-II, q. 10, a.2, Respondeo.

[10] Ibid., I-II, q. 10, a. 4, Respondeo.

[11] Ibid., I-II, q. 6, a. 1, Respondeo.

[12] Ibid., I-II, q. 6, a. 4, Respondeo.

[13] *Ibid.*, I-II, q. 6, a. 3, Respondeo; I-II, q. 6, a. 4, Respondeo; and I-II, q. 6, a. 6, Respondeo.

[14] *Ibid.*, I-II, q. 6, a. 6, Respondeo.

[15] *Ibid.*, I-II, q. 6, a. 7.

[16] *Ibid.*, I-II, q. 6, a. 8, Respondeo.

[17] *Ibid.*, I-II, qq. 11-17.

[18] *Ibid.*, I-II, q. 12. St. Thomas contends that willing is not an act of ordering but a tending towards something. Hence acts of will are ordered, or directed, by the human mind. See I-II, q. 12, a. 1, ad 3.

[19] *Ibid.*, I-II, q. 14, a. 1, Respondeo.

[20] *Ibid.*, I-II, q. 14, a. 4, Respondeo.

[21] *Ibid.*, I-II, q. 14, a. 2, Respondeo.

[22] *Ibid.*, I-II, q. 14, a. 6, Respondeo.

[23] *Ibid.*, I-II, q. 15.

[24] *Ibid.*, I-II, q. 13.

[25] *Ibid.*, I-II, q. 13, a. 6, Respondeo.

[26] *Ibid.*, I-II, q. 17.

[27] *Ibid.*, I-II, q. 16, a. 2, Respondeo.

[28] *Ibid.*, I-II, q. 17, a. 5, ad 3.

[29] *Ibid.*, I-II, q. 17.

[30] *Ibid.*, I-II, q. 17, a. 6, Respondeo.

[31] *Ibidem.*

[32] *Ibid.*, I-II, q. 17, a. 7, Respondeo.

[33] *Ibidem.*

[34] *Ibid.*, I-II, q. 17, a. 7, ad 1 and ad 2.

[35] *Ibid.*, I-II, q. 11.

[36] *Ibid.*, II-II, q. 27, a. 6, Respondeo.

[37] *Ibid.*, I-II, q. 18, a. 6, Respondeo.

[38] *Ibidem.*

[39] *Ibidem.*

[40] *Ibid.*, I-II, q. 19, a. 3, Respondeo.

[41] *Ibid.*, I-II, q. 19, a. 4, Respondeo.

[42] *Ibid.*, I-II, q. 19, a. 5, Respondeo.

[43] *Ibidem.* St. Thomas goes so far as to say here that, while believing in Christ is good because it is necessary for salvation, it is bad if it is against reason.

[44] *Ibid.*, I-II, q. 19, a. 6, Respondeo.

[45] *Ibidem.*

[46] *Ibid.*, I-II, q. 20.

[47] *Ibid.*, I-II, q.21, a. 1, Respondeo.

[48] *Ibid.*, I-II, q. 20, a. 4, Respondeo.

[49] *Ibid.*, I-II, q. 18, a. 8, Respondeo.

[50] *Ibid.*, I-II, q. 18, a. 10 and a. 11.

[51] *Ibid.*, I-II, q. 18, a. 9, Respondeo.

[52] *Ibid.*, I-II, q. 6, a. 1, Respondeo; and I-II, q. 19, a. 6, Respondeo.

[53] *Ibid.*, I-II, q. 19, a. 10, Respondeo.

[54] *Ibidem.*

[55] *Ibid.*, I-II, q. 13, a. 3, Respondeo.

[56] *Ibid.*, I-II, q. 91.

[57] *Ibid.*, II-II, q. 23, a. 1, Respondeo.

[58] *Ibid.*, I-II, q. 63, a. 2 Respondeo.

[59] *Ibid.*, I-II, q. 23.

[60] *Ibid.*, I-II, q. 24, a. 1 and a. 2.

[61] *Ibid.*, I-II, q. 23, a. 8, ad 3.

CHAPTER 7

[1] *S.t.*, II-II, q. 81, a. 7, Respondeo.

[2] See St. Augustine's, *De libero arbitrio*.

[3] See *A Simplified Introduction to the Wisdom of St. Thomas*, op.cit., pp. 109-143.

[4] *S.t.*, I, q. 2, ad 1.

[5] *S.c.g.* III, Ch. 40.

[6] *Ibid.*, I-II, q. 2, a. 1, ad 3.

[7] *Ibid.*, I-II, q. 3, a. 8, Respondeo.

[8] *Ibid.*, I-II, q. 2, a. 8, Respondeo.

QUESTIONS FOR STUDY AND DISCUSSION

INTRODUCTION

1. Can genuine knowledge be achieved in the area of morals?

2. Can the subject of morals be unobservable to empirical science and still be knowable?

3. Explain the difference between philosophy and experimental science.

4. Is moral knowledge a scientific knowledge? Is it a philosophical knowledge? Can it be both? Can it be neither?

5. What is a "fact"? What is a "value"?

6. Do facts have value? Are values factual?

7. What is the difference between knowing and demonstrating?

8. Could the thinkers of the seventeenth century have demonstrated to others the reality of experimental science? How?

CHAPTER 1

1. Recount St. Thomas's sevenfold division of reality. What makes one level superior to another?

2. For what reasons is it necessary to hold that there are other ways of observing reality apart from our external senses and scientific instruments?

3. In what way is the reality of science related to a "power psychology"?

4. Explain the importance of a power psychology for the reality of ethics.

5. What is meant by "power"? "instinct"?

6. In what way, for St. Thomas, is creation an order?

7. Explain the difference in the way God exists and the way angels and men exist.

8. Explain the difference between St. Thomas's view of a human being and that of Plato.

9. Recount the order of powers which St. Thomas attributes to a human being. Why does St. Thomas hold that such an order of powers exists?

10. For what reason does the human person occupy the top position within the physical universe of St. Thomas?

CHAPTER 2

1. Explain what St. Thomas means by "moral activity"?

2. Explain how moral activity is a type of natural activity.

3. In what sense are moral acts the same as human acts?

4. What, for St. Thomas, is a free human act? Explain.

5. Explain how distintively human acts are different from animal acts.

6. Explain how the way humans make decisions differs from the way animals make decisions.

7. What does St. Thomas mean by the term "good"? Explain. How is "good" like a spatial notion?

8. Explain how knowledge of good influences all human knowledge.

9. Why is physical science incapable of being an impartial and competent judge of the reality of what people call "good"?

10. For St. Thomas is there a distinguishing human good pursued by all people? Why does he think there is, or is not, such a good?

CHAPTER 3

1. Explain what St. Thomas means by "power" and by "appetite."

2. Explain how the sense appetite differs from the intellectual appetite.

3. How does the propelling appetite differ from the contending appetite?

4. Explain the major roles played by the intellect and the will in moral activity.

5. What does St. Thomas mean by an "emotion"? Identify the propelling emotions and the contending emotions.

6. How do emotions differ from subjective preferences?

7. What role do the emotions play in moral activity?

8. What does St. Thomas mean by a "disposition"? How does it differ from a "habit"?

9. Explain what St. Thomas means by "virtue," "intellectual virtue," and "moral virtue."

10. Identify the intellectual virtues and the "cardinal" moral virtues. Why are the latter called "cardinal" virtues?

11. What are the theological virtues? What are infused virtues?

12. Explain the meaning of "gifts," "fruits," and "beatitudes."

13. Identify the 7 gifts of the Holy Spirit.

14. Identify the 12 fruits of the Holy Spirit.

15. Recount the 8 beatitudes.

16. Explain what, for St. Thomas, gifts, fruits, and beatitudes contribute to moral activity.

CHAPTER 4

1. Explain what St. Thomas means by "love" or "liking." Explain the difference between love of friendship and love of desire.

2. What, for Thomas, are the causes of love? What, for him, are the effects of love?

3. Explain what St. Thomas means by "desire" and "aversion." How does desire differ from love?

4. What does St. Thomas mean by "pleasure"? How does pleasure differ from joy?

5. Why does St. Thomas think intellectual pleasures are more intense than physical pleasures?

6. What, for St. Thomas, are the causes of pleasure? What, for him, are the effects of pleasure?

7. For St. Thomas, is pleasure morally evil? Why or why not?

8. For St. Thomas, are some pleasures unnatural or abnormal? Why or why not?

9. What does St. Thomas mean by pain? How does it differ from sorrow?

10. What, for St. Thomas, are the causes of pain and sorrow? What, for him, are the effects of pain and sorrow?

11. According to St. Thomas, what are the remedies for pain and sorrow? Why do these remedies work?

12. For St. Thomas, is pain morally evil? Why or why not?

13. Explain what St. Thomas means by "hope." How does it differ from despair?

14. For St. Thomas, what causes hope?

15. How, for St. Thomas, is fear like hope? What causes fear? What are the effects of fear?

16. Identify and explain the six kinds of fear cited by St. Thomas.

17. Explain what St. Thomas means by "daring."

18. Explain what St. Thomas means by "anger."

19. For St. Thomas, what are the different types of anger and what is the cause of anger?

20. Recount the effects of anger listed by St. Thomas.

CHAPTER 5

1. What does St. Thomas mean by "law"?

2. What are the six types of law examined by St. Thomas?

3. Explain how Eternal law differs from natural law.

4. How is human law an outgrowth of natural law?

5. Why, for St. Thomas, is a divine law needed beyond natural law?

6. For St. Thomas, should all vices be outlawed? Why or why not?

7. For St. Thomas, what is the role played by grace in moral activity?

8. Can the moral philosophy of St. Thomas be understood outside the context of his theology? Why or why not?

CHAPTER 6

1. How does St. Thomas distinguish a voluntary activity from a violent activity?

2. Explain the difference between "voluntary," "involuntary," and "non-voluntary."

3. What, for St. Thomas, are the three kinds of ignorance related to voluntary activity?

4. Explain the difference between "ignorance of bad choice" and "ignorance of right principles."

5. Explain what St. Thomas means by "intention," "counsel," and "consent."

6. Explain what St. Thomas means by "choice," "command," "employment," and "delight."

7. Why, for St. Thomas, cannot the human will be totally determined?

8. How does one measure a moral act?

9. How does one measure a good moral act?

10. How does one measure the moral goodness of an external act?

11. What role is played by the virtue of charity in the moral teaching of St. Thomas?

CHAPTER 7

1. Explain what St. Thomas means when he says that "natural desires cannot be in vain."

2. Why does St. Thomas think that man has a natural desire for an infinite good?

3. Why, for St. Thomas, does man's natural desire for an infinite good mean that there must really be an infinite good?

BIBLIOGRAPHY

Adler, Mortimer, J. How to Think About God: A Guide for the 20th Century Pagan. New York: Macmillan Publishing Co., Inc., and London: Collier Macmillan Publishers, 1980.

_____. St. Thomas and the Gentiles. Milwaukee: Marquette University Press, 1948.

Aquinas, St. Thomas. The Division and Methods of the Sciences. Tr. Armand A. Maurer. 3rd ed. Toronto: The Pontifical Institute of Mediaeval Studies, 1963.

_____. Expositio super librum Boethii de Trinitate. Ed. Bruno Decker. Leiden: E.J. Brill, 1955.

_____. Quaestiones de veritate, in Quaestiones disputatae. Ed. R. Spiazzi. Turin: Marietti, 1953.

_____. Summa contra gentiles. Editio manualis Leonina. Rome: Marietti, 1946.

_____. Summa theologiae. 5 vols. Ottawa: Institum Studiorum Medievalium, 1941.

Aristotle. Nichomachean Ethics. Trans. Martin Ostwald. Indianapolis and New York: The Bobbs-Merrill Co., Inc., 1962.

Augustine, St. Aurelius. De libero arbitrio, in Sancti Aureli Augustini opera. Ed. William M. Green, Vol. LXXIV. Vienna, 1956.

Bourke, Vernon J. "Is Thomas Aquinas a Natural Law Ethicist?" The Monist, 58 (1974), 52-66.

Chesterton, Gilbert K. The Everlasting Man. New York: Doubleday and Co., Inc., 1955.

Gilson, Etienne. The Christian Philosophy of St. Thomas Aquinas. New York: Random House, 1956.

Hume, David. *An Inquiry Concerning Human Understanding*. Ed. Charles W. Mendel. Indianapolis and New York: The Bobbs-Merrill Co., Inc., 1955.

Owens, Joseph. *An Elementary Christian Metaphysics*. Milwaukee: The Bruce Publishing Co., 1963.

Redpath, Peter A. *A Simplified Introduction to the Wisdom of St. Thomas*. Washington, D.C.: University Press of America, 1980.

Veatch, Henry B. *For an Ontology of Morals: A Critique of Contemporary Ethical Theory*. Evanston: Northwestern University Press, 1971.

_____. *Rational Man*. Bloomington and London: Indiana University Press, 1962.

_____. *Two Logics*. Evanston: Northwestern University Press, 1969.

Weisheipl, J. *Friar Thomas D'Aquino*. New York: Doubleday and Co., Inc., 1974.

INDEX

abnormal, and normal, 73-74, 98-101
action, alteration in as effect of fear, 111-113; alteration in as effect of pleasure, 95-96; as cause of pleasure, 91; of others as cause of pleasure, 92; and purpose of ethics for Aristotle, 79; understanding of, 31
Adler, M., 169 n5, n6
agony, as kind of fear, 110-111
alteration, and fear, 113; and pleasure, 96; in reason as an effect of anger, 118-119; in reason as an effect of pleasure, 95-96; in personality caused by gifts, 73
amazement, as kind of fear, 110-111
angels, existence of, 20-23; unlike man, 23
anger, 60-62, 115-119; cause of 116-118; effects of, 116-118; types of, 116-118
animals, as inferior to humans, 12-15; instinct in, 14, 25-26; 33-40; knowledge as different from humans, 33-40; and moral activity, 28-30
anxiety, as kind of sorrow, 103
appetite, 165-166; concupiscible, 57; contending, emotions of, 61, 80-108; irascible, 57; intellectual, 58-59 propelling, emotions of, 80-108; sensory, 55-57; of will, 31-40, 58, 66-67, 143-161
Aristotle, 79, 83, 178 nl
aversion, 60-62, 86-87
Augustine, St. Aurelius, 82, 90, 123, 133, 163, 173 n31, 178n 8, 179 n37

Bacon, F., 4
bad deeds, as cause of pleasure, 93-94
bathing, as a remedy for pain and sorrow, 106
beatitudes, 71, 75-77
belittlement, as cause of anger, 116-117
bitterness, as kind of anger, 116
bodily agitation, as effect of anger, 118-119
Bourke, V., 2-3, 169 nl

cardinal moral virtues, 68-69
causality, Hume's denial of sensory grasp of, 63; human awareness of, 33-40
change, and fear, 113; and pleasure, 96; in reason as effect of pleasure, 95-96
charity, as end of other virtues, 160-161; and New Law; 133-134; and Ten Commandments, 134; as theological virtue, 70-74
chastity, as fruit of the Holy Spirit, 73
Chesterton, G.K., 97, 226, 180 n59
choice, in animals, 15, 58-59, free, 69, 149-50; and human good, 47-53, 121; measuring the moral value of, 154-156; and natural law, 126-127; reasoning about moral value of, 70, 156-160; and will, 58-59, 149-150
circumstance, and moral reasoning, 159
cold, as effect of fear, 112
command, as feature of moral act, 147, 156; as act of reason, 150-151

199

compassion, of friends as remedy for pain and sorrow, 106-107
concupiscible appetite, 57; emotions of, 61, 80-108
consent, as feature of moral act, 148-149
contemplation, of truth as remedy for pain and sorrow, 106-107
continence, as fruit of the Holy Spirit, 73
contempt, as cause of anger, 116-118
contending emotions, 61, 108-119
contraction, as effect of fear, 111-113
counsel, as feature of moral act, 148; as gift of Holy Spirit, 72
courage, as cause of hope, 109; as gift of the Holy Spirit, 72; moral virtue of, 68-69
creation, order of, 19-23
crying, as remedy for pain and sorrow, 106-107
custom, and morals, 27; and normalcy, 101

daring, 60-62, 113-115; as contrary of fear, 114; as effect of hope, 114; as pursuit of evil, 114
Descartes, R., 4, 6
deliberation, as effect of fear, 111, 113; as feature of moral act, 148
delight, as feature of moral act, 151-152
demonstration, empirio-mathematical, 6-9; meaning of, 6-9
depression, as effect of pain and sorrow, 104-106

desire, 60-62, 86-87; as effect of pleasure, 95; for good as cause of pain, 103-104; and nature, 104
despair, 60-62, 109; as avoidance of good, 114
dilation, spiritual, as effect of pleasure, 94-95
disposition, meaning of, 64; as different from habit, 63-65
distinguishing human good, nature of, 47-53
distinguishing a moral act, 31-40
distinguishing power, meaning of, 12
distinctively human action, 31-47
divine law, 124, 129-135
drunkards, as daring, 114-115; as hopeful, 109

ecstasy, as effect of love, 83-84
embarrassment, as kind of fear, 110-111
emotion, meaning of, 59-61
emotions, 59-62, 79; contending; 108-119; meaning of, 61; propelling, 80-108
employment, as feature of a moral act, 150
enjoyment, as an effect of love, 85
enlargement, spiritual, as effect of pleasure, 94-95
envy, as a kind of sorrow, 103; jealousy of, 84-85
Eternal law, 122, 125
ethical, 27-30; see moral

ethics, cause of contemporary misunderstanding of, 15-16; etymology of, 27; as genuine area of knowledge, 4-10; as related to a power psychology, 15-18; and theology, 135-142; and value judgments, 45-46

evil, as cause of anger, 115; as cause of aversion, 86-87; as cause of hatred, 85-86; daring as pursuit of, 114; fear as avoidance of, 110; pain as union with, 103-104

experience, as cause of hope, 109; and fact, 5, 7; meaning of, 5; restrictive understanding of, 5

fact, and experience, 5, 7; and values, 46

faith, and happiness, 136-137; necessity of for happiness, 134, 140, 141

fear, 60-62, 110-113; as contrary of daring, 114; as gift of Holy Spirit, 72

fervor, as effect of anger, 118-119; as effect of love, 85

flattery, as cause of pleasure, 92

fool, as daring, 114; as hopeful, 109

form, meaning of, 21

freedom, meaning of, 52-53; of choice, 69, 144-147, 149-150; as human, 55; and moral activity, 26, 27, 30; as self-mastered, 53-55, 72; and will, 143-161

freezing, as opposed to melting, 85

fruits, of the Holy Spirit, 71-73

furor, as kind of anger, 116

general sense, 56

gifts of the Holy Spirit, 71-73

Gilson, E., 186 n52

God, and creation, 19-23; existence of and human happiness, 141-142; 163-166; self subsistent, 20

good, and appetitive movements, 113-114; as cause of anger, 115; as cause of hope, 109; as cause of love, 81; as cause of pleasure, 93-95, 104; human, 40-53; meaning of, 41-46

grace, as justifying, 133-134; and law, 76-79; and moral activity, 135-142, 166

habit, meaning of, 65; and natural law, 69, 72, 125-126

happiness, as distinguishing human good, 47-53; as the end of moral action, 40-53, 72-73, 129-130; and the existence of God, 163-166; and law, 121-125, 128-142; as twofold, 69, 70, 155, 163

hatred, 60-62, 85-86

heat, as deserting the heart in fear, 112; relation to hope and fear, 114

hope, 109-110; as cause of pleasure, 92; related to daring, 114; as pursuit of good, 114; as theological virtue, 70, 73

human act, as distinctively human, 31-47, 56; as free activity, 29-40, 121; meaning of, 29-30; as moral activity, 29-31, 56; source of, 31-34; as superior to animal activity, 34-47

human good, nature of, 40-53
human law, limitations of, 123, 128-129; need for, 123; relation to natural law, 128-129
Hume, D., 4-5, 175 n32

ignorance, of bad choice, 147; of right principles, 147
imagination, 56
inclination, 18, 27, 129; and disposition, 64
infused virtue, 69-71
injustice, as cause of anger, 116-118
instinct, 14, 18, 24-26, 29, 47-52, 64-66; meaning of, 18; and power, 18-19
instruction, as cause of hope, 109
intellect, 58; see reason
intellectual, appetite, 31-40, 58-59, 143-152; pleasures as superior to sensory, 89-91; power, 58-59; virtues, 67-68
intention, as feature of moral act, 147-148
irascible appetite, 57

jealousy, as effect of love, 84-85; on behalf of a friend, 84-85; of envy, 84-85
joy, 60-62, 87-102
justice, and anger, 115-118; moral virtue of, 67-69

Kant, I., 4-5
kindness, as fruit of the Holy Spirit, 73
knowledge, as cause of love, 81; as different from learning, philosophy, and science, 4-6; and judgment, 44-45; restrictive understanding of, 5-9; two distinct kinds of, 43-44

langour, as effect of love, 85
law, divine, 124, 129-135; Eternal, 122, 125; general consideration of, 125-135; and grace, 76-77, 121-142; human, 123, 128-129; of lust, 125; meaning of, 121; and moral reasoning, 153-160; natural, 122-123, 125-128; New, 124, 132-135; Old, 124, 129-132; particular consideration of, 125-135
laziness, as kind of fear, 110-111
likeness, as cause of love, 81-82; as cause of pleasure, 92, 94; kinds of, 81-82
liking, 80-85
longsuffering, as fruit of the Holy Spirit, 73
love, 80-86; of desire, 80-81; of friendship, 80-81; of God as intent behind divine law, 142; New Testament law of, 133

mania, as kind of anger, 116
matter, meaning of, 21
measure, 121, 152
measuring, a good moral act, 152-154; a moral act, 152-154
melting, as effect of love, 85
memory, as cause of pleasure, 92; sensory, 56
mildness, as fruit of the Holy Spirit, 73
moderation, as fruit of the Holy Spirit, 73
moral, meaning of, 27-30; virtues, 68-69

moral activity, the nature of, 27-53; distinguishing source of, 31-40; and external factors of, 154-161; and good moral acts, 152-161; mental and volitional factors of, 143-152; measuring, 152-154; measuring as good, 152-154; as natural, 28-31, 55; points of origin of, 55-77; and power psychology, 16-18; as supernatural, 129; terminating point of, 40-47
moral virtues, 68-69; cardinal, 69; infused, 69-71; and rightly ordered reason, 159-160
mutual inhesion, as effect of love, 82-83

natural, meaning of, 28, 98-101; pleasures, meaning of, 99-101; and unnatural, 99-101
natural activity, 28-29; relation to morals of, 28-31, 55; and instinct, 29
natural law, 122-123, 124; and grace, 137-142; limitations of, 123, 128, 129, 131, 137, 160; meaning of, 122-123, 137; not a habit, 125-126; precepts of, 125-128
nature, and cause of actions, 102; of distinguishing human good, 52-53; diversity in operation, 24; of man and his place in the cosmos, 11-30; meaning of, 12, 28, 62, 64, 99-101; of moral activity, 27-53
New Law, 123-124, 132-135
Newton, I., 4
non-voluntary act, 146-147
norm, meaning of, 99
normal, and abnormal, 73-74, 98-102

Old Law, 124, 129-132
order, and creation, 19-23; meaning of, 19; with the person, 23-26

Owens, Joseph, 173 n25

pain, 59-62, 102-108; causes of, 103-104; effects of, 104-106; moral value of, 108; remedies for, 106-108
particular reason, 58
passions, 60
patience, as fruit of the Holy Spirit, 73
Paul, St., 134
peace, as fruit of the Holy Spirit, 73
persuasion, as cause of hope, 108
piety, as gift of the Holy Spirit, 73
pity, as kind of sorrow, 103
Plato, St. Thomas's criticism of, 22-23; view of man, 22
pleasure, 59-62, 87-108; causes of, 91-94; as effect of anger, 118; effects of, 94-97; intellectual, 89-91; moral value of, 97-98; normalcy and abnormalcy of, 98-102
power, and habit, 65-68; and instinct, 18, 52; irresistible, as cause of pain, 103-104; meaning of, 18; psychology and relation to ethics, 15-18; of sense and intellect, 24-26; vegetative, 24-25
powers, and appetites, 55-59; of man, 24-26; under command of reason, 150-152
propelling emotions, 61, 80-108
prudence, moral virtue of, 68

203

rational, humans as, 37
reason, alteration in as cause of pleasure, 95-96; and faith, 140-141; and law, 121; as measure of moral acts, 152-154; and moral acts, 31-40, 56, 58, 143-152; particular, 58; and reality of things, 7; right, 152-160; and will, 66-67; and voluntary acts, 143-147; weakness of, 139-141
reality, and reason, 7; sevenfold division of, 11-23
religion, and virtue, 163
revenge, as cause of anger, 115-118
right, meaning of, 52; reason, 152-160
rudeness, as object of anger, 116

sadness, as cause of pleasure, 92
science, as area of learning, 4; as different from philosophy, 4-5; experimental, 5-9; as gift of the Holy Spirit, 72; intellectual virtue of, 17; and power psychology, 66-68; restrictive understanding of, 5-9; as unable to judge about reality of good, 45-46
scientific method, 8
self-mastered acts, 15, 30, 34, 39, 40, 52-53, 60-63, 68, 72, 79, 121
sense, appetites of, 56-58; powers of, 65-66
shame, as kind of fear, 110-111
sight, sensory pleasure of, 88
similarity, as cause of love, 81-82
sleep, as remedy for pain and sorrow, 106, 108
sorrow, 102-108; as cause of pleasure, 92; effects of, 104-106; remedies for, 106-108
soul, in Plato and St. Thomas, 22-23; powers of, 23-26
spiritual dilation, as effect of pleasure, 94-95

spite, as cause of anger, 116-118
stupidity, as cause of daring, 114; as cause of hope, 109
stupor, as kind of fear, 110-111
success, estimation of as cause of daring, 114; estimation of as cause of hope, 109
superiority, 11-15, 19-23, 26; as cause of anger, 117; and freedom, 26, 52-53

temperance, moral virtue of, 68
terminating point of moral action, 40-47
theological virtues, 69-71, 73
theology, and moral philosophy, 138-142
thirst, as effect of pleasure, 95
torpor, as kind of sorrow, 103
touch, sensory pleasure of, 88
trembling, as effect of fear, 111-113
trustworthiness, as fruit of the Holy Spirit, 73
truth, and demonstration, 8

understanding, intellectual virtue of, 66-68; as gift of the Holy Spirit, 72
union, as effect of love, 82; with evil as cause of pain, 103-104
unnatural, and natural, 99-101
unnatural, meaning of, 99; pleasures, meaning of, 99-101

values, and facts, 46
variation, as cause of pleasure, 91-92
Veatch, H., 170 n10, 173 n27, 179, n34
virtue, meaning of, 67
virtues, 67-77; and gifts, fruits, and beatitudes, 71-77; infused, 69-71; intellectual, 67-68; moral, 68-69; and moral reasoning, 159-160; theological, 69-71, 73
volitional factors of moral acts, 143-152
voluntary act, meaning of, 145-148

warmth, as fruit of the Holy Spirit, 73
wealth, as cause of hope, 109
Weisheipl, J., 2-3; 169 n2
will, and moral acts, 31-40, 56, 66-67, 143-161; and reason, 66-67, 143-161, 188 n18
wisdom, intellectual virtue of, 66-68; as gift of the Holy Spirit, 72
wonder, as cause of pleasure, 94

youth, as daring, 114; as hopeful, 109

Dr. Peter Redpath is Associate Professor of Philosophy at
St. John's University, Staten Island, New York.